PUBLIC POLICY FOR THE SEAS

Norman J. Padelford

The M.I.T. Press
Cambridge, Massachusetts, and London, England

MIT Press
0262660016
PADELFORD
PUBLIC PO REV ED

Third Printing, August 1971

ISBN 0 262 66001 6 (paperback)

Library of Congress catalog card number: 74-115761

Cover: The Tongue of the Ocean, Bahamas, as seen from Gemini V.

TABLE OF CONTENTS

ILLUSTRATIONS

INTRODUCTION

The passage of the Marine Resources and Engineering Development Act of 1966 marked a turning point in United States policy toward marine affairs. With the passage of this Act, the Congress laid the basis for a long-range program calling for greater use of the resources of the seas.

The oceans afford, as the Congress acknowledged, an asset of "immense potential significance" for mankind. Increased utilization of the marine resources is now becoming possible through new developments in vehicles, structures and technology. As these capabilities expand, the role of public policy in relation to the seas becomes increasingly significant.

The objectives set forth by the Congress in 1966 encompass a broad span of national interests. They look to expansion of knowledge of the seas, enhancement of commerce, navigation and national security, rehabilitation of commercial fisheries, encouragement of private investment for exploring and developing the mineral wealth in the oceans, advancement of education and training in marine science and engineering, and improvement of the capabilities, performance and use of vehicles and instruments for exploring the marine environment, recovering its resources and transmitting energy.

These declarations reflect the determination of the Congress to have the country retain a leading role in marine activities. In addition it called for cooperation of the United States with other nations, groups of nations, and international organizations when this is found to be in the national interest.

The present collection of source materials, documents and cases has been assembled to facilitate study of policy issues relating to increased use of the marine environment.

The primary focus of this volume is on United States policy toward the oceans, this being the first concern of ocean engineers in this country. Numerous documents are included, nevertheless, relating to the policies of other states and to measures of international cooperation where these are particularly relevant to American interests or activities, or are instructive of other approaches to specific situations.

The author is grateful to friends and colleagues for numerous suggestions relating to the book. I am particularly indebted to Professor Alfred H. Keil, Chairman of the Department of Naval Architecture and Marine Engineering at M.I.T., for the invitation to conduct a seminar on Ocean Policy. This served as a spur to collect the materials contained in this volume. Professor Philip Mandel of the same Department, and Professor Eugene Skolnikoff, colleague in the Department of Political Science and formerly Special Assistant to the President's Science Advisory Commitee in Washington, together with Professor Harvey Sapolsky also of the Political Science Department, offered helpful suggestions on the contents. To Captain W.J.L. Parker, Coast Guard, I am indebted for interpretations of the scope of responsibilities which rest upon this helpful service to mariners.

Many streams of thought initiated by students in the Ocean Engineering course have gone into the organization of this volume. One of the satisfactions of teaching is the companionship of younger scholars eager to extend their knowledge and the help they invariably afford in untangling complicated problems. From these young men, drawn from a dozen disciplines and representing the principal national services, I have learned much and am indebted for their ideas.

Acknowledgment is made with gratitude to the National Science Foundation, the Ford Foundation and to M.I.T. for financial underwriting of the costs of preparing the materials for this book. To Priscilla W. Scott and Mrs. Margo Conk I am especially grateful for help in editing and preparing the book for publication.

Norman J. Padelford

Cambridge, Massachusetts
December 1969

CHAPTER ONE

NEW GOALS FOR NATIONAL POLICY

Introductory Note

Interest in the oceans has been a factor in American politics since colonial days. The seas have afforded a livelihood to many, supported an active foreign trade, provided communications, and surrounded the New World with a shield behind which the nation could develop.

These and other related concerns such as freedom of the seas have continued to occupy the country's attention to such an extent that today nearly thirty agencies of the Federal Government are concerned with maritime affairs.

The achievements of engineering and scientific ingenuity harnessed to national purpose in World War II fashioned an image of science and technology not only as an endless frontier, but as being capable of almost limitless accomplishments. More recent developments such as the application of nuclear power to the propulsion of submarines, the construction of armadas of guided intercontinental ballistic missiles, the launching of man into space, and the fabrication of vehicles capable of transporting man to the bottom of the deepest trenches of the ocean, have preserved the image while adding fresh dimensions to national strength.

Rapid strides in science and engineering abroad have helped to close many of the gaps opened by World War II. American merchant tonnage on the seas has fallen from first to fifth place. Other nations have developed shipbuilding facilities that currently far outproduce American yards. The Soviet Union has for some years had the world's largest fleet of submarines, and is now in the vanguard of tonnage in high seas fishing fleets. The American fish catch has dropped to sixth place among the principal nations. Thus, the picture has mixed shadings of light and dark as the world proceeds into the final third of the 20th century.

Among the intriguing facets of the marine scene are the discoveries of mineral and fuel resources on the ocean floor. As geological surveying, exploratory drilling, and research have been proceeding, it has become apparent that the oceans contain, on the seabeds and in the rock formations underlying the continental shelves, important reserves which may relieve feared shortages.

How to extract these ores and energy sources economically is the challenge that is confronting technology and industry today. On the legal and political side are questions pertaining to the terms under which exploration and exploitation can take place, the arrangements which will govern activities conducted beneath the high seas, and the jurisdictions under which these resources lie. These are issues engaging the attention of policy makers, lawyers, scientists, and industrialists of many countries. The answers are by no means certain, for the questions are often exceedingly complex involving the interests and responsibilities of several agencies and countries.

Among the principal issues confronting decision makers today, none is more important than that of determining the general direction in which national policy should be moving in relation to the oceans. Should it be headed, as the principles of the Great Society programs suggest, in the direction of mounting massive national attacks upon unlocking the mineral and food resources of the oceans ? Should it alternatively, as conservatives advocate, adopt a hands-off position, leaving private enterprise the option to get what it can, where it will and with such means as it is able to command ? Or should policy strive toward some mid-ground, recognizing that the mineral wealth of the seas is a treasure bequeathed to mankind by nature which should be regulated in ways to ensure equitable sharing, but exploitation of which is left to industry much as in the case of land-based resources ?

Finding acceptable solutions to these problems is not easy within composite societies. It is even more difficult in the world community where there are sharply differing concepts of the roles of the state and of private enterprise, capital and labor. What is likely to result from the political process will be a compromise solution. Whether this will be an orderly and systematic compromise with the results testable by logical means remains to be seen.

In the United States the initiative for a fresh appraisal of the roles of science and engineering in relation to national goals and policy in marine affairs came in the mid-1950's from the Office of Naval Research and Development which appealed to the National Academy of Sciences for support and ideas. The Academy's Committee on Oceanography in a far-sighted report in 1959 called for a ten-year national effort to extend research and knowledge of the seas, to draw additional manpower into oceanology and engineering, and to develop radically new vehicles for underwater activity.

Responding to the scientists' recommendations, President Eisenhower established an Inter-Agency Committee on Oceanography to coordinate Government activities. President Kennedy followed with a bold request to the Congress to authorize construction of fifty-two research vessels, establishment of thirty laboratories, and allot at least $138 million annually for research and marine education over a ten year period. Portions of this were approved under the subsequent urgings of President Johnson following the tragedy of the U.S.S. Thresher and the less difficult recovery of an unarmed H-bomb off the coast of Spain. Both of these events, as well as the later disappearance of the U.S.S. Scorpion, revealed the nation's limited capability to locate and retrieve objects in the deep seas.

It was not until 1966 that the Congress was able to reach agreement on broad-fronted legislation. Although the Marine Resources and Engineering Development Act has ambiguities, which reflect the haste and compromising in the final stages of its passage, it does lay down an important series of objectives. It focuses leadership in ocean affairs in the hands of the President, and makes the National Council on Marine Resources and Engineering Development an advisory body to the President.

The principles set forth by the Congress in the 1966 Act are a landmark in marine policy, for they enact a general policy directed toward increased utilization of the resources of the oceans. Moreover, they indicate the Congressional intention to provide support for research, education and technological improvements in marine engineering. The objectives incorporated into this Act reflect Congress' desire to maintain the nation's position as a leader in ocean science and engineering. The effectiveness of these goals will depend much upon the willingness of later Congresses to follow through with necessary implementing legislation and appropriations, but at least a creative beginning has been made.

Time alone can tell to what extent the chosen instrument of the National Council on Marine Resources and Engineering Development, as authorized, is able to move the

TABLE I.—*Federal agencies having marine science activities*

Agency	*Missions*
Department of Defense:	All phases of oceanography relating to national security.
Navy, Army Corps of Engineers, Advanced Research Projects Agency.	Undersea technology.
	Statutory Civilian Responsibilities:
	Great Lakes, river, harbor, coastal and ocean charting and forecasting.
	Great Lakes, river, harbor, coastal development, restoration, and preservation.
Department of State	United States' participation in international organizations.
	Support of International Fisheries Commissions.
Agency for International Development	Foreign assistance.
Department of Commerce:	Environmental prediction and description.
Environmental Sciences Services Administration,	Charting and mapping coastal and deep-ocean waters.
Martime Administration	Central responsibility for air/sea interaction program.
	Research on shipbuilding and ship operations.
	Marine transportation systems.
Department of the Interior:	Management, conservation, and development of marine natural resources.
Geological Survey, Federal Water Pollution Control Administration, Bureau of Commercial Fisheries, Bureau of Sport Fisheries and Wildlife, Bureau of Mines, Bureau of Land Management, National Park Service, Bureau of Outdoor Recreation, Office of Saline Water.	Measurement and enforcement of water quality standards.
	Preservation and development of coastal areas.
	Identification and development of technology for evaluation of mineral resources.
Department of Transportation:	Safety at sea.
Coast Guard	Delineation and prediction of ice masses.
	Oceanographic services.
Department of Health, Education, and Welfare:	Relation of marine organisms to health and pollution.
Public Health Service, Office of Education	Marine science and engineering education—fellowships, grants.
Atomic Energy Commission	Effects of radioactivity in the marine environment.
	Development of marine nuclear technology.
National Science Foundation	Basic and academic oceanography.
	Graduate and undergraduate training in marine science and engineering.
	Sea-Grant program.
Smithsonian Institution	Identification, classification, and ecology of marine organisms; investigations of the geophysical factors of oceanic environment.
National Aeronautics and Space Administration	Feasibility, design, and engineering of spacecraft and sensors for ocean observations

multitude of Federal agencies, the various State governments, industry, and the universities in unified cadence toward common goals. In naming the Vice-President chairman of this organ, the Congress signified its desire that this body should operate at the highest level of authority and be given strong momentum. Its accomplishments to date include obtaining agreement within the Executive branch on fresh priorities for national action; stepping up scientific investigations within the oceans; stimulating the production of new deep water research vehicles; instituting studies relating to the legal regime of the seas; and extending international cooperation in marine research and surveying.

The procedures to be employed in reaching decisions on ocean policy questions pose some difficulties. Systems analysis may seem to be an appropriate method to use in this connection, but it must be remembered that the ends are not limited to a single function or purpose. Should the concern revolve around improving a service or increasing a product ? Perhaps it should in part, but there are other less tangible elements such as increasing knowledge and extending international cooperation which have to be considered. Facilitating certain missions and tasks must also be kept in mind, such as extending capability in deep submergence, making more food available to needy peoples, learning more about bodily reactions to long exposure in the dark,cold, saline surroundings of the deep seas. Again, the limitations of budget, of legal authority, and of public acceptability have to be kept in view. In short, it is doubtful that a single operational concept or mode of analysis can totally satisfy all of the conditions that must be considered in making decisions pertaining to increased utilization of the resources of the oceans. As the environment is in itself an aggregate of many elements, so the mode of attack on the problems relating to greater use of the seas must entail multi-dimensional forms of analysis.

Many of the problems and tasks associated with utilization of the seas relate primarily to land-based concerns and to the shores. Others are focused in contiguous sea areas and on the continental shelves, while some involve activities in the high seas. Difficulties arising from man's desire to make use of the marine environment often require consideration of bilateral and multilateral relationships; involve treaty rights and obligations; or come under prescriptions of international law.

What has been lacking heretofore, and is now particularly needed, is a policy strategy for dealing with the multiplicity of ocean concerns in the total air-water-land-sea bottom environment. The country has too long dealt in a piecemeal manner with its interests in and actions toward fisheries, the merchant marine, safety of life at sea, control of submerged lands, coastal and harbor improvements, resource development, naval strength and national security, smuggling, and the like. There is a need to think out the relationships of the various parts to the whole and to our relationships with other countries.

The merit of the choice made by the Congress in selecting a cabinet-level Council under the chairmanship of the Vice-President is that no single outlook or vested interest is likely to dominate policy determination. Moreover, a body of this nature close to the top of national decision making is able to keep its eye on the broader aspects of issues, and to fasten on matters of highest priority. On the whole the Council has succeeded in discharging the mandate given to it.

A third feature of the Marine Resources and Engineering Development Act was its establishment of a Marine Science Commission to formulate recommendations for an "adequate" national ocean program, and to present proposals for a permanent administrative structure to coordinate the handling of ocean affairs within the Federal Government. The Congress must eventually decide what to do along both of these lines. This it could not do when acting on the 1966 legislation. However, rather than impede progress at that time, the Congress passed the responsibility of of considering such issues to the Commission headed by ex-President Julius A. Stratton of M.I.T., and in turn gained more time for further Congressional examination of the problems.

It is difficult to see what new viewpoints can be offered on questions which have already received the earnest attention of the National Academy of Sciences, the President's Science Advisory Committee, the Congress, and countless numbers of individuals both within and outside of the Government. Nevertheless, there is always the possibility that one further look at the pieces will find the solution to a puzzle. This, of course, is the hope here. It is to the credit of the President that he asked the principal authors of the 1966 legislation -- Senator Magnuson (Dem.) of Washington and Congressman Alton Lennon (Dem.) of North Carolina -- to sit with the Commission. Having Congressional leaders in on the thinking of the Commission should help to speed up the legislative process of action on the recommendations when they are presented.

The problem as the Commission has visualized it is how to initiate a national program in this area that is adequately coordinated and directed. One possibility suggested by Senator Muskie of Maine is to create a single overall Department of Marine and Atmospheric Affairs. However the formation of such a department would mean that bureaus would have to be moved from existing departments and placed under a new roof. In some instances this might mean that independent agencies would lose their status if their functions were transferred to other hands. Such actions could conceivably have adverse effects on working morale.

Within academic communities interdepartmental centers or laboratories are often established to investigate problems of common interest to scholars in different fields yet employing interdisciplinary techniques. Within the government heirarchy this is not an easy task. Suggestions have been made of a super-powered agency like the Space Agency -- a "wet NASA" as it has been called which would incorporate some of the advantages akin to university centers and laboratories. But this is probably not the answer. It has been proposed that a task force with a supreme commander, comparable to wartime operations in the Pacific, be considered. This at best would be a temporary expedient.

Other possible solutions to the administrative problem might be to concentrate ocean activities within a few agencies joined by a cabinet level council. Alternatively, it has been suggested that the whole be placed under the direction of the Office of Science and Technology in the White House; that ocean affairs be handled by a Comsat-type government corporation; that the present arrangement be made a permanent one, leaving bureaus, agencies, and functions distributed more or less as they are today; and possibly instituting a high level office comparable to an executive vice-president of many corporations to assume direction of ocean policy and activities.

With the interaction that exists between a multiplicity of goals, programs and activities, it is clear that there are a variety of ways in which coordination and direction could be handled. Whether any of these would turn out to be better than the present arrangement is hard to say. In the end the solution that is adopted will have to rest upon a political judgment. This will undoubtedly involve some measure of compromise between the desirable and the feasible. The Congress could do worse than making the National Marine Council a permanent body much as it stands today. It would do well, however, to leave some measure of flexibility in membership to the judgment of the President, much as in the National Security Council where the President may invite whom he will from time to time to sit with a nucleus of constituent members. However the lines of authority are ultimately drawn, it will be desirable to have an arrangement which will afford an adequate voice to science and engineering and at the same time take cognizance of the political equations involved in policy making and public administration. The central figure in the picture should remain the President.

Richard Neustadt has said in his book Presidential Power that the Constitutional Fathers established the United States policy process on the notion of shared powers. Certain powers were given to the Executive; others to the Congress. Still others were left to be worked out by experience. In the passage of the Marine Resources and Engineering Development Act, as well as in the companion National Sea Grant Colleges and Programs Act, the Congress manifest its determination to shape the broad outlines of national ocean policy. At the same time, it left to the President and the Vice-President, together with their advisers and appointees, the prerogatives of formulating daily policy decisions, issuing directives, making recommendations to the Congress, and carrying on administrative practice. Thus, the partnership has been preserved as we move toward new goals in national policy.

The National Sea Grant Colleges and Programs Act, which was passed some three months after the Marine Resources and Engineering Development Act, was declared to be an amendment to the prior Act. By the terms of this law the Congress broadened the list of purposes which it sought to achieve with respect to the seas. In particular it recorded its determination to provide Federal support for education, training,and research designed to promote gainful use of marine resources and increased utilization of the seas for national purposes. To this end it authorized the National Science Foundation to act as a granting authority for initiating and supporting so-called sea grant colleges, research projects, and programs consisting of "instruction, practical demonstrations, publications, and otherwise " -- a broad canopy of opportunity. The National Council on Marine Resources and Engineering Development was at the same time empowered to advise the Foundation with respect to policies, procedures and operations in carrying out the Act in the discretion of the President. The provision of funds to implement the terms of this Act must be made by subsequent sessions of the Congress as its judgment deems best.

The readings which follow in this chapter are directed to the broad lines of national policy as they have been drawn in recent times. For further readings see Hubert H. Humphrey, "Opportunity to Move Ahead," Journal of Undersea Technology, January 1967, pp. 22-25; Edward Wenk, "Policy of Marine Council Explained," Journal of Ocean Industry , June 1967, pp. 12-14; National Academy of Sciences and National Research Council, Oceanography 1966: Achievements and Opportunities (Washington, 1967),pp.153-183; Marine Science Affairs-- A Year of Plans and Progress, Second Report of the President to the Congress on Marine Resources and Engineering Development, Washington, March 1968; International Decade of Ocean Exploration, A Report of the National Council on Marine Resources and Engineering Development, Executive Office of the President, May 1968.

MARINE RESOURCES AND ENGINEERING DEVELOPMENT ACT

Public Law 89-454
89th Congress, S. 944
June 17, 1966

Be it enacted... That this Act may be cited as the "Marine Resources and Engineering Development Act of 1966".

Declaration of Policy and Objectives

Sec. 2. (a) It is hereby declared to be the policy of the United States to develop, encourage, and maintain a coordinated, comprehensive, and long-range national program in marine science for the benefit of mankind to assist in protection of health and property, enhancement of commerce, transportation, and national security, rehabilitation of our commercial fisheries, and increased utilization of these and other resources.

(b) The marine science activities of the United States should be conducted so as to contribute to the following objectives:

(1) The accelerated development of the resources of the marine environment.

(2) The expansion of human knowledge of the marine environment.

(3) The encouragement of private investment enterprise in exploration, technological development, marine commerce, and economic utilization of the resources of the marine environment.

(4) The preservation of the role of the United States as a leader in marine science and resource development.

(5) The advancement of education and training in marine science.

(6) The development and improvement of the capabilities, performance, use, and efficiency of vehicles, equipment, and instruments for use in exploration, research, surveys, the recovery of resources, and the transmission of energy in the marine environment.

(7) The effective utilization of the scientific and engineering resources of the Nation, with close cooperation among all interested agencies, public and private, in order to avoid unnecessary duplication of effort, facilities, and equipment, or waste.

(8) The cooperation by the United States with other nations and groups of nations and international organizations in marine science activities when such cooperation is in the national interest.

The National Council on Marine Resources and Engineering Development

Sec. 3. (a) There is hereby established, in the Executive Office of the President, the National Council on Marine Resources and Engineering Development (hereinafter called the "Council") which shall be composed of --

(1) The Vice President, who shall be Chairman of the Council.
(2) The Secretary of State
(3) The Secretary of the Navy
(4) The Secretary of the Interior
(5) The Secretary of Commerce
(6) The Chairman of the Atomic Energy Commission
(7) The Director of the National Science Foundation
(8) The Secretary of Health, Education, and Welfare
(9) The Secretary of the Treasury

(b) The President may name to the Council such other officers and officials as he deems advisable.

(c) The President shall from time to time designate one of the members of the Council to preside over meetings of the Council during the absence, disability, or unavailability of the Chairman.

(d) Each member of the Council, except those designated pursuant to subsection (b), may designate any officer of his department or agency appointed with the advice and consent of the Senate to serve on the Council as his alternate in his unavoidable absence.

(e) The Council may employ a staff to be headed by a civilian executive secretary who shall be appointed by the President and shall receive compensation at a rate established by the President at not to exceed that of level II of the Federal Executive Salary Schedule. The executive secretary, subject to the direction of the Council, is authorized to appoint and fix the compensation of such personnel, including not more than seven persons who may be appointed without regard to civil service laws or the Classification Act of 1949 and compensated at not to exceed the highest rate of grade 18 of the General Schedule of the Classification Act of 1949, as amended, as may be necessary to perform such duties as may be prescribed by the President.

(f) The provisions of this Act with respect to the Council shall expire one hundred and twenty days after the submission of the final report of the Commission pursuant to section 5 (h).

Responsibilities

Sec. 4. (a) In conformity with the provisions of section 2 of this Act, it shall be the duty of the President with the advice and assistance of the Council to --

(1) survey all significant marine science activities, including the policies, plans, programs, and accomplishments of all departments and agencies of the United States engaged in such activities;

(2) develop a comprehensive program of marine science activities, including, but not limited to, exploration, description and prediction of the marine environment, exploitation and conservation of the resources of the marine environment, marine engineering, studies of air-sea interaction, transmission of energy, and communications to be conducted by departments and agencies of the United States, independently or in cooperation with such non-Federal organizations as States, institutions and industry;

(3) designate and fix responsibility for the conduct of the foregoing marine science activities by departments and agencies of the United States;

(4) insure cooperation and resolve differences arising among departments and agencies of the United States with respect to marine science activities under this Act, including differences as to whether a particular project is a marine science activity;

(5) undertake a comprehensive study, by contract or otherwise, of the legal problems arising out of the management, use, development, recovery, and control of the resources of the marine environment;

(6) establish long-range studies of the potential benefits to the United States economy, security, health, and welfare to be gained from marine resources, engineering, and science, and the costs involved in obtaining such benefits; and

(7) review annually all marine science activities conducted by departments and agencies of the United States in light of the policies, plans, programs, and priorities developed pursuant to this Act.

(b) In the planning and conduct of a coordinated Federal program the President and the Council shall utilize such staff, interagency, and non-Government advisory arrangements as they may find necessary and appropriate and shall consult with departments and agencies concerned with marine science activities and solicit the views of non-Federal organizations and individuals with capabilities in marine sciences.

Commission on Marine Science, Engineering, and Resources

Sec. 5. (a) The President shall establish a Commission on Marine Science, Engineering, and Resources (in this Act referred to as the "Commission"). The Commission shall be composed of fifteen members appointed by the President, including individuals drawn from Federal and State governments, industry, universities, laboratories and other institutions engaged in marine scientific or technological pursuits, but not more than five members shall be from the Federal Government. In addition the Commission shall have four advisory members appointed by the President from among the Members of the Senate and the House of Representatives. Such advisory members shall not participate, except in an advisory capacity, in the formulation of the findings and recommendations of the Commission. The President shall select a Chairman and Vice Chairman from among such fifteen members. The Vice Chairman shall act as Chairman in the latter's absence.

(b) The Commission shall make a comprehensive investigation and study of all aspects of marine science in order to recommend an overall plan for an adequate national oceanographic program that will meet the present and future national needs. The Commission shall undertake a review of existing and planned marine science activities of the United States in order to assess their adequacy in meeting the objectives set forth under section 2(b), including but not limited to the following:

(1) Review the known and contemplated needs for natural resources from the marine environment to maintain our expanding national economy.

(2) Review the surveys, applied research programs, and ocean engineering projects required to obtain the needed resources from the marine environment.

(3) Review the existing national research programs to insure realistic and adequate support for basic oceanographic research that will enhance human welfare and scientific knowledge.

(4) Review the existing oceanographic and ocean engineering programs, including education and technical training, to determine which programs are required to advance our national oceanographic competence and stature and which are not adequately supported.

(5) Analyze the findings of the above reviews, including the economic factors involved, and recommend an adequate national marine science program that will meet the present and future national needs without unnecessary duplication of effort.

(6) Recommend a Governmental organizational plan with estimated cost.

(c) Members of the Commission appointed from outside the Government shall each receive $100 per diem when engaged in the actual performance of duties of the Commission and reimbursement of travel expenses, including per diem in lieu of subsistence, as authorized in section 5 of the Administrative Expenses Act of 1946, as amended (5U.S.C. 73b-2), for persons employed intermittently. Members of the Commission appointed from within the Government shall serve without additional compensation to that received for their services to the Government but shall be reimbursed for travel expenses, including per diem in lieu of subsistence, as authorized in the Act of June 9, 1949, as amended (5U.S.C. 835-842).

(d) The Commission shall appoint and fix the compensation of such personnel as it deems advisable in accordance with the civil service laws and the Classification Act of 1949, as amended. In addition, the Commission may secure temporary and intermittent services to the same extent as is authorized for the departments by section 15 of the Administrative Expenses Act of 1946 (60 Stat. 810) but at rates not to exceed $100 per diem for individuals.

(e) The Chairman of the Commission shall be responsible for (1) the assignment of duties and responsibilities among such personnel and their continuing supervision, and (2) the use and expenditures of funds available to the Commission. In carrying out the provisions of this subsection, the Chairman shall be governed by the general policies of the Commission with respect to the work to be accomplished by it and the timing thereof.

(f) Financial and administrative services (including those related to budgeting, accounting, financial reporting, personnel, and procurement) may be provided the Commission by the General Services Administration, for which payment shall be made in advance, or by reimbursement from funds of the Commission in such amounts as may be agreed upon by the Chairman of the Commission and the Administrator of General Services: Provided, That the regulations of the General Services Administration for the collection of indebtedness of personnel resulting from erroneous payments (5U.S.C. 46d) shall apply to the collection of erroneous payments made to or on behalf of a Commission employee, and regulations of said Administrator for the administrative control of funds (31 U.S.C. 665(g) shall apply to appropriations of the Commission: And provided further, That the Commission shall not be required to prescribe such regulations.

(g) The Commission is authorized to secure directly from any executive department, agency, or independent instrumentality of the Government any information it deems necessary to carry out its functions under this Act; and each such department, agency, and instrumentality is authorized to cooperate with the Commission and, to the extent permitted by law, to furnish such information to the Commission, upon request made by the Commission.

(h) The Commission shall submit to the President, via the Council, and to the Congress not later than eighteen months after the establishment of the Commission as provided in subsection (a) of this section, a final report of its findings and recommendations. The Commission shall cease to exist thirty days after it has submitted its final report.

International Cooperation

Sec. 6. The Council, under the foreign policy guidance of the President and as he may request, shall coordinate a program of international cooperation in work done pursuant to this Act, pursuant to agreements made by the President with the advice and consent of the Senate.

Reports

Sec. 7. (a) The President shall transmit to the Congress in January of each year a report, which shall include (1) a comprehensive description of the activities and the accomplishments of all agencies and departments of the United States in the field of marine science during the preceding fiscal year, and (2) an evaluation of such activities and accomplishments in terms of the objectives set forth pursuant to this Act.

(b) Reports made under this section shall contain such recommendations for legislation as the President may consider necessary or desirable for the attainment of the objectives of this Act, and shall contain an estimate of funding requirements of each agency and department of the United States for marine science activities during the succeeding fiscal year.

Definitions

Sec. 8. For the purposes of this Act the term "marine science" shall be deemed to apply to oceanographic and scientific endeavors and disciplines, and engineering and technology in and with relation to the marine environment; and the term "marine environment" shall be deemed to include (a) the oceans, (b) the Continental Shelf of the United States, (c) the Great Lakes, (d) seabed and subsoil of the submarine areas adjacent to the coasts of the United States to the depth of two hundred meters, or beyond that limit, to where the depths of the superjacent waters admit of the exploitation of the natural resources of such areas, (e) the seabed and subsoil of similar submarine areas adjacent to the coasts of islands which comprise United States territory, and (f) the resources thereof. ...

DECISION MAKING RESPONSIBILITIES FOR

MARINE SCIENCE AFFAIRS

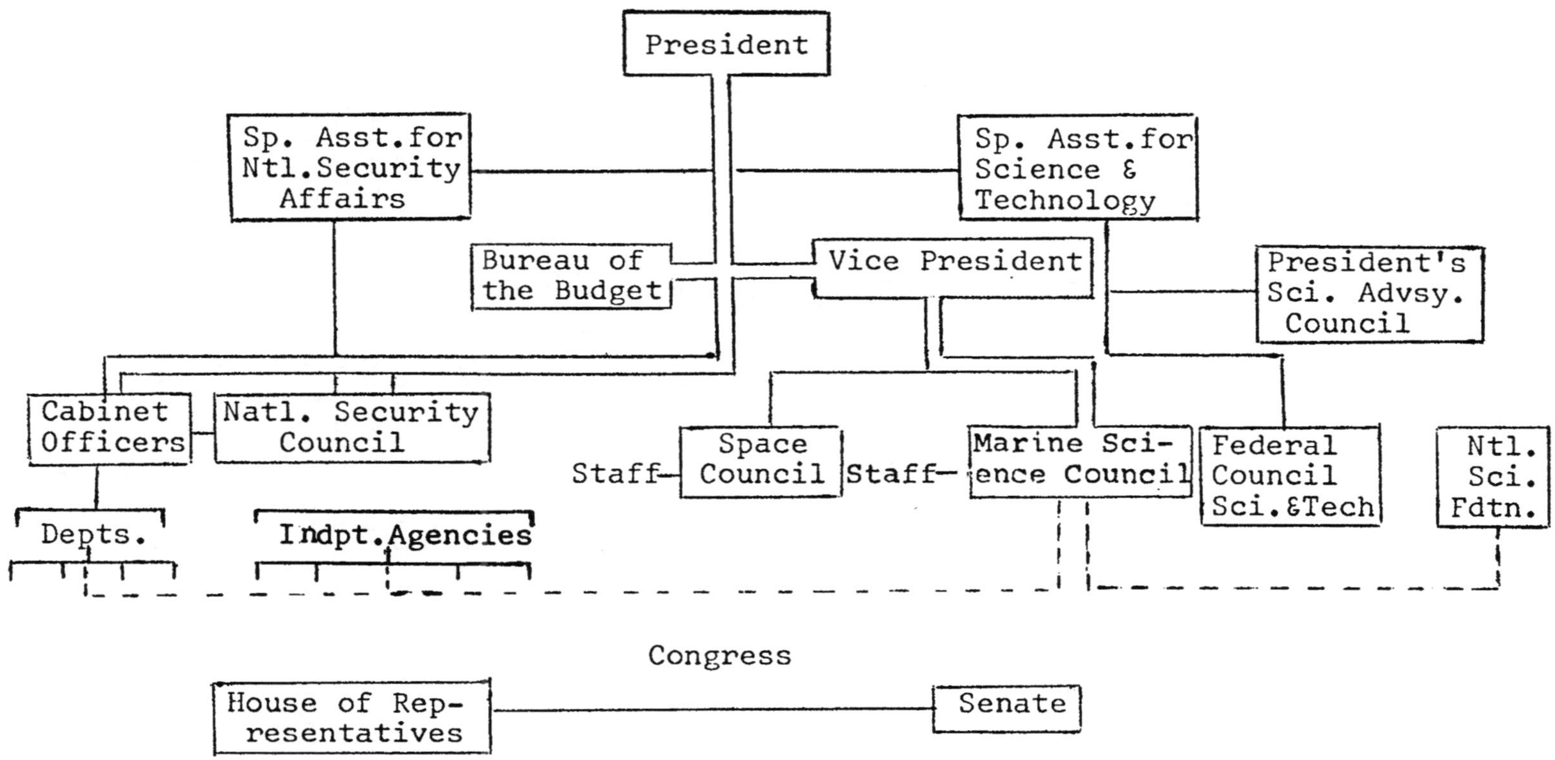

Comttee. on Appropriations
Armed Services
Agriculture
Foreigh Affrs.
Govt. Operations
Interior & Insul.Affs.
Mercht.Marine & Fisheries
Public Works

Commttee. on Appropriations
Armed Services
Agricult.& Forestry
Foreign Relations
Govt. Operations
Interior & Insul. Affs.
Interstate & For.Commerce
Public Works

NATIONAL SEA GRANT COLLEGES AND PROGRAMS ACT

Public Law 89-688,
89th Congress, H.R. 16559,
October 15, 1966

Be it enacted ... That the Marine Resources and Engineering Development Act of 1966 is amended by adding at the end thereof the following new title:

"TITLE II - SEA GRANT COLLEGES AND PROGRAMS

"Declaration of Purpose

"Sec. 202. The Congress hereby finds and declares ---

"(a) that marine resources, including animal and vegetable life and mineral wealth, constitute a far-reaching and largely untapped asset of immense potential significance to the United States; and

"(b) that it is in the national interest of the United States to develop the skilled manpower, including scientists, engineers, and technicians, and the facilities and equipment necessary for the exploitation of these resources; and

"(c) that aquaculture, as with agriculture on land, and the gainful use of marine resources can substantially benefit the United States, and ultimately the people of the world, by providing greater economic opportunities, including expanded employment and commerce; the enjoyment and use of our marine resources; new sources of food; and new means for the development of marine resources; and

"(d) that Federal support toward the establishment, development, and operation of programs by sea grant colleges and Federal support of other sea grant programs designed to achieve the gainful use of marine resources, offer the best means of promoting programs toward the goals set forth in clauses (a), (b), and (c), and should be undertaken by the Federal Government; and

"(e) that in view of the importance of achieving the earliest possible institution of significant national activities related to the development of marine resources, it is the purpose of this title to provide for the establishment of a program of sea grant colleges and education, training, and research in the fields of marine science, engineering, and related disciplines.

"Grants and Contracts For Sea Grant Colleges and Programs

"Sec. 203. (a) The provisions of this title shall be administered by the National Science Foundation (hereafter in this title referred to as the 'Foundation').

"(b) (1) For the purpose of carrying out this title, there is authorized to be appropriated to the Foundation for the fiscal year ending in June 30, 1967, not to exceed the sum of $5,000,000, for the fiscal year ending June 30, 1968, not to exceed the sum of $15,000,000, and for each subsequent fiscal year only such sums as the Congress may hereafter specifically authorize by law.

"(2) Amounts appropriated under this title are authorized to remain available until expended.

"Marine Resources

"Sec. 204. (a) In carrying out the provisions of this title the Foundation shall (1) consult with those experts engaged in pursuits in the various fields related to the development of marine resources and with all departments and agencies of the Federal Governmnet (including the United States Office of Education in all matters relating to education) interested in, or affected by, activities in any such fields, and (2) seek advice and counsel from the National Council on Marine Resources and Engineering Development as provided by section 205 of this title.

"(b) The Foundation shall exercise its authority under this title by ---

"(1) initiating and supporting programs at sea grant colleges and other suitable institutes, laboratories, and public or private agencies for the education of participants in the various fields relating to the development of marine resources;

"(2) initiating and supporting necessary research programs in the various fields relating to the development of marine resources with preference given to research aimed at practices, techniques, and design of equipment applicable to the development of marine resources; and

"(3) encouraging and developing programs consisting of instruction, practical demonstrations, publications, and otherwise, by sea grant colleges and other suitable institutes, laboratories, and public or private agencies through marine advisory programs with the object of imparting useful information to persons currently employed or interested in the various fields related to the development of marine resources, the scientific community, and the general public.

"(c) Programs to carry out the purposes of this title shall be accomplished through contracts with, or grants to suitable public or private institutions of higher education, institutes, laboratories, and public or private agencies which are engaged in, or concerned with, activities in the various fields related to the development of marine resources, for the establishment and operation by them of such programs.

"(d) (1) The total amount of payments in any fiscal year under any grant to or contract with any participant in any program to be carried out by such participant under this title shall not exceed 66 2/3 per centum of the total cost of any such program. For purposes of computing the amount of the total cost of any such program furnished by any participant in any fiscal year, the Foundation shall include in such computation an amount equal to the reasonable value of any buildings, facilities, equipment, supplies, or services provided by such participant with respect to such program (but not the cost of value of land or of Federal contributions).

"(2) No portion of any payment by the Foundation to any participant in any program to be carried out under this title shall be applied to the purchase or rental of any land or the rental, purchase, construction, preservation, or repair of any building, dock, or vessel.

"(3) The total amount of payments in any fiscal year by the Foundation to participants within any State shall not exceed 15 per centum of the total amount appropriated to the Foundation for the purposes of this title for such fiscal year.

"(e) In allocating funds appropriated in any fiscal year for the purposes of this title the Foundation shall endeavor to achieve maximum participation by sea grant colleges and other suitable institutes, laboratories, and public or private agencies throughout the United States, consistent with the purposes of this title.

"(f) In carrying out its functions under this title, the Foundation shall attempt to support programs in such a manner as to supplement and not duplicate or overlap any existing and related Government activities.

"(g) Except as otherwise provided in this title,the Foundation shall, in carrying out its functions under this title, have the same powers and authority it has under the National Science Foundation Act of 1950 to carry out its functions under that Act.

"(h) The head of each department, agency, or instrumentality of the Federal Government is authorized, upon request of the Foundation, to make available to the Foundation, from time to time, on a reimbursable basis, such personnel, services, and facilities as may be necessary to assist the Foundation in carrying out its functions under this title.

"(i) For the purposes of this title --

"(1) the term 'development of marine resources' means scientific endeavors relating to the marine environment, including, but not limited to, the fields oriented toward the development, conservation, or economic utilization of the physical, chemical, geological, and biological resources of the marine environment; the fields of marine commerce and marine engineering; the fields relating to exploration or research in, the recovery of natural resources from, and the transmission of energy in, the marine environment; the fields of oceanography and oceanology; and the fields with respect to the study of the economic, legal, medical, or sociological problems arising out of the management, use, development, recovery, and control of the natural resources of the marine environment;

"(2) the term 'marine environment' means the oceans; the Continental Shelf of the United States; the Great Lakes; the seabed and subsoil of the submarine areas adjacent to the coasts of the United States to the depth of two hundred meters, or beyond that limit, to where the depths of the superjacent waters admit of the exploitation of the natural resources of the area; the seabed and subsoil of similar submarine areas adjacent to the coasts of islands which comprise United States territory; and the natural resources thereof;

"(3) the term 'sea grant college' means any suitable public or private institution of higher education supported pursuant to the purposes of this title which has major programs devoted to increasing our Nation's utilization of the world's marine resources; and

"(4) the term 'sea grant program' means (A) any activities of education or research related to the development of marine resources supported by the Foundation by contracts with or grants to institutions of higher education either initiating, or developing existing, programs in fields related to the purposes of this title, (B) any activities of education or research related to the development of marine resources supported by the Foundation by contracts with or grants to suitable institutes, laboratories, and public or private agencies, and (C) any programs of advisory services oriented toward imparting information in fields related to the development of marine resources supported by the Foundation, by contracts with or grants to suitable institutes, laboratories, and public or private agencies.

"Advisory Functions

"Sec. 205. The National Council on Marine Resources and Engineering Development established by section 3 of title I of this Act shall, as the President may request --

"(1) advise the Foundation with respect to the policies, procedures, and operations of the Foundation in carrying out its functions under this title;

"(2) provide policy guidance to the Foundation with respect t contracts or grants in support of programs conducted pursuant to this title, and make such recommendations thereon to the Foundation as may be appropriate; and

"(3) submit an annual report on its activities and its recommendations under this section to the Speaker of the House of Representatives, the Committee on Merchant Marine and Fisheries of the House of Representatives, the President of the Senate, and the Committee on Labor and Public Welfare of the Senate...."

NEW OCEAN RESEARCH TOOL - USNS SILAS BENT

Courtesy U.S. Naval Oceanographic Office

CHAPTER TWO

TERRITORIAL WATERS AND CONTIGUOUS ZONES

Introductory Note

States customarily extend their jurisdiction over a belt of marginal waters off their shores which has become known as the territorial sea. Foreign war ships are generally forbidden to enter these waters or ports without prior permission, and public vessels must have clearance to go into or remain in such areas. Innocent passage through territorial waters is normally tolerated except when national defense requirements make it necessary to establish security zones, or when vessels engage in activities in violation of local laws. By contrast, the high seas are as the Supreme Court of the United States has declared "common to all nations and foreign to none, and every nation having vessels there has power to regulate them and also to seize them for a violation of its laws" (Maul v. United States, 1927, 274 U.S. 501).

So-called defensive sea areas were widely employed during World War I. Such areas were authorized by Act of Congress on March 4, 1917, and thirty-three zones of this nature were set up between 1917-18. These were discontinued in 1919. Similar areas were again instituted in World War II as a protective measure.

By the Anti-Smuggling Act of August 5, 1935, the Congress authorized the President to establish Customs Enforcement Areas when he had reason to believe attempts were being made to violate the revenue or customs laws of the United States. These areas may extend as much as fifty miles from shore, and laterally one hundred miles. Five such zones have been set up at one time or another to deter smuggling or to stop gambling ship operations. In no place were these extended more than twelve miles from low water, however. All were terminated in 1946.

Expansion of national jurisdiction has been occurring in recent years as various states have found it desirable or necessary to proclaim rights in what have been called contiguous zones. Such claims have been asserted mainly for the purpose of conserving fishery resources and restricting fishing rights in these areas to local fishermen. In most instances these zones have been limited to waters lying between the three and twelve mile lines. President Truman, for example, in a proclamation dated September 28, 1945, reserved the coastal fisheries of certain areas off the United States to American fishermen. This was followed twenty years later by formal enactment of legislation establishing a contiguous fishing zone between the three mile and twelve mile lines. Other nations have made similar reservations. Some states have claimed sovereignty as far out as 200 miles from their shores and insisted that foreign fishermen have explicit authorization from local port officials to operate in these waters.

Not long ago the terminal line of territorial waters was generally accepted as being three miles from shore. This line, hallowed by tradition and celebrated by courts, dates back to 1702 when the Dutch jurist Cornelius Van Bynkershoek argued that national jurisdiction should extend only so far as the territorial sorereign was able to extend his sway. In his day the major weapon of defense was the cannon, whose fire was limited to three miles. This distance then became a rule of convenience adopted by the smaller and weaker states to restrain the pretensions of the great naval powers of the time--Britain and Spain--who claimed rights to rule the seas. Eventually Britain recognized the advantage of claiming a measurable line that could be policed.

As the Supreme Court of the United States said in the case of the Cunard Steamship Company v. Mellon in 1923: "It is now settled in the United States and recognized elsewhere that the territory subject to its jurisdiction includes the land areas under its dominion and control, the ports, harbors, bays and other enclosed arms of the sea along its coast and a marginal belt of the sea extending from the coast line outward a marine league, or three geographical miles" (262 U.S. 100).

The trend for nations to claim larger marginal belts is illustrated in the Table of Maritime Jurisdiction Claimed by States. Now more nations adhere to the twelve mile line than to the older three mile limit. There is some logic in this movement in as much as many states have for some time insisted on the right to enforce their customs and revenue laws within four leagues of their shores. The United States is included in this group notwithstanding its general championship of the three mile rule for territorial waters.

Divisions still exist among states not only on the extent and nature of national jurisdiction, but also over the activities that may be performed within territorial waters and contiguous zones. To prevent misunderstandings and difficulties, the United States advises all oceanographers that they should obtain foreign clearance before attempting to undertake any research or surveying projects in the territorial waters or over the continental shelves of other states. In the hope of resolving differences between countries, moves have been made to convene a new Law of the Sea Conference to try to reach further agreement regarding territorial waters and contiguous zones. Meanwhile, a considerable measure of uncertainty may continue to exist as nations increasingly interpose themselves in affairs of the seas.

The readings that follow illustrate a few of the ways in which states have extended their jurisdiction over portions of the seas and over vessels and persons thereon.

For further discussion the reader is referred to L. G. Parks, "The Law Of and Under the Sea," U.S. Naval Institute Proceedings, February 1966, pp. 54-60; Capt. G. E. Carlisle, "Three Mile Limit: Obsolete Concept," ibid., February 1967, pp. 25-33; U.S. Naval War College, International Law Documents, 1948-49, especially pp. 159-180; Myres S. McDougal and William T. Burke, The Public Order of the Oceans: A Contemporary International Law of the Sea (New Haven, Yale University Press,

1962); Lewis M. Alexander (ed.), <u>The Law of the Sea: Offshore Boundaries and Zones</u> (Columbus, Ohio State Press, 1967).

TERRITORIAL WATERS OF THE UNITED STATES

Manchester vs. Massachusetts

U.S. Supreme Court, 1891

139 U.S. 258

... "We think it must be regarded as established that, as between nations, the minimum limit of territorial jurisdiction of a nation over tide waters is a marine league from its coast; that bays wholly within its territory not exceeding two marine leagues in width at the mouth are within this limit; and that included in this territorial jurisdiction is the right of control over fisheries, whether the fish be migratory, free-swimming fish, or free moving fish, or fish attached to or embedded in the soil. The open sea within this limit is, of course, subject to the common right of navigation; and all governments, for the purpose of self-protection in time of war or for the prevention of frauds on its revenue, exercise an authority beyond this limit."

NAVIGATION AND NAVIGABLE WATERS OF THE

UNITED STATES

United States Code
Title 33
Chapter 1

Sec. 2.10-1 High Seas

(a) For the purpose of describing Coast Guard jurisdiction generally ... the Act of May 10, 1956 (46 U.S.C. 390) and other laws relating to navigation, navigable waters or vessel inspection, the term "high seas" shall be considered to be those parts of a sea or ocean which are not included in the territorial sea or in the internal waters of a nation.

(b) For the purposes of the Rules of the Road ... the term "high seas" shall be construed to be the waters upon which the "Rules of the Road - International" shall apply.

(c) For the purposes of describing Coast Guard jurisdiction with respect to criminal offenses under Title 18, U.S. Code, the term "high seas" as defined in Section 7 of Title 18, U.S. Code, includes the territorial sea as well as the seas beyond the territorial sea which are "out of the jurisdiction of any particular State."

Sec. 2.10-5 Navigable Waters of the United States

(a) As used in the Federal Boating Act of 1958 (46 U.S.C. 527 a and 527 e), ... and other laws, the term "navigable waters of the United States" shall be construed to mean those waters of the United States, including the territorial seas adjacent thereto, the general character of which, either by themselves or by uniting with other waters, form a continuous waterway on which boats or vessels may navigate or travel between two or more States, or to or from foreign nations...

Sec. 2.10-10 Waters Subject to the Jurisdiction of the United States

(a) As used in Sec. 2 of Title 14, U.S. Code, the term "waters subject to the jurisdiction of the United States," for purposes of enforcement of navigation and vessel inspection laws and regulations administered by the Coast Guard, means the navigable waters of its territories and possessions.

Sec. 2.15-1 Coast Guard Determination

(a) In the administration and enforcement of laws enacted by Congress the Coast Guard is frequently called upon to make determinations with respect to jurisdiction. It should be understood that such determinations represent the Coast Guard's view until the status of the waters is determined conclusively through judicial or legislative proceedings.

CUSTOMS WATERS, ENFORCEMENT PROVISIONS

CUSTOMS ENFORCEMENT AREA

TARIFF ACT OF 1930

Public Law 361
June 17, 1930
46 Stat. 708
United States Code,
Title 19

Part I - Definitions

Sec. 1401 Customs Waters

Officer of the Customs

(l) The term "officer of the customs" means any officer of the Customs Service or any commissioned, warrant or petty officer of the Coast Guard, or agent or other person authorized by law or by the Secretary of the Treasury, or appointed in writing by a Collector, to perform the duties of an officer of the Customs Service.

Customs Waters

(m) The term "customs waters" means, in the case of a foreign vessel subject to a treaty or other arrangement between a foreign government and the United States enabling or permitting the authorities of the United States to board, examine, search, seize, or otherwise to enforce upon such vessel upon the high seas the laws of the United States, the waters within such distance of the coast of the United States as the said authorities are or may be so enabled or permitted by such treaty or arrangement and, in the case of every other vessel, the waters within four leagues of the coast of the United States.

Hovering Vessel

(n) The term "hovering vessel" means any vessel which is found or kept off the coast of the United States within or without the customs waters, if, from the history, conduct, character, or location of the vessel it is reasonable to believe that such vessel is being used or may be used to introduce or promote or facilitate the introduction or attempted introduction of merchandise into the United States in violation of the laws respecting the revenue. June 17, 1930, c. 497, Title lV, Sec. 401. 46 Stat. 708.

Part V - Enforcement Provisions

Sec. 1581 Boarding Vessels

(a) Any **officer** of the customs may at any time go on board of any vessel **or** vehicle at any place in the United States or within the **customs** waters or, as he may be authorized, within a **customs-enforcement** area established under sections 1701 and 1703 1711 of this title, or at any other authorized place, without as well as within his district, and examine the manifest and other documents and papers and examine, inspect, and search the vessel or vehicle and every part thereof and any person, trunk, package, or cargo on board, and to this end may hail and stop such vessel or vehicle, and use all necessary force to compel compliance.

(b) Officers of the Department of the Treasury and other persons authorized by such department may ... board such vessel in the enforcement of the navigation laws, and arrest or, in case of escape or attempted escape, pursue and arrest any person engaged in the breach or violation of the navigation laws.

(c) Any master of a vessel being examined as herein provided, who presents any forged, altered, or false document or paper to the examining officer, knowing the same to be forged, altered, or false and without revealing the fact shall, in addition to any forfeiture to which in consequence the vessel may be subject, be liable to a fine of not more than $5,000 nor less than $500.

(d) Any vessel ... [failing] to comply shall become subject to pursuit and the master, owner, operator, or person in charge thereof shall be liable to a penalty of not more than $5,000 nor less than $1,000.

(e) ... such vessel or vehicle, or the merchandise or any part thereof shall be liable to forfeiture or to secure any fine or penalty, the same shall be seized and any person who has engaged in such breach shall be arrested ...

(g) Any vessel, within or without the customs waters, from which any merchandise is being, or has been, unlawfully introduced into the United States by means of any boat belonging to, or owned, controlled, or managed in common with, said vessel, shall be deemed to be employed within the United States and, as such, subject to the provisions of this section. June 17, 1930, c.497, Title IV, Sec. 581, 46 Stat. 747.

Sec. 1701 Customs-Enforcement Areas

(a) Whenever the President finds and declares that at any place or within any area on the high seas adjacent to but outside customs waters any vessel or vessels hover or are being kept off the coast of the United States and that, by virtue of the presence of such vessel or vessels at such place or within such area, the unlawful introduction or removal into or from the United States of any merchandise or person is being or may be occasioned, promoted, or threatened, the place or area so found and declared shall constitute a customs-enforcement area... No customs-enforcement area shall include any waters more than one hundred nautical miles from the place or immediate area where the President declares such vessel or vessels are hovering... and... shall not include any waters more than fifty nautical miles outwards from the outer limit of customs waters... The provisions of law applying to the high seas adjacent to customs waters of the United States shall be enforced in a customs-enforcement area upon any vessel, merchandise, or person found therein... August 5, 1935, c.438, Title I, Sec. 1, 49 Stat. 517.

AUTHORITY OF THE UNITED STATES COAST GUARD

United States Code
Title 14
Chap. 1

Sec. 2 Primary Duties

The Coast Guard shall enforce or assist in the enforcement of all applicable Federal laws upon the high seas and waters subject to the jurisdiction of the United States; shall administer laws and promulgate and enforce regulations for the promotion of safety of life and property on the high seas and on waters subject to the jurisdiction of the United States covering all matters not specifically delegated by law to some other executive department; shall develop, establish, maintain, and operate, with due regard to the requirements of national defense, aids to maritime navigation, ice breaking facilities, and rescue facilities for the promotion of safety on and over the high seas and waters subject to the jurisdiction of the United States; shall engage in oceanographic research on the high seas and in waters subject to the jurisdiction of the United States; and shall maintain a state of readiness to function as a specialized service of the Navy in time of war. Aug. 4, 1949, c. 393. 63 Stat. 496.

Chap. 5

Sec. 89 Law Enforcement

(a) The Coast Guard may make inquiries, examinations, inspections, searches, seizures, and arrests upon the high seas and waters over which the United States has jurisdiction, for the preservation, detection, and suppression of violations of laws of the United States. For such purposes, commissioned, warrant, and petty officers may at any time go on board of any vessel subject to the jurisdiction, or to the operation of any law, of the United States, address inquiries to those on board, examine the ship's documents and papers, and examine, inspect, and search the vessel and use all necessary force to compel compliance. When from such inquiries, examinations, inspection, or search it appears that a breach of the laws of the United States rendering a person liable to arrest is being, or has been committed, by any person, such person shall be arrested or, if escaping to shore, shall be immediately pursued and arrested on shore, or other lawful and appropriate action shall be taken; or if it shall appear that a breach of the laws of the United States has been committed so as to render such vessel, or the merchandise, or any part thereof, on board of, or brought into the United States by, such vessel, liable to forfeiture, or so as to render such vessel liable to a fine or penalty and if necessary to secure such fine or penalty, such vessel or such merchandise, or both, shall be seized. Aug. 4, 1949, c. 393. 63 Stat. 502.

Sec. 90 Ocean Stations

(a) The Coast Guard is authorized to operate and maintain floating ocean stations for the purpose of providing search and rescue, communication, and air navigation facilities, and meteorological services in such ocean areas as are regularly traversed by aircraft of the United States. Aug. 4, 1949, c. 393. 63 Stat. 502.

Sec. 94 Oceanographic Research

The Coast Guard shall conduct such oceanographic research, use such equipment or instruments, and collect and analyse such oceanographic data, in cooperation with other agencies of the Government, or not, as may be in the national interest. P.L. 87-396, Oct. 5, 1961. 75 Stat. 827.

ADMIRALTY AND MARITIME JURISDICTION

OF THE UNITED STATES

United States Code
Title 19 A

Sec. 740 Extension of Jurisdiction

The admiralty and maritime jurisdiction of the United States shall extend to and include all cases of damage or injury, to persons or property, caused by a vessel on navigable water, notwithstanding that such damage or injury be done or consumated on land. June 19, 1948, c.526, 62 Stat. 496.

Note

The jurisdiction of the Federal Government over navigable waterways is based on Article I, Section 8 of the United States Constitution giving the Congress the power to regulate commerce with foreign nations and among the several States, and to make all laws necessary for carrying into execution all powers vested by the Constitution in the United States. It is also based on Article III, Section 2, providing that " The judicial power shall extend to ... all cases of admiralty and maritime jurisdiction..."

COOK v. UNITED STATES (THE MAZEL TOV)

Supreme Court of the United States, 1933

288 U.S. 102

[The Mazel Tov, a British registered vessel, was seized by United States Coast Guard officers 11.5 miles off the coast of Massachusetts and taken into Providence, R.I. where proceedings were instituted against the vessel and its master under Sections 584 and 594 of the Customs laws.

The vessel had cleared from the French island of St. Pierre and was ostensibly bound for Nassau, B.W.I. with an unmanifested cargo of liquor. For some time prior to her stoppage and seizure the vessel had been cruising slowly off the U.S. coast with apparent intent of transshipping the liquor to other boats to be taken into the United States in contravention of the Prohibition laws. At the time of seizure apparently no liquor had been unloaded. The record showed no evidence of radio or other communication with shore. The speed of the vessel did not exceed ten miles an hour.

The District Court dismissed the libel on exceptions being taken to the jurisdiction of the Coast Guard to seize the vessel more than one hour's sailing time from the shore under the terms of the United States-British Liquor Treaty of 1924. On appeal the Circuit Court of Appeals reversed the action. It held that the treaty which established the one hour sailing rule did not create a "change in the customs-revenue laws of the United States wherein Congress had fixed a four league protective zone."

On further appeal to the United States Supreme Court, Cook, the master, argued that the terms of the treaty had superceded the customs laws with respect to liquor and that the Coast Guard lacked the right to seize the Mazel Tov more than one hour of her sailing time from the shore.

The pertinent provisions of the Liquor Treaty were as follows:

"Article I. The High Contracting Parties declare that it is their firm intention to uphold the principle that

3 marine miles extending from the coastline outwards and measured from low-water mark constitute the proper limits of territorial waters.

"Article II. (1) His Britannic Majesty agrees that he will raise no objection to the boarding of private vessels under the British flag outside the limits of territorial waters by the authorities of the United States, its territories or possessions in order that enquiries may be addressed to those on board and an examination be made of the ship's papers for the purpose of ascertaining whether the vessel or those on board are endeavoring to import or have imported alcoholic beverages into the United States, its territories or possessions in violation of the laws there in force. When such enquiries and examination show a reasonable ground for suspicion, a search of the vessel may be instituted.

"(2) If there is reasonable cause for belief that the vessel has committed or is committing or attempting to commit an offense against the laws of the United States, its territories or possessions prohibiting the importation of alcoholic beverages, the vessel may be seized and taken into a port of the United States, its territories or possessions for adjudication in accordance with such laws.

"(3) The rights conferred by this article shall not be exercised at a greater distance from the coast of the United States, its territories or possessions than can be traversed in one hour by the vessel suspected of endeavoring to commit the offense. In cases, however, in which the liquor is intended to be conveyed to the United States, its territories or possessions by a vessel other than the one boarded and searched, it shall be the speed of such other vessel and not the speed of the vessel boarded, which shall determine the distance from the coast at which the right under this article can be exercised.

"Article III. No penalty or forfeiture under the laws of the United States shall be applicable or attached to alcoholic liquors or to vessels or persons by reason of the carriage of such liquors, when such liquors are listed as sea stores or cargo destined for a port foreign to the United States, its territories or possessions on board British vessels voyaging to or from ports of the United States, or its territories or possessions or passing through the territorial waters thereof, and such carriage shall be as now provided by law with respect to the transit of such liquors through the Panama Canal, provided that such liquors shall be kept under seal continuously while the vessel on which they are carried remains within said territorial waters and that no part of such liquors shall at any time or place be unladen within the United States, its territories or possessions."]

MR. JUSTICE BRANDEIS delivered the opinion of the Court as follows:

The Government insists that the Treaty did not have the effect of so modifying Section 581 of the [Tariff] Act of 1922; and that, if it did, the re-enactment of Section 581 without change, by the Act of 1930, removed the alleged modification. ...

It is suggested on behalf of the Government that the power to search and seize within the twelve-mile zone conferred upon officers of the Coast Guard by Section 581 of the Tariff Act of 1922, was unaffected by the Treaty, save that the British Government agreed not to protest where the seizure was within an hour's sailing distance of the coast. The argument is that the Treaty settled the validity of the seizure only for those cases where it was made within the limits described in the Treaty; and that since this seizure was made beyond one hour's sailing distance from the coast the Treaty did not apply. In construing the Treaty its history should be consulted.... Both its language and its history show that the high contracting parties did not intend so to limit its operation.... The history reveals that serious differences had arisen between the two Governments in that connection; and that, for the purpose of resolving them, the parties determined to deal completely with the subject of search and seizure. beyond our territorial limits, of British vessels suspected of smuggling liquors.

Prior to the Eighteenth Amendment the United States had never attempted, in connection with the enforcement of our customs laws, to board foreign vessels beyond the three-mile limit except where consent was implied from the fact that the vessel, being hailed, answered that she was bound for the United States, or where a vessel had been discovered violating our laws within the three-mile limit and, while endeavoring to escape, was hotly pursued. Although Hovering Acts conferring authority to board and search vessels, foreign and domestic, "within four leagues of the coast," had existed since the foundation of our Government, see Act of August 4,1790,c.35,Section 31, 1 Stat.145,164, the authority therein conferred had, prior to the Tariff Act of 1922, been in terms limited to inbound vessels; and no statute had purported to confer authority to seize foreign vessels beyond our territorial waters for violation of any of our laws, except in those few instances in which Congress acted pursuant to specific treaties. But soon after the Eighteenth Amendment took effect (January 16,1920), vessels of British registry were found to be engaged in smuggling intoxicating liquors into the United States in violation of our laws. In the effort to prevent such violations British vessels were being boarded, searched and seized beyond the three-mile limit; and by Section 581 of the Tariff Act of 1922 Congress undertook to sanction such action through enlarging the authority to board, search and seize beyond the three-mile limit so as to include foreign vessels although not inbound.

Both before and after the passage of the Tariff Act of 1922 it was the consistent policy of our Government to release, upon protest, all British vessels seized beyond the three-mile limit and not bound to the United States, unless it appeared that the hovering vessel had, by means of her own small boats and crew, assisted in landing there contraband goods. Our Government deemed that exception an essential to the enforcement of our laws and consistent with the principles of international law. But the British Government declined to acquiesce in the propriety of the exception; declared that our practice of seizing vessels under those circumstances was not in harmony with the law of nations; protested against the seizure of any British vessel outside of the three-mile limit; and stated that insistence upon the practice would be regarded as creating "a very serious situation."

With a view to removing the British objections, the Secretary of State proposed, on June 26,1922, that a treaty be entered into "under which the authorities of each nation would be authorized to exercise beyond the three-mile limit of territorial waters a measure of control over vessels belonging to the other" and which would include specifically "reciprocal provisions authorizing the authorities of each Government to exercise a right of search of vessels of the other beyond the three-mile limit of territorial waters to the extent of twlve miles from the shore." The British Government declined definitely to entertain any such proposal.

The decision rendered by this Court on April 30,1923, in Cunard Steamship Co. v. Mellon, 262 U.S. 100, led to the resumption of negotiations. It was there decided that the National Prohibition Act applied to all merchant vessels, foreign or domestic, within the territorial waters of the United States, and that the carrying of intoxicating liquors, either as cargo or as sea stores, through the territorial waters or into the ports and harbors of the United States is forbidden by that Act and the Eighteenth Amendment. The embarrassment to British vessels and trade threatened by this decision was serious. Recognizing the urgent need of some arrangement between the two Governments which would permit the conduct by the British of legitimate trade and remove this obstacle to the operation of their vessels in the accustomed manner, the Secretary of State submitted to Great Britain, on June 11, 1923, the draft of a treaty designed to remove the friction between the two Governments. The draft did not refer specifically to intoxicating liquors. Article I provided in general terms, that the authorities of each country should "within the distance of twelve geographical miles from its coasts" be permitted to board and search private vessels of the other to ascertain whether such vessels were engaged in an attempt to violate its laws "prohibiting or regulating the unloading near, or importation into its territories of any article"; and "if there is reasonable cause for belief" that the vessel is so engaged to seize it. Article II, likewise, in general terms, provided that articles on private vessels of either nation listed as sea stores, or as cargo destined to a foreign port, the importation of which is prohibited, might be brought within the territorial waters of the other on condition that they be sealed "upon arrival of the vessel so destined within twelve geographical miles of the coasts" and be kept sealed continuously thereafter while within the territorial waters.

This proposal of the Secretary of State also failed to meet with the approval of the British Government because it was regarded as involving an extension of the limits of territorial waters. The negotiations were, however, continued; and ultimately the British Government submitted a counter-proposal, which sought to achieve the same results by different means. The British draft provided that the high contracting parties should declare "their firm intention to uphold the principle that three marine miles measured from low water mark constitute the proper limits of territorial waters"; and avoiding all language which could possibly indicate a contrary purpose, it made no reference to the twelve-mile limit. Moreover, the arrangement, instead of applying generally to merchandise subject to prohibitory or regulatory laws, was to be limited specifically to intoxicating liquors; and no reciprocal rights were to be conferred. Each country was to secure the immunity required to satisfy its peculiar need. The need of the United States was to be met by providing that His Britannic Majesty "will raise no objection to the boarding," etc., outside the territorial waters at no "greater distance from the coast of the United States than can be traversed in one hour by the vessel suspected of" smuggling. The need of Great Britain was to be met by our allowing "British vessels voyaging to or from the ports or passing through the waters of the United States to have on board alcoholic liquors listed as sea stores or as cargo destined for a foreign port, provided that such liquor is kept under seal while within the jurisdiction of the United States."

The draft of treaty submitted by the British Government was accepted with a few purely verbal changes....

The Treaty, being later in date than the Act of 1922, superceded, so far as inconsistent with the terms of the Act, the authority which had been conferred by Section 581 upon officers of the Coast Guard to board, search and seize beyond our territorial waters.... For in a strict sense the Treaty was self-executing, in that no legislation was necessary to authorize executive action pursuant to its provisions.

The purpose of the provisions for seizure in Section 581, and their practical operation as an aid in the enforcement of the laws prohibiting alcoholic liquors, leave no doubt that the territorial limitations there established were modified by the Treaty. This conclusion is supported by the course of administrative practice. Shortly after the Treaty took effect, the Treasury Department issued amended instructions for the Coast Guard which pointed out, after reciting the provisions of Section 581, that "in cases of special treaties, the provisions of those treaties shall be complied with," and called attention particularly to the recent treaties dealing with the smuggling of intoxicating liquors. The Commandant of the Coast Guard, moreover, was informed in 1927, as the Solicitor General states, that all seizures of British vessels captured in the rum-smuggling trade should be within the terms of the Treaty and that seizing officers should be instructed to produce evidence, not that the vessel was found within the four-league limit, but that she was apprehended within one hour's sailing distance from the coast.

The Treaty was not abrogated by re-enacting Section 581 in the Tariff Act of 1930 in the identical terms of the Act of 1922. A treaty will not be deemed to have been abrogated or modified by a later statute unless such purpose on the part of Congress has been clearly expressed.... Here, the contrary appears. The committee reports and the debates upon the Act of 1930, like the re-enacted section itself, make no reference to the Treaty of 1924. Any doubt as to the construction of the section should be deemed resolved by the consistent departmental practice existing before its re-enactment....

Searches and seizures in the enforcement of the laws prohibiting alcoholic liquors are governed, since the 1930 Act, as they were before, by the provisions of the Treaty. Section 581, with its scope narrowed by the Treaty, remained in force after its re-enactment in the Act of 1930. The section continued to apply to the boarding, search and seizure of all vessels of all countries with which we had no relevant treaties. It continued also, in the enforcement of our customs laws not related to the prohibition of alcoholic liquors, *to govern the boarding of vessels of those* countries with which we had entered into treaties like that with Great Britain....

The decree of the Circuit Court of Appeals is reversed.

Mr. JUSTICE SUTHERLAND and Mr. JUSTICE BUTLER are of opinion that in respect of British vessels engaged in smuggling intoxicating liquor into the United States the treaty of 1924 was not intended to cut down the rights claimed by the United States under the hovering statutes in force since the organization of our government, but that it was the purpose of both countries to extend and enlarge such rights to enable the United States more effectively to enforce its liquor laws and that therefore the decree of the Circuit Court of Appeals should be affirmed.

PRESIDENTIAL PROCLAMATION WITH RESPECT TO COASTAL FISHERIES IN CERTAIN AREAS OF THE HIGH SEAS

September 28, 1945

(10 Federal Register 12304)

Whereas for some years the Government of the United States of America has viewed with concern the inadequacy of present arrangements for the protection and perpetuation of the fishery resources contiguous to its coasts, and in view of the potentially disturbing effect of this situation, has carefully studied the possibility of improving the jurisdictional basis for conservation measures and international cooperation in this field; and

Whereas such fishery resources have a special importance to coastal communities as a source of livelihood and to the nation as a food and industrial resource; and

Whereas the progressive development of new methods and techniques contributes to intensified fishing over wide sea areas and in certain cases seriously threatens fisheries with depletion; and

Whereas there is an urgent need to protect coastal fishery resources from destructive exploitation, having due regard to conditions peculiar to each region and situation and to the special rights and equities of the coastal State and of any other State which may have established a legitimate interest therein;

NOW,THEREFORE, I, HARRY S. TRUMAN, President of the United States of America, do hereby proclaim the following policy of the United States of America with respect to coastal fisheries in certain areas of the high seas:

In view of the pressing need for conservation and protection of fishery resources, the Government of the United States of America regards it as proper to establish conservation zones in those areas of the high seas contiguous to the coasts of the United States wherein fishing activities have been or in the future may be developed and maintained on a substantial scale. Where such activities have been or shall hereafter be developed and maintained by its nationals alone, the United States regards it as proper to establish explicitly bounded conservation zones in which fishing activities shall be subject to the regulation and control of the United States. Where such activities have been or shall hereafter be legitimately developed, maintained jointly by nationals of the United States and nationals of other States, explicitly bounded conservation zones may be established under agreements between the United

States and such other States; and all fishing activities in such zones shall be subject to regulation and control as provided in such agreements. The right of any State to establish conservation zones off its shores in accordance with the above principles is conceded, provided that corresponding recognition is given to any fishing interests of nationals of the United States which may exist in such areas. The character as high seas of the areas in which such conservation zones are established and the right to their free and unimpeded navigation are in no way thus affected. ...

ACT TO PROHIBIT FOREIGN FISHING VESSELS IN THE TERRITORIAL WATERS OF THE UNITED STATES

Public Law 88-308
May 20, 1964
78 Stat. 194
United States Code,
Title 16

It is unlawful for any vessel, except a vessel of the United States, or for any master or other person in charge of such vessel, to engage in the fisheries within territorial waters of the United States, its territories and possessions and the Commonwealth of Puerto Rico, or within any waters in which the United States has the same rights in respect to fisheries as it has in its territorial waters or to engage in the taking of any Continental Shelf fishery resource which pertains to the United States except as provided in this act, or as expressly provided by an international agreement to which the United States is a party. However, sixty days after written notice to the President of the Senate and the Speaker of the House of Representatives of intent to do so, the Secretary of the Treasury may authorize a vessel other than a vessel of the United States to engage in fishing for designated species within the territorial waters of the United States or within any waters in which the United States has the same rights in respect to fisheries as it has in its territorial waters or for resources of the Continental Shelf which appertain to the United States upon certification by the Secretaries of State and of Interior that such permission would be in the national interest and upon concurrence of any State, Commonwealth, territory, or possession directly affected. The authorization in this section may be granted only after a finding by the Secretary of the Interior that the country of registry, documentation, or licensing extends substantially the same fishing privileges for fishery vessels of the United States. Notwithstanding any other provision of law, the Secretary of State, with the concurrence of the Secretaries of Treasury and of Interior, may permit a vessel, other than a vessel of the United States, owned or operated by an international organization of which the United States is a member, to engage in fishery research within the territorial waters of the United States or within any waters in which the United States has the same rights in respect to fisheries as it has in its territorial waters, or for resources of the Continental Shelf which appertain to the United States and to land its catch in a port of the United States in accordance with such conditions as the Secretary may prescribe whenever they determine such action is in the national interest.

(Persons violating this act shall be fined not more than $10,000 or imprisoned for not more than one year or both, and vessels and their apparel and cargo shall be subject to forfeiture.)

AN ACT

TO ESTABLISH A CONTIGUOUS FISHERY ZONE BEYOND THE TERRITORIAL SEA OF THE UNITED STATES[1]

Approved October 14, 1966

Be it enacted by the Senate and House of Representatives of the United States of America in Congress assembled, That there is established a fisheries zone contiguous to the territorial sea of the United States. The United States will exercise the same exclusive rights in respect to fisheries in the zone as it has in its territorial sea, subject to the continuation of traditional fishing by foreign states within this zone as may be recognized by the United States.

Sec. 2. The fisheries zone has as its inner boundary the outer limits of the territorial sea and as its seaward boundary a line drawn so that each point on the line is nine nautical miles from the nearest point in the inner boundary.

Sec. 3. Whenever the President determines that a portion of the fisheries zone conflicts with the territorial waters or fisheries zone of another country, he may establish a seaward boundary for such portion of the zone in substitution for the seaward boundary described in section 2.

Sec. 4. Nothing in this Act shall be construed as extending the jurisdiction of the States to the natural resources beneath and in the waters within the fisheries zone established by this Act or as diminishing their jurisdiction to such resources beneath and in the waters of the territorial seas of the United States.

1. Public Law 89-658, 88th Cong., S. 2218; 80 Stat. 908.

CONVENTION ON THE TERRITORIAL SEA AND THE CONTIGUOUS ZONE

Signed at Geneva, April 29, 1958[1]

PART I: TERRITORIAL SEA

Section I. General

Article 1

1. The sovereignty of a state extends, beyond its land territory and its internal waters, to a belt of sea adjacent to its coast, described as the territorial sea.

2. This sovereignty is exercised subject to the provisions of these articles and to other rules of international law.

Article 2

The sovereignty of a coastal state extends to the airspace over the territorial sea as well as to its bed and subsoil.

Section II. Limits of the Territorial Sea

Article 3

Except where otherwise provided in these articles, the normal baseline for measuring the breadth of the territorial sea is the low-water line along the coast as marked on large-scale charts officially recognized by the coastal state.

1. U.N. Doc. A/CONF.13/L.52

Article 4

1. In localities where the coastline is deeply indented and cut into, or if there is a fringe of islands along the coast in its immediate vicinity, the method of straight baselines joining appropriate points may be employed in drawing the baseline from which the breadth of the territorial sea is measured.

2. The drawing of such baselines must not depart to any appreciable extent from the general direction of the coast, and the sea areas lying within the lines must be sufficiently closely linked to the land domain to be subject to the régime of internal waters.

3. Baselines shall not be drawn to and from low-tide elevations, unless lighthouses or similar installations which are permanently above sea level have been built on them.

4. Where the method of straight baselines is applicable under the provisions of paragraph 1, account may be taken, in determining particular baselines, of economic interests peculiar to the region concerned, the reality and the importance of which are clearly evidenced by a long usage.

5. The system of straight baselines may not be applied by a state in such a manner as to cut off from the high seas the territorial sea of another state.

6. The coastal state must clearly indicate straight baselines on charts, to which due publicity must be given.

Article 5

1. Waters on the landward side of the baseline of the territorial sea form part of the internal waters of the state.

2. Where the establishment of a straight baseline in accordance with Article 4 has the effect of enclosing as internal waters areas which previously had been considered as part of the territorial sea or of the high seas, a right of innocent passage, as provided in Articles 14 to 23, shall exist in those waters.

Article 6

The outer limit of the territorial sea is the line every point of which is at a distance from the nearest point of the baseline equal to the breadth of the territorial sea.

Article 7

1. This article relates only to bays the coasts of which belong to a single state.

2. For the purposes of these articles, a bay is a well-marked indentation whose penetration is in such proportion to the width of its mouth as to contain landlocked waters and constitute more than a mere curvature of the coast. An indentation shall not, however, be regarded as a bay unless its area is as large as, or larger than, that of the semi-circle whose diameter is a line drawn across the mouth of that indentation.

3. For the purpose of measurement, the area of an indentation is that lying between the low-water mark around the shore of the indentation and a line joining the low-water marks of its natural entrance points. Where, because of the presence of islands, an indentation has more than one mouth, the semi-circle shall be drawn on a line as long as the sum total of the lengths of the lines across the different mouths. Islands within an indentation shall be included as if they were part of the water area of the indentation.

4. If the distance between the low-water marks of the natural entrance points of a bay does not exceed twenty-four miles, a closing line may be drawn between these two low-water marks, and the waters enclosed thereby shall be considered as internal waters.

5. Where the distance between the low-water marks of the natural entrance points of a bay exceeds twenty-four miles, a straight baseline of twenty-four miles shall be drawn within the bay in such a manner as to enclose the maximum area of water that is possible with a line of that length.

6. The foregoing provisions shall not apply to so-called "historic" bays, or in any case where the straight baseline system provided for in Article 4 is applied.

Article 8

For the purpose of delimiting the territorial sea, the outermost permanent harbour works which form an integral part of the harbour system shall be regarded as forming part of the coast.

Article 9

Roadsteads which are normally used for the loading, unloading and anchoring of ships, and which would otherwise be situated wholly or partly outside the outer limit of the territorial sea, are included in the territorial sea. The coastal state must clearly demarcate such roadsteads and indicate them on charts together with their boundaries, to which due publicity must be given.

Article 10

1. An island is a naturally-formed area of land, surrounded by water, which is above water at high tide.

2. The territorial sea of an island is measured in accordance with the provisions of these articles.

Article 11

1. A low-tide elevation is a naturally-formed area of land which is surrounded by and above water at low-tide but submerged at high tide. Where a low-tide elevation is situated wholly or partly at a distance not exceeding the breadth of the territorial sea from the mainland or an island, the low-water line on that elevation may be used as the baseline for measuring the breadth of the territorial sea.

2. Where a low-tide elevation is wholly situated at a distance exceeding the breadth of the territorial sea from the mainland or an island, it has no territorial sea of its own.

Article 12

1. Where the coasts of two states are opposite or adjacent to each other, neither of the two states is entitled, failing agreement between them to the contrary, to extend its territorial sea beyond the median line every point of which is equidista from the nearest points on the baselines from which the breadth of the territorial seas of each of the two states is measured. The provisions of this paragraph shall not apply, however, where it is necessary by reason of historic title or other special circumstances to delimit the territorial seas of the two states in a way which is at variance with this provision.

2. The line of delimitation between the territorial seas of two states lying opposite to each other or adjacent to each other shall be marked on large-scale charts officially recognized by the coastal states.

Article 13

If a river flows directly into the sea, the baseline shall be a straight line across the mouth of the river between points on the low-tide line of its banks.

SECTION III. RIGHT OF INNOCENT PASSAGE

Sub-section A. Rules applicable to all ships

Article 14

1. Subject to the provisions of these articles, ships of all states, whether coastal or not, shall enjoy the right of innocent passage through the territorial sea.

2. Passage means navigation through the territorial sea for the purpose either of traversing that sea without entering internal waters, or of proceeding to internal waters, or of making for the high seas from internal waters.

3. Passage includes stopping and anchoring, but only insofar as the same are incidental to ordinary navigation or are rendered necessary by *force majeure* or by distress.

4. Passage is innocent so long as it is not prejudicial to the peace, good order or security of the coastal state. Such passage shall take place in conformity with these articles and with other rules of international law.

5. Passage of foreign fishing vessels shall not be considered innocent if they do not observe such laws and regulations as the coastal state may make and publish in order to prevent these vessels from fishing in the territorial sea.

6. Submarines are required to navigate on the surface and to show their flag.

Article 15

1. The coastal state must not hamper innocent passage through the territorial sea.

2. The coastal state is required to give appropriate publicity to any dangers to navigation, of which it has knowledge, within its territorial sea.

Article 16

1. The coastal state may take the necessary steps in its territorial sea to prevent passage which is not innocent.

2. In the case of ships proceeding to internal waters, the coastal state shall also have the right to take the necessary steps to prevent any breach of the conditions to which admission of those ships to those waters is subject.

3. Subject to the provisions of paragraph 4, the coastal state may, without discrimination amongst foreign ships, suspend temporarily in specified areas of its territorial sea the innocent passage of foreign ships if such suspension is essential for the protection of its security. Such suspension shall take effect only after having been duly published.

4. There shall be no suspension of the innocent passage of foreign ships through straits which are used for international navigation between one part of the high seas and another part of the high seas or the territorial sea of a foreign state.

Article 17

Foreign ships exercising the right of innocent passage shall comply with the laws and regulations enacted by the coastal state in conformity with these articles and other rules of international law and, in particular, with such laws and regulations relating to transport and navigation.

Sub-section B. Rules applicable to merchant ships

Article 18

1. No charge may be levied upon foreign ships by reason only of their passage through the territorial sea.

2. Charges may be levied upon a foreign ship passing through the territorial sea as payment only for specific services rendered to the ship. These charges shall be levied without discrimination.

Article 19

1. The criminal jurisdiction of the coastal state should not be exercised on board a foreign ship passing through the territorial sea to arrest any person or to conduct any investigation in connexion with any crime committed on board the ship during its passage, save only in the following cases:

(a) If the consequences of the crime extend to the coastal state; or
(b) If the crime is of a kind to disturb the peace of the country or the good order of the territorial sea; or
(c) If the assistance of the local authorities has been requested by the captain of the ship or by the consul of the country whose flag the ship flies; or
(d) If it is necessary for the suppression of illicit traffic in narcotic drugs.

2. The above provisions do not affect the right of the coastal state to take any steps authorized by its laws for the purpose of an arrest or investigation on board a foreign ship passing through the territorial sea after leaving internal waters.

3. In the cases provided for in paragraphs 1 and 2 of this article, the coastal state shall, if the captain so requests, advise the consular authority of the flag state before taking any steps, and shall facilitate contact between such authority and the ship's crew. In cases of emergency this notification may be communicated while the measures are being taken.

4. In considering whether or how an arrest should be made, the local authorities shall pay due regard to the interests of navigation.

5. The coastal state may not take any steps on board a foreign ship passing through the territorial sea to arrest any person or to conduct any investigation in connexion with any crime committed before the ship entered the territorial sea, if the ship, proceeding from a foreign port, is only passing through the territorial sea without entering internal waters.

Article 20

1. The coastal state should not stop or divert a foreign ship passing through the territorial sea for the purpose of exercising civil jurisdiction in relation to a person on board the ship.

2. The coastal state may not levy execution against or arrest the ship for the purpose of any civil proceedings, save only in respect of obligations or liabilities assumed or incurred by the ship itself in the course or for the purpose of its voyage through the waters of the coastal state.

3. The provisions of the previous paragraph are without prejudice to the right of the coastal state, in accordance with its laws, to levy execution against or to arrest, for the purpose of any civil proceedings, a foreign ship lying in the territorial sea, or passing through the territorial sea after leaving internal waters.

Sub-section C. Rules applicable to government ships other than warships

Article 21

The rules contained in Sub-sections A and B shall also apply to government ships operated for commercial purposes.

Article 22

1. The rules contained in Sub-section A and in Article 18 shall apply to government ships operated for non-commercial purposes.

2. With such exceptions as are contained in the provisions referred to in the preceding paragraph, nothing in these articles affects the immunities which such ships enjoy under these articles or other rules of international law.

Sub-section D. Rule applicable to warships

Article 23

If any warship does not comply with the regulations of the coastal state concerning passage through the territorial sea and disregards any request for compliance which is made to it, the coastal state may require the warship to leave the territorial sea.

PART II: CONTIGUOUS ZONE

Article 24

1. In a zone of the high seas contiguous to its territorial sea, the coastal state may exercise the control necessary to:

(a) Prevent infringement of its customs, fiscal, immigration or sanitary regulations within its territory or territorial sea;
(b) Punish infringement of the above regulations committed within its territory or territorial sea.

2. The contiguous zone may not extend beyond twelve miles from the baseline from which the breadth of the territorial sea is measured.

3. Where the coasts of two states are opposite or adjacent to each other, neither of the two states is entitled, failing agreement between them to the contrary, to extend its contiguous zone beyond the median line every point of which is equidistant from the nearest points on the baselines from which the breadth of the territorial seas of the two states is measured.

PART III: FINAL ARTICLES

Article 25

The provisions of this Convention shall not affect conventions or other international agreements already in force, as between states parties to them.

Article 26

This Convention shall, until 31 October 1958, be open for signature by all States Members of the United Nations or of any of the specialized agencies, and by any other state invited by the General Assembly to become a party to the Convention.

Article 27

This Convention is subject to ratification. The instruments of ratification shall be deposited with the Secretary-General of the United Nations.

Article 28

This Convention shall be open for accession by any states belonging to any of the categories mentioned in Article 26. The instruments of accession shall be deposited with the Secretary-General of the United Nations.

Article 29

1. This Convention shall come into force on the thirtieth day following the date of deposit of the twenty-second instrument of ratification or accession with the Secretary-General of the United Nations.

2. For each state ratifying or acceding to the Convention after the deposit of the twenty-second instrument of ratification or accession, the Convention shall enter into force on the thirtieth day after deposit by such state of its instrument of ratification or accession.

MARITIME JURISDICTION CLAIMED BY

VARIOUS STATES

Breadth of Fishery Jurisdiction Claimed if other than Territorial Sea is shown in parentheses ( )

Claims to Continental Shelf indicated by (CS)

Claims based on Archipelago Principle indicated by #

<u>3 Miles</u> (34 States)

Australia (12)
Barbados
Belgium (12)
Canada (12)
China-Taiwan
Costa Rica (200)
Cuba
Dahomey (12)
Denmark (12)
Dominican Republic (15)
Fed. Repub. of Germany (12)
France (12)
Gambia
Guyana
Ireland (12)
Japan
Jordan
Kenya
Malaysia
Malta
Mauritius
Morocco (12)
Muscat & Oman
Nauru
Netherlands (12)
New Zealand (12)
Nicaragua (200) (CS)
Philippines (12) #
Poland
Singapore
Trinidad & Tobago
United Kingdom (12)
United States (12) (CS)
Vietnam (South) (10.8)

<u>4 Miles</u> (4 States)

Finland
Iceland (12)
Norway (12)
Sweden (12)

<u>5 Miles</u> (1 State)

Cambodia (12) (CS)

<u>6 Miles</u> (17 States)

Brazil (12)
Ceylon (100)
Greece
Haiti
India (100)
Israel
Italy (12)
Ivory Coast (12)

6 Miles contd.

Lebanon
Maldive Islands
Portugal (12)
Senegal (12)
South Africa (12)
Spain (12)
Tunisia (12)
Turkey (12)
Uruguay (12)

9 Miles (1 State)

Mexico (12)

10 Miles (2 States)

Albania (12)
Yugoslavia

12 Miles (39 States)

Algeria
Bulgaria
Burma
Colombia
Communist China
Cyprus
Ethiopia
Gabon
Ghana (100)
Guatemala
Honduras (200)
Iceland
Indonesia #
Iran
Iraq
Jamaica
Korea (20 200) (CS)
Kuwait
Liberia
Libya
Malagasy
Mauritania
Nigeria
Pakistan (100)
Rumania
Saudi Arabia
Sierre Leone
Somalia
Sudan
Syria
Tanzania
Thailand
Togo
Ukrainian S.S.R.
U.S.S.R.
United Arab Republic
Venezuela
Vietnam (North)
Yemen

18 Miles (1 State)

Cameroon

50 Kilometers (1 State)

Chile (200)

130 Miles (1 State)

Guinea

<u>200 Miles</u> (5 States)

Argentina (CS)
Ecuador
El Salvador
Panama (CS)
Peru

<u>Unknown or Unspecified</u>

Congo (both)
Dem. Repub. of Germany
Monaco
W. Samoa

Compiled from information supplied to the Committee on Commerce, United States Senate, by the Department of State. Senate Report No. 1280, 89th Congress, 2nd Sess. (June 15, 1966), pp. 12-13 and p. 5; and to the Committee on Merchant Marine and Fisheries, House of Representatives, by the same. House Report No. 2086, 89th Congress, 2nd Sess. (September 26, 1966), pp. 6-7. Revised by Department of State, February 15, 1968. See also list furnished to the Australian House of Representatives by the Minister of External Affairs, March 9, 1967. <u>Current Notes on International Affairs</u>, Vol. 38, No. 3, March 1967, pp. 118-120. Published by the Australian Ministry of External Affairs.

Diagram A

IDEALIZED TOPOGRAPHIC PROFILE OF
CONTINENTAL SHELF
(Vertical Scale Exaggerated)

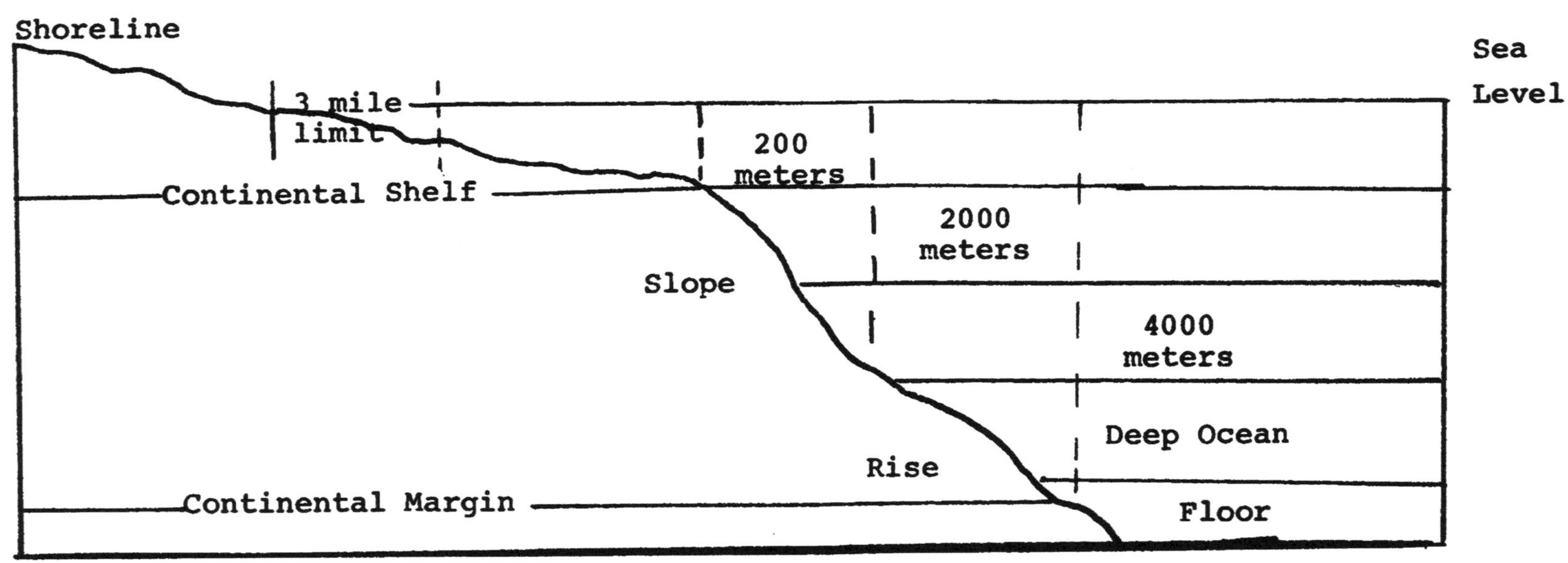

CHAPTER THREE

THE CONTINENTAL SHELF

Introductory Note

In addition to the territorial sea and contiguous fishing zones, states in the past twenty years have been recognizing the importance of the continental shelf as an area vital to national welfare and security.

The continental shelf refers to the seabed lying beyond territorial waters. It is a continuation of the geological land mass of the continents and is usually composed of rock formations similar to those found on the shore. The term now has both physical and legal connotations, which it gained upon incorporation into a special convention signed at the Geneva Law of the Sea Conference in 1958.

Argentina and Spain appear to have been among the first nations to call public attention to the shelves as significant appendages of the state. During World War I these countries proclaimed national control of the waters above their continental shelves to protect their neutrality. The Soviet Union followed with a claim in the Arctic based upon the continental shelf.

Threatened by German and Japanese belligerent activities off the Americas, the United States and the American Republics agreed at Panama in 1939 to establish a security zone extending around the American Hemisphere which in effect reserved the waters of the continental shelf, and considerably more as well, to peaceful activity preserving their neutrality. This did not prevent hostile vessels from coming within the reserved area, but it did fortify the legal and moral hand of the Americans in taking measures to preserve their neutrality and security when these waters were threatened by foreign ships.

With petroleum operations already underway by 1945 off Long Beach, California, and with the detection of oil and sulphur resources in the Gulf of Mexico off Louisiana and Texas, President Harry S. Truman took the precautionary step of proclaiming exclusive United States jurisdiction and control of the resources of the seabed and subsoil of the continental shelf off the coast of the United States on September 28, 1945. The President was careful, however, to safeguard the right of navigation in the waters above the shelf.

This move prompted a series of acts elsewhere. A number of Latin American countries asserted jurisdiction over their continental shelves. Ecuador, Peru and Chile went to the extent of claiming sovereignty over a belt of water extending 200 miles from their shores in order to preserve the anchovy fisheries for their own economic benefit. Notwithstanding strong diplomatic protests by the United States and others, these governments have continued to seize and arrest foreign fishing vessels which enter their waters without prior official permission.

Faced with the prospect of a fencing off of national "lakes" in the high seas, eighty-six nations met in 1958 in Geneva to try to resolve some of the disputes relating to sovereignty and jurisdictional rights in the seas. It was soon established that a majority of states were prepared to agree on the right of states to exercise sovereignty over the seabed and subsoil of the continental shelf lying contiguous to their own coasts. The problem came in defining the shelf with sufficient accuracy to make this a meaningful concept. A legal definition appears in Article I of the Convention on the Continental Shelf, but it has left many questions unresolved. Article I declares:

> "For the purposes of these articles the term "continental shelf" is used as referring (a) to the seabed and subsoil of the submarine areas adjacent to the coast but outside the area of the territorial sea, to a depth of 200 meters or, beyond that limit, to where the depth of the superjacent waters admits of the exploitation of the natural resources of the said area; (b) to the seabed and subsoil of similar areas adjacent to the coasts of islands."

In short, it was agreed that the resources of the continental shelf belong to and may be exploited exclusively by the coastal state and its nationals or by such persons and firms as the state permits to operate in this area.

A Bulletin by the Geographer of the Department of State entitled <u>Sovereignty of the Sea</u>, describes the problems which exist in the horizontal projection of jurisdictional rights.

> "On and below the surface of the sea offshore claims run into three dimensions where jurisdiction over the seabed differs from that of the superjacent water. For example, a coastal state may have the right to drill for petroleum in a submarine area for which no fishing rights obtain to that state. In turn, the vertical dimension of offshore rights above sea level may differ from those on and below the surface of the sea. Here <u>airspace</u> must be added to a full inventory of offshore zones, superimposed as it is over the entire surface pattern.
>
> "Rights in airspace offer none of the flexibility found on and below the water surface . . . No right of innocent passage prevails as for surface craft, a situation giving rise to the possibility of hostile action against planes counter to regulations in marginal sea areas where tension prevails."

In the physical sense the continental shelf is the land mass which extends from the coast into the sea to where it falls into the abyssal deep. Oceanographers recognize two parts to the shelf: the slope and the continental rise. The slope is that part of the shelf which stretches outward from the shore to a point where it drops into the deeps. The rise is that portion of the shelf which extends from the drop-off point to the abyssal floor.

In employing the 200 meter depth line for the demarcation of the shelf, the Geneva conferees selected what was then considered to be the average outer edge of the continental shelf; where the slope usually begins to drop off into deeper water. Since that time surveys have shown that the breaking point is often not precise, and that the angles of the slopes vary considerably. Furthermore, it has been found that continental shelves exist at much greater depths, the Sahul Shelf off the coast of northern Australia being 550 meters.

In speaking of the outer edge of the continental shelf there is some confusion among scientists, industrialists and lawyers whether this refers to the breaking-point of the slope, or to where the shelf touches the floor of the abyssal deep, in other words, at the outer terminus of the rise.

There is no doubt of the right of the coastal state to explore and exploit any resources found on its continental shelf. Each country may require licenses for mining or other operations conducted on the shelf, such as placing platforms, stationing vehicles, sinking shafts, or extracting materials from the seabed. There is some difference of opinion as to the right of a nation to issue licenses which would allow activities to be conducted on the rise. However, following the language of the Geneva Convention and the implications of the Outer Continental Shelf Lands Act, the U.S. Department of Interior has been granting licenses that do extend to the continental rise. Members of the American Petroleum Institute, which includes most of the major petroleum companies, have been advocating that the industry should take a concerted position on the right to exploit resources clear to the foot of the rise where the shelf joins the abyssal ocean floor.

Judging from the language of the latter half of Article I of the Geneva Convention, this area would appear to belong to the coastal state, assuming technology permits the oil and mining companies to exploit the resources located there. In any event, there is no international agreement which denies coastal nations the right to exert their jurisdiction over both the slope and the rise of the continental shelf.

Horizontally, continental shelves extend varying distances seaward from the shores, although thirty miles is given as an average length. Off Long Island the outer edge of the slope runs nearly 75 miles. The width of the shelf is measured in hundreds of miles off the coast of Argentina, while along the west coast of South America the land plunges to great depths leaving little trace of anything resembling a shelf. North of Siberia in the Bering Strait area the shelf stretches some 800 miles with less than 100 fathoms of depth.

In summation, each coastal state has sovereign rights which extend from its shoreline to the outer limit of territorial waters. It may exert control over fishing in a contiguous zone. A nation may also exercise exclusive power over the seabed and subsoil of the continental shelf to its terminus. Foreign vessels may navigate freely, however, in the waters above the shelf, particularly outside of the territorial sea, and, if this portion of the ocean has not been declared to be a "defensive sea area", may engage in oceanographic research concerning such matters as temperature, currents, salinity, noise, sea life, and the like. Foreign fishing fleets may also fish in these waters if there is no international agreement restricting their activity in this neighborhood. Boundary lines in the shelf are settled by mutual agreement between adjoining states.

The readings in this chapter touch on the basic legal positions of the United States with respect to the continental shelf. The text of the Geneva Convention on the Continental Shelf is contained in Chapter Four.

For other readings see Lewis M. Alexander (ed.), The Law of the Sea: Offshore Boundaries and Zones (Columbus, Ohio State University Press, 1967); Myres S. McDougal and William T. Burke, The Public Order of the Oceans (New Haven, Yale University Press, 1962); G. Etzel Pearcy, "Geographical Aspects of the Law of the Sea," Annals of the Association of American Geographers, Vol. 49, March 1959; Henry Reiff, The United States and the Treaty Law of the Sea (Minneapolis, University of Minnesota Press, 1959); Aaron L. Shalowitz, Shore and Sea Boundaries, Vol. I (1963), Vol. II (1964), U.S. Department of Commerce, Coast and Geodetic Survey, Washington; Department of State, Sovereignty of the Sea, Geographic Bulletin No.3, April 1965.

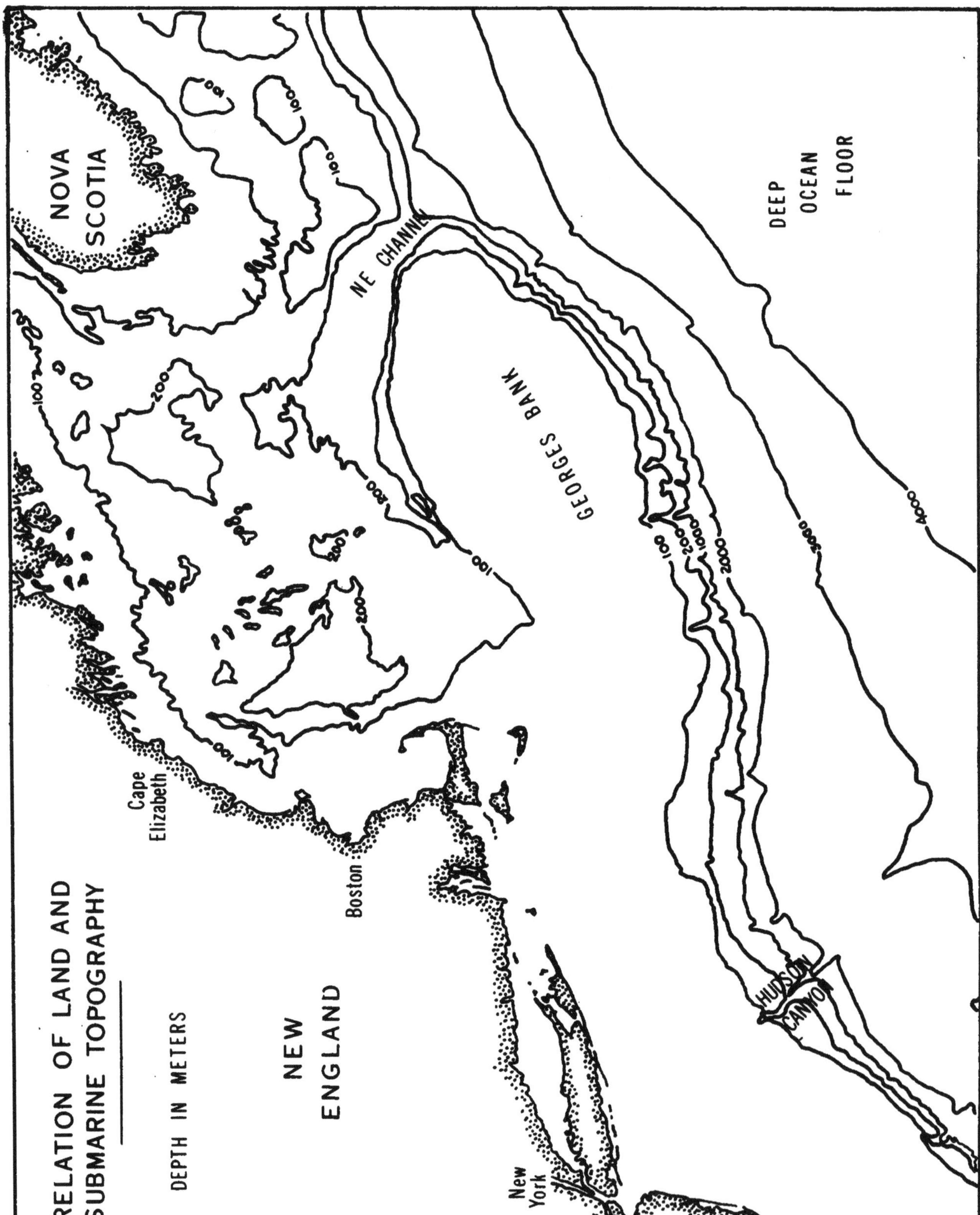

(after U.S. Geological Survey Map I-451)

UNITED STATES

PROCLAMATION OF PRESIDENT TRUMAN CLAIMING JURISDICTION OVER RESOURCES OF THE CONTINENTAL SHELF

September 28,1945[1]

Whereas the Government of the United States of America, aware of the long-range world-wide need for new sources of petroleum and other minerals, holds the view that efforts to discover and make available new supplies of these resources should be encouraged; and

Whereas its competent experts are of the opinion that such resources underlie many parts of the continental shelf off the coasts of the United States of America, and that with modern technological progress their utilization is already practicable or will become so at an early date; and

Whereas recognized jurisdiction over these resources is required in the interest of their conservation and prudent utilization when and as development is undertaken; and

Whereas it is the view of the Government of the United States that the exercise of jurisdiction over the natural resources of the subsoil and sea bed of the continental shelf by the contiguous nation is reasonable and just, since the effectiveness of measures to utilize or conserve these resources would be contingent upon cooperation and protection from the shore, since the continental shelf may be regarded as an extension of the land-mass of the coastal nation and thus naturally appurtenant to it, since these resources frequently form a seaward extension of a pool or deposit lying within the territory, and since self-protection compels the coastal nation to keep close watch over activities off its shores which are of a nature necessary for utilization of these resources;

NOW, THEREFORE, I, HARRY S. TRUMAN, President of the United States of America, do hereby proclaim the following policy of the United States of America with respect to the natural resources of the subsoil and sea bed of the continental shelf.

Having concern for the urgency of conserving and prudently utilizing its natural resources, the Government of the

United States regards the natural resources of the subsoil and sea bed of the continental shelf beneath the high seas but contiguous to the coasts of the United States as appertaining to the United States, subject to its jurisdiction and control. In cases where the continental shelf extends to the shores of another State, or is shared with an adjacent State, the boundary shall be determined by the United States and the State concerned in accordance with equitable principles. The character as high seas of the waters above the continental shelf and the right to their free and unimpeded navigation are in no way thus affected. ...

1. Federal Register, Vol. X, p. 12303.

UNITED STATES SUBMERGED LANDS ACT

AN ACT

TO CONFIRM THE TITLE OF STATES TO LANDS BENEATH NAVIGABLE WATERS WITHIN STATE BOUNDARIES AND TO CONFIRM UNITED STATES JURISDICTION AND CONTROL OVER RESOURCES OF THE SEABED AND THE CONTINENTAL SHELF SEAWARD OF STATE BOUNDARIES

Approved May 22, 1953 [1]

Be it enacted... That this Act may be cited as the "Submerged Lands Act."

TITLE I

DEFINITION

SECTION 2. WHEN USED IN THIS ACT. --

(a) The term "lands beneath navigable waters" means --

(1) all lands within the boundaries of each of the respective States which are covered by nontidal waters that were navigable under the laws of the United States at the time such State became a member of the Union, or acquired sovereignty over such lands and waters thereafter, up to the ordinary high water mark as heretofore or hereafter modified by accretion, erosion, and reliction;

(2) all lands permanently or periodically covered by tidal waters up to but not above the line of mean high tide and seaward to a line three geographical miles distant from the coast line of each such State and to the boundary line of each such State where in any case such boundary as it existed at the time such State became a member of the Union, or as heretofore approved by Congress, extends seaward (or into the Gulf of Mexico) beyond three geographical miles, and

(3) all filled in, made, or reclaimed lands which formerly were lands beneath navigable waters, as hereinabove defined;

(b) The term "boundaries" includes the seaward boundaries of a State or its boundaries in the Gulf of Mexico or any of the Great Lakes... but in no event shall the term "boundaries" or the term "lands beneath navigable waters" be interpreted as extending from the coast line more than three geographical miles into the Atlantic Ocean or the Pacific Ocean, or more than three marine leagues into the Gulf of Mexico;

(c) The term "coast line" means the line of ordinary low water along that portion of the coast which is in direct contact with the open sea...

(d) The terms "grantees" and Lessees" include... all political subdivisions, municipalities, public and private corporations... to lands beneath navigable waters... Provided, however, That nothing herein shall be construed as conferring upon said grantees or lessees any greater rights or interests other than are described herein and in their respective grants from the State, or its predecessor sovereign;

(e) The term "natural resources" includes, without limiting the generality thereof, oil, gas, and all other minerals, and fish, shrimp, oysters, clams, crabs, lobsters, sponges, kelp, and other marine animal and plant life but does not include water power, or the use of water for the production of power;

(f) The term "lands beneath navigable waters" does not include the beds of streams in lands now or heretofore constituting a part of the public lands of the United States if such streams were not meandered in connection with the public survey of such lands under the laws of the United States and if the title to the beds of such streams was lawfully patented or conveyed by the United States or any State to any person;

(g) The term "State" means any State of the Union;

(h) The term "person" includes, in addition to a natural person, an association, a State, a political subdivision of a State, or a private, public, or municipal corporation.

TITLE II

LANDS BENEATH NAVIGABLE WATERS WITHIN STATE BOUNDARIES

SECTION 3. RIGHTS OF THE STATES. --

(a) It is hereby determined and declared to be in the public interest that (1) title to and ownership of the lands beneath navigable waters within the boundaries of the respective States, and the natural resources within such lands and waters, and (2) the right and power to manage, administer, lease, develop, and use the said lands and natural resources all in accordance with applicable State law be, and they are hereby, subject to the provisions hereof, recognized, confirmed, established, and vested in and assigned to the respective States or the persons who were on June 5, 1950, entitled thereto under the law of the respective States in which the land is located, and the respective grantees, lessees, or successors in interest thereof;

(b) (1) The United States hereby releases and relinquishes unto said States and persons aforesaid, except as otherwise reserved herein, all right, title, and interest of the United States, if any it has, in and to all said lands, improvements, and natural resources; (2) the United States hereby releases and relinquishes all claims of the United States, if any it has, for money or damages arising out of any operations of said States or persons pursuant to State authority upon or within said lands and navigable waters;...

(c) The rights, powers, and titles hereby recognized, confirmed, established, and vested in and assigned to the respective States and their grantees are subject to each lease executed by a State, or its grantee, which was in force and effect on June 5, 1950... Provided, however, that, if oil or gas was not being produced from such lease on and before December 11, 1950, or if the primary term of such lease has expired since December 11, 1950, then for a term from the effective date hereof equal to the term remaining unexpired on December 11, 1950...[payment provisions].

(d) Nothing in this Act shall affect the use, development, improvement, or control by or under the constitutional authority of the United States of said lands and waters for the purposes of navigation or flood control or the production of power, or be construed as the release or relinquishment of any rights of the United States arising under the constitutional authority of Congress to regulate or improve navigation, or to provide for flood control, or the production of power;...

SECTION 4. SEAWARD BOUNDARIES. --

The seaward boundary of each original coastal State is hereby approved and confirmed as a line three geographical miles distant from its coast line or, in the case of the Great Lakes, to the international boundary...

SECTION 5. EXCEPTIONS FROM OPERATION OF SECTION 3 OF THIS ACT.—

There is excepted from the operation of Section 3 of this Act -

(a) all tracts or parcels of land together with all accretions thereto, resources therein, or improvements thereon, title to which has been lawfully and expressly acquired by the United States from any State or from any person in whom title had vested under the law of the State or of the United States, and all lands which the United States lawfully holds under the law of the State; all lands expressly retained by or ceded to the United States when the State entered the Union (otherwise than by a general retention or cession of lands underlying the marginal sea); all lands acquired by the United States by eminent domain proceedings, purchase, cession, gift, or otherwise in a proprietary capacity; all lands filled in, built up, or otherwise reclaimed by the United States for its own use; and any right the United States has in lands presently and actually occupied by the United States under claim of right;

(b) such lands beneath navigable waters held, or any interest in which is held by the United States for the benefit of any tribe, band, or group of Indians or for individual Indians; and

(c) all structures and improvements constructed by the United States in the exercise of its navigational servitude.

SECTION 6. POWERS RETAINED BY THE UNITED STATES. --

(a) The United States retains all its navigational servitude and rights in and powers of regulation and control of said lands and navigable waters for the constitutional purposes of commerce, navigation, national defense, and international affairs, all of which shall be paramount to, but shall not be deemed to include, proprietary rights of ownership or the rights of management, administration, leasing, use, and development of the lands and natural resources which are specifically recognized, confirmed, established, and vested in and assigned to the respective States and others by Section 3 of this Act.

(b) In time of war or when necessary for national defense, and the Congress or the President shall so prescribe, the United States shall have the right of first refusal to purchase at the prevailing market price, all or any portion of the said natural resources, or to acquire and use any portion of said lands by proceeding in accordance with due process of law and paying just compensation therefor.

... SECTION 9

Nothing in this Act shall be deemed to affect in any wise the rights of the United States to the natural resources of that portion of the subsoil and seabed of the Continental Shelf lying seaward and outside of the area of lands beneath navigable waters, as defined in Section 2 hereof, all of which natural resources appertain to the United States, and the jurisdiction and control of which by the United States is hereby confirmed...

1. Public Law 31, 83rd Congress, 1st Session. 67 Stat. 29.

UNITED STATES OUTER CONTINENTAL SHELF LANDS ACT

AN ACT

TO PROVIDE FOR THE JURISDICTION OF THE UNITED STATES OVER THE SUBMERGED LANDS OF THE OUTER CONTINENTAL SHELF

Approved August 7, 1953[1]

Be it enacted... That this Act may be cited as the "Outer Continental Shelf Lands Act."

SECTION 2. DEFINITIONS. - WHEN USED IN THIS ACT.-

(a) The term "Outer Continental Shelf" means all submerged lands lying seaward and outside of the area of lands beneath navigable waters as defined in Section 2 of the Submerged Lands Act... and of which the subsoil and seabed appertain to the United States and are subject to its jurisdiction and control;

(b) The term "Secretary" means the Secretary of the Interior;

(c) The term "mineral lease" means any form of authorization for the exploration for, or development or removal of deposits of, oil, gas, or other minerals...

SECTION 3. JURISDICTION OVER OUTER CONTINENTAL SHELF.-

(a) It is hereby declared to be the policy of the United States that the subsoil and seabed of the outer Continental Shelf appertain to the United States and are subject to its jurisdiction, control, and power of disposition as provided in this Act.

(b) This Act shall be construed in such manner that the character as high seas of the water above the outer Continental Shelf and the right to navigation and fishing therein shall not be affected.

SECTION 4. LAWS APPLICABLE TO OUTER CONTINENTAL SHELF.-

(a) (1) The Constitution and laws and civil and political jurisdiction of the United States are hereby extended to the subsoil and seabed of the outer Continental Shelf and to all artificial islands and fixed structures which may be erected thereon for the purpose of exploring for, developing, removing, and transporting resources therefrom, to the same extent as if the outer Continental Shelf were an area of exclusive Federal jurisdiction located within a State: Provided, however, That mineral leases on the outer Continental Shelf shall be maintained or issued only under the provisions of this Act.

(2)...the civil and criminal laws of each adjacent State ... are hereby declared to be the law of the United States for that portion of the subsoil and seabed of the outer Continental Shelf, and artificial islands and fixed structures erected thereon, which would be within the area of the State if its boundaries were extended seaward to the outer margin of the outer Continental Shelf, and the President shall determine and publish in the Federal Register such projected lines extending seaward and defining each such area...

(3) The provisions of this section for adoption of State law as the law of the United States shall never be interpreted as a basis for claiming any interest in or jurisdiction on behalf of any State for any purpose over the seabed and subsoil of the outer Continental Shelf, or the property and natural resources thereof or the revenues therefrom.

(b) The United States district courts shall have original jurisdiction of cases and controversies arising out of or in connection with any operations conducted on the outer Continental Shelf for the purpose of exploring for, developing, removing or transporting by pipeline the natural resources, or involving rights to the natural resources of the subsoil and seabed of the outer Continental Shelf...

SECTION 5. ADMINISTRATION OF LEASING OF THE OUTER CONTINENTAL SHELF.-

(a) (1) The Secretary [of the Interior] shall administer the provisions of this Act relating to the leasing of the outer Continental Shelf, and shall prescribe such rules and regulations as may be necessary to carry out such provisions...

(2) Any person who knowingly and willfully violates any rule or regulation prescribed by the Secretary for the prevention of waste, the conservation of the natural resources, or the protection of correlative rights shall be deemed guilty of a misdemeanor and punishable by a fine of not more than $2,000 or by imprisonment for not more than six months, or by both...

(c) Rights-of-way through the submerged lands of the outer Continental Shelf, whether or not such lands are included in a lease maintained or issued pursuant to this Act, may be granted by the Secretary for pipeline purposes for the transportation of oil, natural gas, sulphur, or other mineral under such regulations and upon such conditions as to the application therefor and the survey, location and width thereof as may be prescribed by the Secretary, and upon the express condition that such oil or gas pipelines shall transport or purchase without discrimination, oil or natural gas produced from said submerged lands in the vicinity of the pipeline in such proportionate amounts as the Federal Power Commission, in the case of gas, and the Interstate Commerce Commission, in the case of oil, may, after a full hearing with due notice thereof to the interested parties, determine to be reasonable, taking into account, among other things, conservation and the prevention of waste...

SECTION 7. CONTROVERSY OVER JURISDICTION.-

In the event of a controversy between the United States and a State as to whether or not lands are subject to the provisions of this Act, the Secretary is authorized... to negotiate and enter into agreements with the State, its political subdivision or grantee or a lessee thereof, respecting operations under existing mineral leases and payment and impounding of rents, royalties, and other sums payable thereunder, or with the State, its political subdivision or grantee, respecting the issuance or nonissuance of new mineral leases pending the settlement or adjudication of the controversy...

SECTION 8. LEASING OF OUTER CONTINENTAL SHELF.-

(a) In order to meet the urgent need for further exploration and development of the oil and gas deposits of the submerged lands of the outer Continental Shelf, the Secretary is authorized to grant to the highest responsible qualified bidder...oil and gas leases on submerged lands of the outer Continental Shelf...

(b) An oil and gas lease issued by the Secretary pursuant to this section shall (1) cover a compact area not exceeding five thousand seven hundred and sixty acres... (2) be for a period of five years and as long thereafter as oil or gas may be produced from the area in paying quantities, or drilling or well reworking operations as approved by the Secretary are conducted thereon, (3) require the payment of a royalty of not less than 12 1/2 per centum, in the amount or value of the production saved, removed, or sold from the lease, and (4) contain such rental provisions and such other terms and provisions as the Secretary may prescribe...

(c) In order to meet the urgent need for further exploration and development of the sulphur deposits in the submerged lands of the outer Continental Shelf, the Secretary is authorized to grant to the qualified persons offering the highest cash bonuses on a basis of competitive bidding sulphur leases on submerged lands of the outer Continental Shelf ...

(d) A sulphur lease issued by the Secretary pursuant to this section shall (1) cover an area of such size and dimensions as the Secretary may determine, (2) be for a period of not more than ten years and so long thereafter as sulphur may be produced from the area in paying quantities or drilling, well reworking, plant construction, or other operations for the production of sulphur, as approved by the Secretary, are conducted thereon, (3) require the payment to the United States of such royalty as may be specified in the lease but not less than 5 per centum of the gross production or value of the sulphur at the wellhead, and (4) contain such rental provisions and such other terms and provisions as the Secretary may by regulation prescribe at the time of offering the area for lease...

SECTION 11. GEOLOGICAL AND GEOPHYSICAL EXPLORATIONS.-

Any agency of the United States and any person authorized by the Secretary may conduct geological and geophysical explorations in the outer Continental Shelf, which do not interfere with or endanger actual operations under any lease maintained or granted pursuant to this Act, and which are not unduly harmful to aquatic life in such area.

SECTION 12. RESERVATIONS.-

(a) The President of the United States may, from time to time, withdraw from disposition any of the unleased lands of the outer Continental Shelf.

(b) In time of war, or when the President shall so prescribe, the United States shall have the right of first refusal to purchase at the market price all or any portion of any mineral produced from the outer Continental Shelf.

(c) All leases issued under this Act... shall contain or be construed to contain a provision whereby authority is vested in the Secretary, upon a recommendation of the Secretary of Defense, during a state of war or national emergency,... to suspend operations under any lease...

(d) The United States reserves and retains the right to designate by and through the Secretary of Defense, with the approval of the President, as areas restricted from exploration and operation that part of the outer Continental Shelf needed for national defense; and so long as such designation remains in effect no exploration or operations may be conducted on any part of the surface of such area except with the concurrence of the Secretary of Defense...

(e) All uranium, thorium, and all other materials determined pursuant to paragraph (1) of subsection (b) of Section 5 of the Atomic Energy Act of 1946, as amended, to be peculiarly essential to the production of fissionable material, contained, in whatever concentration, in deposits in the subsoil or seabed of the outer Continental Shelf are hereby reserved for the use of the United States.

(f) The United States reserves and retains the ownership of and the right to extract all helium... contained in gas produced from any portion of the outer Continental Shelf ...

1. Public Law 212, 83rd Congress, 1st Session. 67 Stat.462

DECLARATION OF PRESIDENT OF CHILE CLAIMING JURISDICTION OVER SEAS TO A DISTANCE OF 200 MILES[1]

June 25, 1947

Considering:

1. That the Governments of the United States of America, of Mexico, and of the Argentine Republic, by presidential declarations made on 28 September 1945, 29 October 1945, and 11 October 1946 respectively, have proclaimed in a categorical manner the sovereignty of those States over the continental shelf adjacent to their coasts, and over the adjacent sea to the full extent necessary to conserve for those States the ownership of the natural riches known or to be discovered in the future.

2. That they have expressly proclaimed the rights of those States to protect, conserve, regulate, and supervise fishing, in order to prevent illicit activities from threatening to diminish or wipe out the considerable riches of that type which are contained in the continental seas and which are indispensable for the welfare and progress of their respective peoples, measures whose justice is indisputable.

3. That particularly in the case of the Republic of Chile there is a manifest advantage in issuing an analogous proclamation of sovereignty, not only because of the fact that the exploitation of resources contained in the continental shelf which are essential to the national life is already under way, as is the case with the coal mines, which are being worked and will continue to expand into the territory which is covered by water, but also even more important, because owing to its topography and lack of mediterranean extension, the country's life is bound up with the sea and with all the present and future riches contained in the sea, to a greater degree than in the case of any other nation.

4. That an international consensus recognizes that each country has the right to consider as national territory the whole extent of the adjacent epicontinental sea and continental shelf.

5. That the State has the obligation to protect and supervise the exploitation of the resources contained in its maritime, terrestrial, and aerial territory.

The President of the Republic declares:

1. The Government of Chile confirms and proclaims the national sovereignty over the whole continental shelf adjacent to the continental and insular coasts of the national territory whatever its depth may be, claiming, consequently, all the natural riches which exist on, in, or under said shelf, known or to be discovered.

2. The Government of Chile confirms and proclaims the national sovereignty over the seas adjacent to its coasts, whatever their depth may be, to the full extent necessary to reserve, protect, conserve, and utilise the natural resources and wealth of whatever nature, found on, in, or under said seas, placing under Government supervision the fishing and marine hunting industries in order to prevent this type of resources from being exploited to the prejudice of the inhabitants of Chile and diminished or destroyed to the detriment of the country and of the American Continent.

3. Demarcation of the zones of protection of maritime hunting and fishing in the continental and inland seas which are under the control of the Government of Chile will be made in virtue of this declaration of sovereignty, whenever the Government considers it suitable, by ratifying, amplifying, or in any manner modifying the said demarcations in conformity with the knowledge, discoveries, studies, and interests of Chile which may be made known in the future; at present said protection and control are declared over all the sea included between the perimeter formed by the coast and a mathematical parallel projected out to sea at a distance of two hundred marine miles from the continental coasts of Chile. With respect to the Chilean islands, this demarcation will be made by marking out a sea zone contiguous to the coasts of these islands, projected parallel to these coasts for two hundred marine miles from the whole circumference.

4. The present declaration of sovereignty does not disregard similar legitimate rights of other States, on the basis of reciprocity, and does not affect rights of free navigation on the high seas.

Santiago, 25 June 1947.

Gabriel Gonzalez Videla,
President of the Republic.

1. Translation from El Mercurio, Santiago de Chile, 29 June 1947, appearing in U.S. Naval War College, International Law Documents, 1948-49 (Washington: Government Printing Office, 1950), pp. 188-190.

UNITED STATES NOTE OF PROTEST TO CHILE REGARDING THE EXTENT OF TERRITORIAL WATERS CLAIMED ALONG THE COASTS OF CHILE, ECUADOR AND PERU [1]

July 2,1948

"I have the honor to refer to the Decree issued by the President of the Republic of Chile on June 25, 1947 concerning the conservation of the resources of the continental shelf and the epicontinental seas and to advise that I have been instructed by my Government to make certain reservations with respect to the rights and interests of the United States of America.

"The United States Government has carefully studied this declaration of the President of the Republic of Chile. The Declaration cites the Proclamations of the United States of September 28,1945 in the Preamble. My Government is accordingly confident that His Excellency, the President of the Republic of Chile, in issuing the Declaration, was actuated by the same long-range considerations with respect to the wise conservation and utilization of natural resources as motivated President Truman in proclaiming the policy of the United States relative to the natural resources of the subsoil and seabed of the continental shelf and its policy relative to coastal fisheries in certain areas of the high seas. The United States Government, aware of the inadequacy of past arrangements for the effective conservation and perpetuation of such resources, views with utmost sympathy the considerations which led the Chilean Government to issue its Declaration.

"At the same time, the United States Government notes that the principles underlying the Chilean Declaration differ in large measure from those of the United States Proclamations and appear to be at variance with the generally accepted principles of international law. In these respects, the United States Government notes in particular (1) the Chilean Declaration confirms and proclaims the national sovereignty of Chile over the continental shelf and over the seas adjacent to the coast of Chile outside the generally accepted limits of territorial waters, and (2) the Declaration fails, with respect to fishing, to accord appropriate and adequate recognition to the rights and interests of the United States in the high seas off the coasts of Chile. In view of these considerations, the United States Government wishes to indicate to the Chilean Government that it reserves the rights and interests of the United States so far as concerns any effects of the Declaration of June 25, 1947, or of any measures designed to carry that Declaration into execution.

"The reservations thus made by the United States Government are not intended to have relation to or to prejudge any Chilean claim with reference to the Antarctic Continent or other land areas.

"The Government of the United States of America is similarly reserving its rights and interests with respect to decrees issued by the Governments of Argentina and Peru which purport to extend their sovereignty beyond the generally accepted limits of territorial domain."

1. Text in U.S. Naval War College, _International Law Situations and Documents_, 1956, pp.450-451.

FORM OF LEASE FOR DRILLING AND MINING ON CONTINENTAL SHELF

Form 3380–1
(February 1966)
(formerly 4–1255)

UNITED STATES
DEPARTMENT OF THE INTERIOR
BUREAU OF LAND MANAGEMENT

OIL AND GAS LEASE OF SUBMERGED LANDS
UNDER THE OUTER CONTINENTAL SHELF LANDS ACT

Office	
Serial Number	
Cash Bonus	
Rental Rate	
Minimum Royalty Rate	Royalty Rate

This indenture of lease entered into and effective as of , by and between the United States of America, hereinafter called the Lessor, by the Director, Bureau of Land Management, and

hereinafter called the Lessee, under, pursuant, and subject to the terms and provisions of the Outer Continental Shelf Lands Act of August 7, 1953 (67 Stat. 462; 43 U.S.C., Sec. 1331, *et seq.*), hereinafter referred to as the Act, and to all lawful and reasonable regulations of the Secretary of the Interior (hereinafter referred to as the Secretary) when not inconsistent with any express and specific provisions herein, which are made a part hereof:

WITNESSETH:

Sec. 1. Rights of Lessee. That the Lessor, in consideration of a cash bonus and of the rents and royalties to be paid, and the conditions and covenants to be observed as herein set forth, does hereby grant and lease to the Lessee the exclusive right and privilege to drill for, mine, extract, remove and dispose of all oil and gas deposits except helium gas in or under the following-described area of the Outer Continental Shelf (as that term is defined in the Act):

containing acres, more or less (hereinafter referred to as the leased area), together with:

(*a*) the nonexclusive right to conduct within the leased area geological and geophysical explorations which are not unduly harmful to aquatic life;

(*b*) the right to drill water wells within the leased area and use free of cost, and to dispose of, water produced from such wells; and

(*c*) the right to construct or erect and to maintain within the leased area all artificial islands, platforms, fixed or floating structures, sea walls, docks, dredged channels and spaces, buildings, plants, telegraph or telephone lines and cables, pipelines, reservoirs, tanks, pumping stations, and other works and structures necessary or convenient to the full enjoyment of the rights granted by this lease, for a period of 5 years and as long thereafter as oil or gas may be produced from the leased area in paying quantities, or drilling or well reworking operations, as approved by the Secretary, are conducted thereon; subject to any unitization or pooling agreement heretofore or hereafter approved by the Secretary which affects the leased area or any part thereof, the provisions of such agreements to govern the leased area or part thereof subject thereto where inconsistent with the terms of this lease.

Sec. 2. Obligations of Lessee. In consideration of the foregoing, the Lessee agrees:

(*a*) *Rentals and royalties.* (1) To pay rentals and royalties as follows:

Rentals. To pay the Lessor on or before the first day of each lease year commencing prior to a discovery of oil or gas on the leased area, a rental of per acre or fraction thereof.

Minimum royalty. To pay the Lessor in lieu of rental at the expiration of each lease year commencing after discovery a minimum royalty of per acre or fraction thereof or, if there is production, the difference between the actual royalty paid during the year and the prescribed minimum royalty, if the actual royalty paid is less than the minimum royalty.

Royalty on production. To pay the Lessor a royalty of percent in amount or value of production saved, removed, or sold from leased area. Gas of all kinds (except helium and gas used for purposes of production from and operations upon the leased area or unavoidably lost) is subject to royalty.

(2) It is expressly agreed that the Secretary may establish reasonable minimum values for purposes of computing royalty on products obtained from this lease, due consideration being given to the highest price paid for a part or for a majority of production of like quality in the same field, or area, to the price received by the Lessee, to posted prices, and to other relevant matters. Each such determination shall be made only after due notice to the Lessee and a reasonable opportunity has been afforded the Lessee to be heard.

(3) When paid in value, such royalties on production shall be due and payable monthly on the last day of the month next following the month in which the production is obtained. When paid in production, such royalties shall be delivered at pipeline connections or in tanks provided by the Lessee. Such deliveries shall be made at reasonable times and intervals and, at the Lessee's option, shall be effected either (i) on or immediately adjacent to the leased area, without cost to the Lessor, or (ii) at a more convenient point closer to shore or on shore, in which event the Lessee shall be entitled to reimbursement for the reasonable cost of transporting the royalty substance to such delivery point. The Lessee shall not be required to provide storage for royalty taken in kind in excess of tankage required when royalty is paid in value. When payments are made in production the Lessee shall not be held liable for the loss or destruction of royalty oil or other liquid products in storage from causes over which the Lessee has no control.

(4) Rentals or minimum royalties may be reduced and royalties on the entire leasehold or any deposit, tract, or portion thereof segregated for royalty purposes may be reduced if the Secretary finds that, for the purpose of increasing the ultimate recovery of oil or gas and in the interest of conservation of natural resources, it is necessary, in his judgment, to do so in order to promote development, or because the lease cannot be successfully operated under the terms fixed herein.

(*b*) *Bonds.* To maintain at all times the bond required prior to the issuance of this lease and to furnish such additional security as may be required by the Lessor if, after operations or production have begun, the Lessor deems such additional security to be necessary.

(*c*) *Cooperative or unit plan.* Within 30 days after demand, to subscribe to and to operate under such reasonable cooperative or unit plan for the development and operation of the area, field, or pool, or part thereof, embracing lands included herein as the Secretary may determine to be practicable and necessary or advisable in the interest of conservation which plan shall adequately protect the rights of all parties in interest, including the United States.

(*d*) *Wells.* (1) To drill and produce such wells as are necessary to protect the Lessor from loss by reason of production on other properties or, in lieu thereof, with the consent of the oil and gas supervisor, to pay a sum determined by the supervisor as adequate to compensate the Lessor for failure to drill and produce any such well. In the event that this lease is not being maintained in force by other production of oil or gas in paying quantities or by other approved drilling or reworking operations, such payments shall be considered as the equivalent of production in paying quantities for all purposes of this lease.

(2) After due notice in writing, to drill and produce such other wells as the Secretary may reasonably require in order that the leased area or any part thereof may be properly and timely developed and produced in accordance with good operating practice.

(3) At the election of the Lessee, to drill and produce other wells in conformity with any system of well spacing or production allotments affecting the area, field, or pool in which the leased area or any part thereof is situated, which is authorized or sanctioned by applicable law or by the Secretary.

(e) Payments. To make all payments to the Lessor by check, bank draft or money order payable as indicated herein unless otherwise provided by regulations or by direction of the Secretary. Rental, royalties, and other payments shall be made payable to the United States Geological Survey and tendered to the Oil and Gas Supervisor, *except* that filing charges, bonuses, and first year's rental shall be made payable to the Bureau of Land Management and remitted to the Manager of the appropriate field office of that Bureau.

(f) Contracts for disposal of products. To file with the Oil and Gas Supervisor, Geological Survey, not later than 30 days after the effective date thereof, copies of all contracts for the disposal of lease products; provided that the Supervisor may relieve the Lessee of this requirement, in which event the contracts shall be made available for inspection by the Supervisor upon his request. Nothing in any such contract or in any approval thereof by the Supervisor shall be construed or accepted as modifying any of the provisions of this lease, including, but not limited to, provisions relating to gas waste, taking royalty in kind, and the method of computing royalties due as based on a minimum valuation and in accordance with the regulations applicable to this lease.

(g) Statements, plats, and reports. At such times and in such form as the Lessor may prescribe, to furnish detailed statements and reports showing the amounts and quality of all products saved, removed, and sold from the leased area, the proceeds therefrom, and the amount used for production purposes or unavoidably lost; also a plat showing development work and improvements on or with regard to the leased area.

(h) Inspection. To keep open at all reasonable times for the inspection of any duly authorized representative of the Lessor, the leased area and all wells, improvements, machinery and fixtures thereon and all books, accounts, and records relative to operations and surveys or investigations on or with regard to the leased area or under the lease.

(i) Diligence. To exercise reasonable diligence in drilling and producing the wells herein provided for; to carry on all operations in accordance with approved methods and practices including those provided in the operating and conservation regulations for the Outer Continental Shelf; to remove all structures when no longer required for operations under the lease to sufficient depth beneath the surface of the waters to prevent them from being a hazard to navigation; to carry out at expense of the Lessee all lawful and reasonable orders of the Lessor relative to the matters in this paragraph, and that on failure of the Lessee so to do the Lessor shall have the right to enter on the property and to accomplish the purpose of such orders at the Lessee's cost: *Provided,* That the Lessee shall not be held responsible for delays or casualties occasioned by causes beyond the Lessee's control.

(j) Freedom of purchase. To accord all workmen and employees directly engaged in any of the operations under this lease complete freedom of purchase.

(k) Equal Opportunity clause. During the performance of this contract the lessee agrees as follows:

(1) The lessee will not discriminate against any employee or applicant for employment because of race, creed, color, or national origin. The lessee will take affirmative action to ensure that applicants are employed, and that employees are treated during employment, without regard to their race, creed, color, or national origin. Such action shall include, but not be limited to the following: employment, upgrading, demotion, or transfer; recruitment or recruitment advertising; layoff or termination; rates of pay or other forms of compensation; and selection for training, including apprenticeship. The lessee agrees to post in conspicuous places, available to employees and applicants for employment, notices to be provided by the contracting officer setting forth the provisions of this nondiscrimination clause.

(2) The lessee will, in all solicitations or advertisements for employees placed by or on behalf of the lessee, state that all qualified applicants will receive consideration for employment without regard to race, creed, color, or national origin.

(3) The lessee will send to each labor union or representative of workers with which he has a collective bargaining agreement or other contract or understanding, a notice, to be provided by the agency contracting officer, advising the labor union or workers' representative of the lessee's commitments under Section 202 of Executive Order No. 11246 of September 24, 1965, and shall post copies of the notice in conspicuous places available to employees and applicants for employment.

(4) The lessee will comply with all provisions of Executive Order No. 11246 of September 24, 1965, and of the rules, regulations, and relevant orders of the Secretary of Labor.

(5) The lessee will furnish all information and reports required by Executive Order No. 11246 of September 24, 1965, and by the rules, regulations, and orders of the Secretary of Labor, or pursuant

thereto, and will permit access to his books, records, and accounts by the contracting agency and the Secretary of Labor for purposes of investigation to ascertain compliance with such rules, regulations, and orders.

(6) In the event of the lessee's noncompliance with the nondiscrimination clauses of this contract or with any of such rules, regulations, or orders, this contract may be cancelled, terminated or suspended in whole or in part and the lessee may be declared ineligible for further Government contracts in accordance with procedures authorized in Executive Order No. 11246 of September 24, 1965, and such other sanctions may be imposed and remedies involved as provided in Executive Order No. 11246 of September 24, 1965, or by rule, regulation, or order of the Secretary of Labor, or as otherwise provided by law.

(7) The lessee will include the provisions of Paragraphs (1) through (7) in every subcontract or purchase order unless exempted by rules, regulations, or orders of the Secretary of Labor issued pursuant to Section 204 of Executive Order No. 11246 of September 24, 1965, so that such provisions will be binding upon each subcontractor or vendor. The lessee will take such action with respect to any subcontract or purchase order as the contracting agency may direct as a means of enforcing such provisions including sanctions for noncompliance: *Provided, however,* That in the event the lessee becomes involved in, or is threatened with, litigation with a subcontractor or vendor as a reults of such direction by the contracting agency, the lessee may request the United States to enter into such litigation to protect the interests of the United States.

(l) Assignment of lease. To file for approval with the Bureau of Land Management, within 90 days from the date of final execution, any instrument of transfer of this lease, or any interest therein, including assignments of record title, operating agreements, and subleases. Carried working interests, overriding royalty interests, or payments out of production, may be created or transferred without requirement for filing or approval. Instruments required to be filed shall take effect upon approval as of the first day of the lease month following the date of filing unless at the request of the parties an earlier date is specified in such approval.

Sec. 3. Reservations to Lessor. The Lessor reserves:

(a) Geological and geophysical exploration; rights-of-way. The right to authorize the conduct of geological and geophysical exploration in the leased area which does not interfere with or endanger actual operations under this lease, and the right to grant such easements or rights-of-way upon, through, or in the leased area as may be necessary or appropriate to the working of other lands containing the deposits described in the Act, and to the treatment and shipment of products thereof by or under authority of the United States, its Lessees or Permittees, and for other public purposes, subject to the provisions of Section 5*(c)* of the Act where they are applicable and to all lawful and reasonable regulations and conditions prescribed by the Secretary thereunder.

(b) Leases of sulfur and other mineral. The right to grant sulfur leases and leases of any mineral other than oil, gas, and sulfur within the leased area or any part thereof, subject to the provisions of Section 8*(c)*, 8*(d)*, and 8*(e)* of the Act and all lawful and reasonable regulations prescribed by the Secretary thereunder; *Provided,* That no such sulfur lease or lease of other mineral shall authorize or permit the Lessee thereunder unreasonably to interfere with or endanger operations under this lease.

(c) Purchase of production. In time of war, or when the President of the United States shall so prescribe, the right of first refusal to purchase at the market price all or any portion of the oil or gas produced from the leased area, as provided in Section 12*(b)* of the Act.

(d) Taking of royalties. All rights, pursuant to clause (3) of Section 8*(b)* of the Act, to take royalties in the amount or value of production.

(e) Fissionable materials. All uranium, thorium, and all other materials determined pursuant to paragraph (1) of subsection *(b)* of Section 5 of the Atomic Energy Act of 1946, as amended, to be peculiarly essential to the production of fissionable materials, contained, in whatever concentration, in deposits in the subsoil or seabed of the leased area or any part thereof, as provided in Section 12*(e)* of the Act.

(f) Helium. Pursuant to Section 12*(f)* of the Act, the ownership and the right to extract helium from all gas produced under this lease, subject to such rules and regulations as shall be prescribed by the Secretary.

(g) Suspension of operations during war or national emergency. Upon recommendation of the Secretary of Defense, during a state of war or national emergency declared by the Congress or President of the United States after August 7, 1953, the authority of the Secretary to suspend any or all operations under this lease, as provided in Section 12*(c)* of the Act: *Provided,* That just compensation shall be paid by the Lessor to the Lessee.

(h) Restriction of exploration and operations. The right, as provided in Section 12*(d)* of the Act, to restrict from exploration and operations the leased area or any part thereof which may be designated by and through the Secretary of Defense, with the approval of the President, as, or as part of, an area of the Outer Continental Shelf needed for national defense; and so long as such designation remains in effect no explora-

tion or operations may be conducted on the surface of the leased area or the part thereof included within the designation except with the concurrence of the Secretary of Defense; and if operations or production under this lease within any such restricted area shall be suspended, any payments of rentals, minimum royalty, and royalty prescribed by this lease likewise shall be suspended during such period of suspension of operations and production, and the term of this lease shall be extended by adding thereto any such suspension period, and the Lessor shall be liable to the Lessee for such compensation as is required to be paid under the Constitution of the United States.

Sec. 4. Directional drilling. This lease may be maintained in force by directional wells drilled under the leased area from surface locations on adjacent or adjoining lands not covered by this lease. In such circumstances, drilling shall be considered to have been commenced on the leased area when drilling is commenced on the adjacent or adjoining land for the purpose of directionally drilling under the leased area, and production of oil or gas from the leased area through any directional well surfaced on adjacent or adjoining land or drilling or reworking of any such directional well shall be considered production or drilling or reworking operations (as the case may be) on the leased area for all purposes of this lease. Nothing contained in this paragraph is intended or shall be construed as granting to the Lessee any leasehold interests, licenses, easements, or other rights in or with respect to any such adjacent or adjoining land in addition to any such leasehold interests, licenses, easements, or other rights which the Lessee may have lawfully acquired under the Act or from the Lessor or others.

Sec. 5. Surrender and termination of lease. The Lessee may surrender this entire lease or any officially designated subdivision of the leased area by filing with the Bureau of Land Management, a written relinquishment, in *triplicate*, which shall be effective as of the date of filing, subject to the continued obligation of the Lessee and his surety to make payment of all accrued rentals and royalties and to abandon all wells on the area to be relinquished to the satisfaction of the Oil and Gas Supervisor.

Sec. 6. Removal of property on termination of lease. Upon the expiration of this lease, or the earlier termination thereof as herein provided, the Lessee shall within a period of 1 year thereafter remove from the premises all structures, machinery, equipment, tools, and materials other than improvements needed for producing wells or for drilling or producing on other leases and other property permitted by the Lessor to be maintained on the area.

Sec. 7. Remedies in case of default. *(a)* Whenever the Lessee fails to comply with any of the provisions of the Act or this lease or the applicable regulations in force and effect on the date of issuance of this lease, the lease shall be subject to cancellation as follows:

(1) *Cancellation of nonproducing lease.* If, at the time of such default, no well is producing, or is capable of producing, oil or gas in paying quantities from the leased area, whether such well be drilled from a surface location within the leased area or be directionally drilled from a surface location on adjacent or adjoining lands, this lease may be cancelled by the Secretary (subject to the right of judicial review as provided in Section 8*(j)* of the Act) if such default continues for the period of 30 days after mailing of notice by registered letter to the Lessee at the Lessee's record post office address.

(2) *Cancellation of producing lease.* If, at the time of such default, any well is producing, or is capable of producing, oil or gas in paying quantities from the leased area, whether such well be drilled from a surface location within the leased area or be directionally drilled from a surface location on adjacent or adjoining lands, this lease may be cancelled by an appropriate proceeding in any United States district court having jurisdiction under the provisions of Section 4*(b)* of the Act if such default continues for the period of 30 days after mailing of notice by registered letter to the Lessee at the Lessee's record post office address.

(b) Other remedies. If any such default continues for the period of 30 days after mailing of notice by registered letter to the Lessee at the Lessee's record post office address, the Lessor may then exercise any legal or equitable remedy which the Lessor may have; however, the remedy of cancellation of this lease may be exercised only under the conditions and subject to the limitations set out above in paragraph *(a)* of this Section, or pursuant to Section 8*(i)* of the Act.

(c) Effect of waiver of default. A waiver of any particular default shall not prevent the cancellation of this lease or the exercise of any other remedy the Lessor may have by reason of any other cause or for the same cause occurring at any other time.

Sec. 8. Heirs and successors in interest. Each obligation hereunder shall extend to and be binding upon, and every benefit hereof shall inure to, the heirs, executors, administrators, successors, or assigns of the respective parties hereto.

Sec. 9. Unlawful interest. No Member of, or Delegate to, Congress, or Resident Commissioner, after his election or appointment, or either before or after he has qualified, and during his continuance in office, and no officer, agent, or employee of the Department of the Interior, except as provided in 43 CFR 7.4(a) (1), shall be admitted to any share or part in this lease or derive any benefit that may arise therefrom; and the provisions of Section 3741 of the Revised Statutes (41 U.S.C. Sec. 22), as amended, and Sections 431, 432, and 433 of Title 18 of the United Stated Code, relating to contracts made or entered into, or accepted by or on behalf of the United States, form a part of this lease so far as the same may be applicable.

THE UNITED STATES OF AMERICA

____________________ By____________________

(Signature of Lessee) (Authorized Officer)

____________________ ____________________

(Signature of Lessee) (Title)

____________________ ____________________

(Signature of Lessee) (Date)

____________________ ____________________

(Signature of Lessee)

If this lease is executed by a corporation, it must bear the corporate seal

GPO 855-238

CONVENTION ON THE CONTINENTAL SHELF

Signed at Geneva, April 29, 1958 [1]

Article 1

For the purposes of these articles, the term "continental shelf" is used as referring (a) to the seabed and subsoil of the submarine areas adjacent to the coast but outside the area of the territorial sea, to a depth of 200 metres or, beyond that limit, to where the depth of the superjacent waters admits of the exploitation of the natural resources of the said area; (b) to the seabed and the subsoil of similar submarine areas adjacent to the coasts of islands.

Article 2

1.The coastal state exercises over the continental shelf sovereign rights for the purpose of exploring it and exploiting its natural resources.

2. The rights referred to in paragraph 1 of this article are exclusive in the sense that if the coastal state does not explore the continental shelf or exploit its natural resources, no one may undertake these activities, or make a claim to the continental shelf, without the express consent of the coastal state.

3. The rights of the coastal state over the continental shelf do not depend on occupation, effective or notional, or on any express proclamation.

4. The natural resources referred to in these articles consist of the mineral and other non-living resources of the seabed and subsoil together with living organisms belonging to sedentary species, that is to say, organisms which, at the harvestable stage, either are immobile on or under the

1. U.N. Doc. A/CONF. 13/L.55

seabed or are unable to move except in constant physical contact with the seabed or the subsoil.

ARTICLE 3

The rights of the coastal state over the continental shelf do not affect the legal status of the superjacent waters as high seas, or that of the airspace above those waters.

ARTICLE 4

Subject to its right to take reasonable measures for the exploration of the continental shelf and the exploitation of its natural resources, the coastal state may not impede the laying or maintenance of submarine cables or pipelines on the continental shelf.

ARTICLE 5

1. The exploration of the continental shelf and the exploitation of its natural resources must not result in any unjustifiable interference with navigation, fishing or the conservation of the living resources of the sea, nor result in any interference with fundamental oceanographic or other scientific research carried out with the intention of open publication.

2. Subject to the provisions of paragraphs 1 and 6 of this article, the coastal state is entitled to construct and maintain or operate on the continental shelf installations and other devices necessary for its exploration and the exploitation of its natural resources, and to establish safety zones around such installations and devices and to take in those zones measures necessary for their protection.

3. The safety zones referred to in paragraph 2 of this article may extend to a distance of 500 metres around the installations and other devices which have been erected, measured from each point of their outer edge. Ships of all nationalities must respect these safety zones.

4. Such installations and devices, though under the jurisdiction of the coastal state, do not possess the status of islands. They have no territorial sea of their own, and their presence does not affect the delimitation of the territorial sea of the coastal state.

5. Due notice must be given of the construction of any such installations, and permanent means for giving warning of their presence must be maintained. Any installations which are abandoned or disused must be entirely removed.

6. Neither the installations or devices, nor the safety zones around them, may be established where interference may be caused to the use of recognized sea lanes essential to international navigation.

7. The coastal state is obliged to undertake, in the safety zones, all appropriate measures for the protection of the living resources of the sea from harmful agents.

8. The consent of the coastal state shall be obtained in respect of any research concerning the continental shelf and undertaken there. Nevertheless, the coastal state shall not normally withhold its consent if the

request is submitted by a qualified institution with a view to purely scientific research into the physical or biological characteristics of the continental shelf, subject to the proviso that the coastal state shall have the right, if it so desires, to participate or to be represented in the research, and that in any event the results shall be published.

Article 6

1. Where the same continental shelf is adjacent to the territories of two or more states whose coasts are opposite each other, the boundary of the continental shelf appertaining to such states shall be determined by agreement between them. In the absence of agreement, and unless another boundary line is justified by special circumstances, the boundary is the median line, every point of which is equidistant from the nearest points of the baselines from which the breadth of the territorial sea of each state is measured.

2. Where the same continental shelf is adjacent to the territories of two adjacent states, the boundary of the continental shelf shall be determined by agreement between them. In the absence of agreement, and unless another boundary line is justified by special circumstances, the boundary shall be determined by application of the principle of equidistance from the nearest points of the baselines from which the breadth of the territorial sea of each state is measured.

3. In delimiting the boundaries of the continental shelf, any lines which are drawn in accordance with the principles set out in paragraphs 1 and 2 of this article should be defined with reference to charts and geographical features as they exist at a particular date, and reference should be made to fixed permanent identifiable points on the land.

Article 7

The provisions of these articles shall not prejudice the right of the coastal state to exploit the subsoil by means of tunnelling irrespective of the depth of water above the subsoil.

Article 8

This Convention shall, until 31 October 1958, be open for signature by all States Members of the United Nations or of any of the specialized agencies, and by any other state invited by the General Assembly to become a party to the Convention.

Article 9

This Convention is subject to ratification. The instruments of ratification shall be deposited with the Secretary-General of the United Nations.

Article 10

This Convention shall be open for accession by any states belonging to any of the categories mentioned in Article 8. The instruments of accession shall be deposited with the Secretary-General of the United Nations.

Article 11

1. This Convention shall come into force on the thirtieth day following the date of deposit of the twenty-second instrument of ratification or accession with the Secretary-General of the United Nations.

2. For each state ratifying or acceding to the Convention after the deposit of the twenty-second instrument of ratification or accession, the Convention shall enter into force on the thirtieth day after deposit by such state of its instrument of ratification or accession.

OCEANIC RESEARCH IN FOREIGN WATERS

Note

Vessels engaged in ocean research are required to observe certain regulations governing clearance for entering foreign territorial waters or engaging in research on the continental shelf. Certain distinctions prevail between public and private vessels in this respect. Public vessels owned, operated or chartered by agencies of the United States Government for a public purpose have a special status as between governments and must adhere strictly to certain rules. They are not operated for any commercial purpose. Private vessels owned and operated by universities, research institutions, or by private parties, may or may not have commercial purposes.

Public vessels are required to have official permission of the host government to enter a foreign port or waters. This is arranged through diplomatic channels; in the case of the United States through the Department of State. Private vessels do not require diplomatic clearance, although this may be advantageous. They must, nevertheless, have formal official authorization from the host government.

No vessel, public or private, may conduct oceanographic research in the territorial waters of another state, or on or above its continental shelf, without clearance from the host government. Operators of private research vessels may seek such permission directly from the host government. The United States Government urges such operators to forward their requests through the Department of State, however, in as much as American Embassies know the channels through which such requests must go. They are in a position to help facilitate clearances and can be of much help in the event changes or emergencies occur requiring some modifcation of plans. Furthermore, most embassies are staffed to be of assistance in arranging contacts with local scientists and organizations that may be interested in the research and be able to give further help.

Requests for clearances must indicate the nature of and reasons for the research, the location where it is desired to be conducted, and the dates to be covered by it. Although the United States recognizes no more than three nautical miles for the territorial sea, it is aware that more extensive claims are held by some states, as indicated in the Table of Maritime Jurisdiction Claimed by Various States given on a subsequent page. It cannot guarantee to assure the immunity of vessels engaging in research off these states when this is done outside of the three mile line but within the distances claimed by these other countries.

Under the terms of the Geneva Convention on the Continental Shelf, coastal states are entitled to exercise sovereign rights in exploring and exploiting the resources of the continental shelf. This is defined to mean the shelf outside of territorial waters to a point where the water is 200 meters deep, or, beyond that limit to a point where "the depth of the superjacent waters admits of the exploitation" of the resources of the area. If the coastal state has capability for exploiting the resources at a depth of 600 meters, its authority to exercise sovereign rights may extend that far irrespective of whether it is actually engaging in such marine operations.

No finite boundary has been drawn or agreed to among states on the outer limits of national jurisdiction over the continental shelves, slope or rise. Until this is done each state is free to establish its own limits, and there is likely to be considerable difference among states on this. Vessels undertaking scientific research along the continental shelves will need to exercise care in inquiring as to local law and understandings, in obtaining the consent of the coastal state for any research concerning the shelf, and in conforming thereto. Parties interested in prospecting for petroleum, gas or other minerals, may be required to obtain a lease for such exploration activities.

Research on the continental shelf has been described in a pamphlet published by the Inter-Agency Committee on Oceanography of the United States Government as including "the removal of shelf samples (such as by coring and dredging) and of living resources which are unable to move at the harvestable stage except in constant physical contact with the shelf." Research in waters above the shelves and on swimming creatures is not affected in as much as this is in the high seas.

The promotion of increased international cooperation in the seas has been declared to be an objective of the United States by the Congress when it passed the Marine Resources and Engineering Development Act of 1966. It has also been stressed by the President, notably at the time of the commissioning of the U.S. oceanographic research vessel Oceanographer. Scientists and engineers engaged in ocean research undertakings are in a particularly good situation to foster international cooperation and goodwill acting as they are in an essentially international environment. Survey and oceanographic research ships can often help promote such cooperation through seeking contacts with members of the overseas scientific community, collaborating with them when possible, and inviting their participation in joint research undertakings. The furtherance of such contacts is a principal objective of the scientific attaches in American embassies abroad.

* * * *

Checklist for Initiating Requests for Foreign Clearance[1]

A. Information requested by the Department of State in connection with any cruise involving foreign port clearances, foreign port calls, foreign territorial waters research, and foreign continental shelf research includes the following:

1. Name of vessel, whether public or private, and affiliation.
2. Itinerary, including all dates as precisely as possible.
3. General purpose of voyage.
4. Reasons for port calls (bunkering, change of personnel, etc.)
5. Any special facilities needed, or particular assistance anticipated.
6. Ship's agent at each port.
7. Name of the master, number in crew, number in scientific party, general information on foreign nationals.
8. Communications frequencies and times watched.
9. Accomodations available for foreign scientists if desired that such information be forwarded by Department of State....
10. Accomodations available for foreign scientists if required as a condition for clearance.
11. Information on whether additional research might be undertaken if requested by foreign scientists or governments. Indicate whether an offer of such research should be made by the Department.

B. Additional information requested by the Department of State in connection with research in foreign territorial waters or on foreign continental shelves:

1. Nature of research, including reason for choosing location in question.
2. Location as precisely as possible.
3. Dates.

C. Notice of changes in plans:

1. Notify Department of State of all changes in schedule of more than a few days.
2. If possible, notify American Embassy or Consulate by ship's radio of emergency requiring last-minute clearances....

F. Timing

1. Information list in A and B should be furnished to the Department of State 60 days prior to commencing a cruise.
2. Material under A and B should be furnished to the Department of State at least 60 days prior to port calls or research work when it cannot be given 60 days prior to a cruise....

1. U.S. Oceanic Research in Foreign Waters. Inter-Agency Committee on Oceanography (Washington,1968), Appendix B.

CHAPTER FOUR

THE SEAS AND INTERNATIONAL LAW

Introductory Note

The oceans embrace 140 million square miles of the Earth's surface. Their vastness is such that it is possible for a vessel to be 1,600 miles from the nearest land or over 3,500 miles from the nearest continent. The Pacific Ocean alone covers 65 million square miles, an area greater than Europe and Asia combined. When the Atlantic, Pacific and Indian Oceans are viewed as a single body of waters they comprise the largest geographic element on the planet.

Since time immemorial man has relied upon the oceans as a source of commerce and food supply, and as a means to power. World fisheries today yield annual catches in the range of 115-125 billion pounds. The mineral wealth of the seas is only now being surveyed on some of the continental shelves. One of the exciting developments of the next twenty-five years will be the extraction of fossil fuel oils and mineral ores from the continental shelves. Aside from these economic assets, the seas serve as a channel of communication between nations, and have on occasion exercised decisive influence upon the outcome of contests of power between states.

As the number of states has increased interest in the seas has heightened. Gone is the time when a religious leader could declare that the oceans were the property of two faithful powers. Since the 17th century nations have accepted the principle of *mare liberum* for the high seas. Yet the rise of new nationalism has brought with it advancing claims to controls at the margins of the seas. Gradually, but perhaps inevitably, the sphere of free seas is dwindling as countries fence off waters for their own sovereignty and control. Although the large majority of states demand free use of the high seas, the width of territorial waters has grown from three to twelve and more miles. This dichotomy has been a source of endless argument among governments and remains an unresolved issue today.

It is possible to organize the world's oceans into a system containing five zones, which run roughly parallel to the coasts. These include: (1) internal waters; (2) the territorial sea; (3) contiguous zones; (4) the continental shelf; and (5) the high seas.

Internal waters refer to bays, indentations, estuaries and river mouths. Like the inland waters of rivers and great lake systems, they are subject to the laws of the land to which they adjoin or separate.

We have spoken about the territorial sea in a preceding chapter. Territorial waters comprise a belt of water which parallels the coast and usually extends to three or twelve miles, depending upon the wishes of the adjacent state. Sovereignty is demanded in these waters with the exception that usage and conventions afford a right of innocent passage for foreign merchant vessels.

Contiguous zones are customarily limited to the breadth of sea between territorial waters and the twelve mile line. Under the United States Customs Enforcement Act this country, however, did reserve a right to extend its jurisdiction for limited times and specific purposes to fifty miles to prevent evasion of its laws. Furthermore, under the Act of Panama in 1939 the American Republics proclaimed a Neutrality Zone around the hemisphere which in places extended to several hundred miles from shore. This highly exceptional arrangement was not recognized by belligerents. For the most part contiguous zones lie close to territorial waters and are restricted to fishery conservation.

Since the geographical situation prevailing along the coasts of states varies considerably, it is not surprising that large differences exist in the practice of countries with respect to jurisdiction in the marginal seas. To date no general agreement has been obtained for establishing uniform jurisdictional limits.

The continental shelf, which has been discussed in the immediately preceding chapter, is now a well-known factor of geopolitics. The United States position is that the coastal state has rights to exercise sovereignty over the resources situated on the seabed and in the subsoil and may exercise control over those who wish to engage in research or exploration on the floor of the slope and rise, or to extract minerals or other resources found on the seabed. Jurisdiction does not extend to the waters lying above the continental shelf outside of territorial limits.

The high seas refer to the waters that lie beyond the outer limit of the territorial sea. Here national jurisdiction approaches zero in time of peace. Surface and submarine navigation may proceed at will on the high seas, although certain regulations have been agreed upon by states to insure safety of navigation, to minimize the risk of accidents, and to provide assistance to vessels in distress. Airplanes may fly over the high seas freely, although again in the interests of safety certain directional flight tracks, riding lights, radio and radar equipment, and rules of the road are employed. Upon, within and over the high seas, as well as on the floor below them beyond the continental shelf, all nations and their nationals are entitled to engage in any activity as long as this does not jeopardize the safety or coequal rights of others.

One can see that as the distance from shore and from the continental landmass increases the measure and force of national jurisdiction tends to decrease, with the exception that the rule of the flag state governs internal matters aboard its vessels regardless of their location upon the seas.

International agreements are often concluded to assure freedom of passage through narrow straits and interoceanic canals and to permit access to ports. Commerce depends upon ability to enter and to leave these restricted ways. As the Geographer of the State Department has said, "the millions of square miles of 'open seas' are not at all open without accessibility to the terminals."

Despite the fact that there are no set divisions between the high seas, the continental shelves and contiguous zones, this does not invalidate the concept of the freedom of the seas. However, within these overlapping areas states may with reason demand that vessels follow specific routes, submit to customs inspections and obtain permission to exploit fisheries and mineral reserves. Nations have also agreed, in the interests of preventing pollution, that vessels may not pump their bilges within fifty miles of shore or dump nuclear wastes. Thus, freedom of the seas is governed by minimal restraints accepted by maritime powers in the interests of safeguarding all users and interested parties.

It will be observed from the Table of Maritime Jurisdiction Claimed by States appearing in Chapter Three that the boundary between territorial waters and the high seas is not universally fixed. There are great differences in the seaward limits of territorial waters, ranging all the way from three miles to two hundred. This factor was taken into consideration in the preparatory work for the Geneva Law of the Sea Conference in 1958. The International Law Commission noted in its report:

1. that international practice is not uniform with regards to the delimitation of the territorial sea;

2. that international law does not permit an extension of the territorial sea beyond twelve miles;

3. that with the absence of international recognition of a set limit for territorial seas some states have claimed more than three miles, while olthers refuse to recognize claims which exceed those of their own;

4. that the breadth of the sea should be fixed by international agreement.

When the Geneva Conference tackled this question, it was not able to agree upon any fixed seaward limit to the territorial sea. The terms of the Convention on the Territorial Seas and Contiguous Zones,which appears in this Chapter,affirm only that the coastal state has sovereignty over a body of marginal water whose breadth is determined by the will of the state.

Because many countries have a stake in maintaining free navigation and are interested in advancing ocean engineering, the law of the sea is a prime topic of discussion. The Geneva Conventions of 1958 made an attempt to reduce practice and unwritten law to conventional terms. Unfortunately, nationalism and world tensions made it difficult to reach accord on the more disputed aspects of rights and obligations. Some authorities feel that another attempt to reach agreement along these lines should be initiated. Perhaps the most that can be expected in the near future, however, is a continuation of the dialogue which has been echoing in the halls of the United Nations since 1966. With the increasing rivalries and differences over fisheries, mineral exploitation privileges, and underwater defense sites, plus the failure of the 1960 attempt to move beyond the limited accord reached in 1958, it appears doubtful that the calling of a general conference would be worthwhile as yet.

Perhaps progress can be attained on a less ambitious level. By encouraging small groups of nations, having mutual interests, to meet with one another perhaps accord can be reached on specific questions such as tuna fishing in the South Pacific, installation of nuclear power plants at specific locations, or the like. States are often willing to agree upon specialized, regional or functional problems despite their difficulty in accepting more generalized regulations.

In addition to the documents included in this Chapter, and the references mentioned in the preceding chapters, readers will find it useful to consult the standard works on international law as they relate to jurisdiction and the seas.

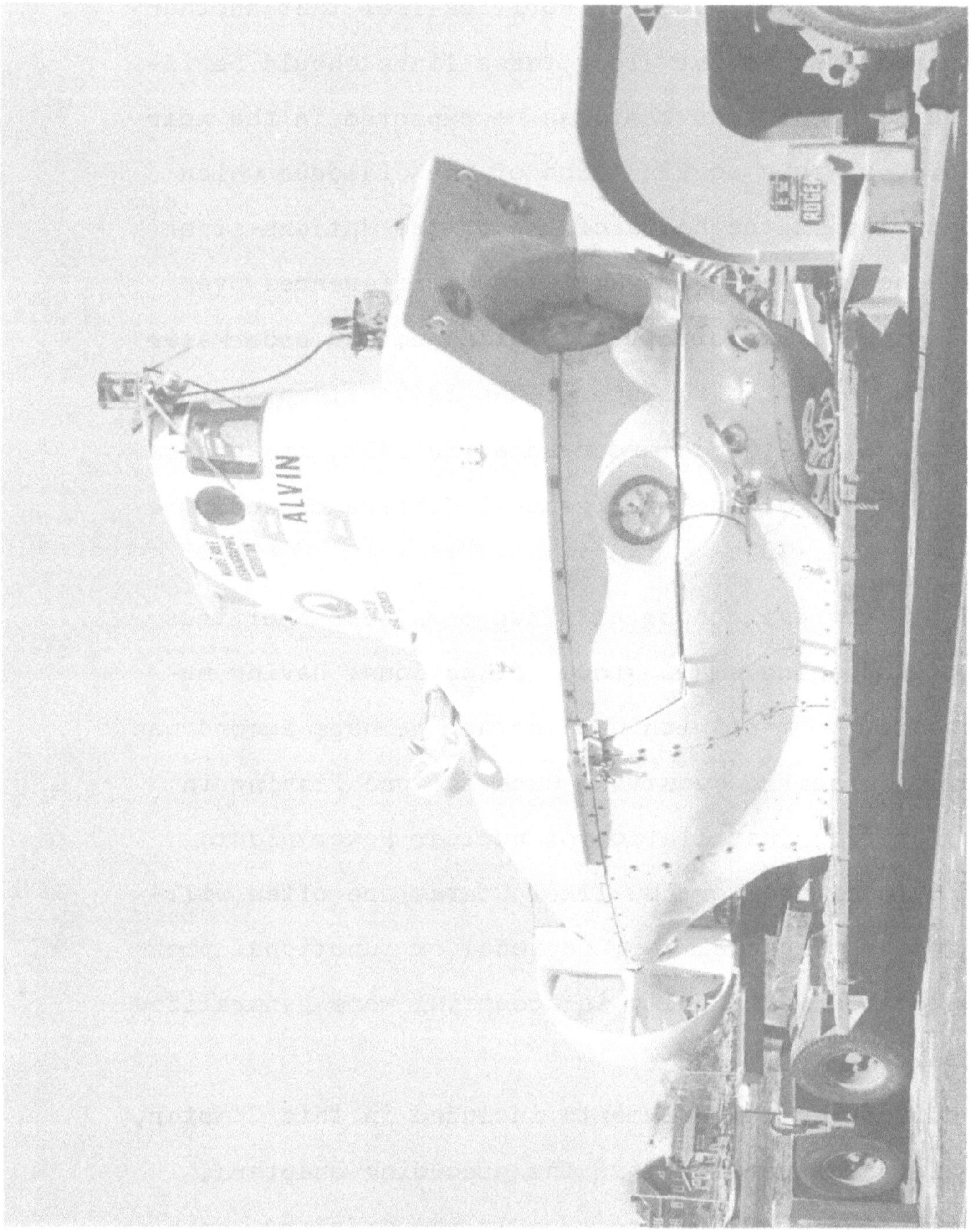

EXPERIMENTAL RESEARCH SUBMARINE - ALVIN

Courtesy Woods Hole Oceanographic Institution

CONVENTION ON THE HIGH SEAS

Signed at Geneva, April 29, 1958 [1]

Article 1

The term "high seas" means all parts of the sea that are not included in the territorial sea or in the internal waters of a state.

Article 2

The high seas being open to all nations, no state may validly purport to subject any part of them to its sovereignty. Freedom of the high seas is exercised under the conditions laid down by these articles and by the other rules of international law. It comprises, *inter alia*, both for coastal and non-coastal states:

(1) Freedom of navigation;
(2) Freedom of fishing;
(3) Freedom to lay submarine cables and pipelines;
(4) Freedom to fly over the high seas.

These freedoms, and others which are recognized by the general principles of international law, shall be exercised by all states with reasonable regard to the interests of other states in their exercise of the freedom of the high seas.

1. U.N. Doc. A/CONF.13/L.53

Article 3

1. In order to enjoy the freedom of the seas on equal terms with coastal states, states having no seacoast should have free access to the sea. To this end states situated between the sea and a state having no seacoast shall by common agreement with the latter and in conformity with existing international conventions accord:

(a) To the state having no seacoast, on a basis of reciprocity, free transit through their territory and

(b) To ships flying the flag of that state treatment equal to that accorded to their own ships, or to the ships of any other states, as regards access to seaports and the use of such ports.

2. States situated between the sea and a state having no seacoast shall settle, by mutual agreement with the latter, and taking into account the rights of the coastal state or state of transit and the special conditions of the state having no seacoast, all matters relating to freedom of transit and equal treatment in ports, in case such states are not already parties to existing international conventions.

Article 4

Every state, whether coastal or not, has the right to sail ships under its flag on the high seas.

Article 5

1. Each state shall fix the conditions for the grant of its nationality to ships, for the registration of ships in its territory, and for the right to fly its flag. Ships have the nationality of the state whose flag they are entitled to fly. There must exist a genuine link between the state and the ship; in particular, the state must effectively exercise its jurisdiction and control in administrative, technical and social matters over ships flying its flag.

2. Each state shall issue to ships to which it has granted the right to fly its flag documents to that effect.

Article 6

1. Ships shall sail under the flag of one state only and, save in exceptional cases expressly provided for in international treaties or in these articles, shall be subject to its exclusive jurisdiction on the high seas. A ship may not change its flag during a voyage or while in a port of call, save in the case of a real transfer of ownership or change in registry.

2. A ship which sails under the flags of two or more states, using them according to convenience, may not claim any of the nationalities in question with respect to any other state, and may be assimilated to a ship without nationality.

Article 7

The provisions of the preceding articles do not prejudice the question of ships employed on the official service of an intergovernmental organization flying the flag of the organization.

Article 8

1. Warships on the high seas have complete immunity from the jurisdiction of any state other than the flag state.
2. For the purposes of these articles, the term "warship" means a ship belonging to the naval forces of a state and bearing the external marks distinguishing warships of its nationality, under the command of an officer duly commissioned by the government and whose name appears in the Navy List, and manned by a crew who are under regular naval discipline.

Article 9

Ships owned or operated by a state and used only on government non-commercial service shall, on the high seas, have complete immunity from the jurisdiction of any state other than the flag state.

Article 10

1. Every state shall take such measures for ships under its flag as are necessary to ensure safety at sea with regard *inter alia* to:

(a) The use of signals, the maintenance of communications and the prevention of collisions;
(b) The manning of ships and labour conditions for crews taking into account the applicable international labour instruments;
(c) The construction, equipment and seaworthiness of ships.

2. In taking such measures each state is required to conform to generally accepted international standards and to take any steps which may be necessary to ensure their observance.

Article 11

1. In the event of a collision or of any other incident of navigation concerning a ship on the high seas, involving the penal or disciplinary responsibility of the master or of any other person in the service of the ship, no penal or disciplinary proceedings may be instituted against such persons except before the judicial or administrative authorities either of the flag state or of the state of which such person is a national.
2. In disciplinary matters, the state which has issued a master's certificate or a certificate of competence or license shall alone be competent, after due legal process, to pronounce the withdrawal of such certificates, even if the holder is not a national of the state which issued them.
3. No arrest or detention of the ship, even as a measure of investigation, shall be ordered by any authorities other than those of the flag state.

ARTICLE 12

1. Every state shall require the master of a ship sailing under its flag, insofar as he can do so without serious danger to the ship, the crew or the passengers:

(a) To render assistance to any person found at sea in danger of being lost;
(b) To proceed with all possible speed to the rescue of persons in distress if informed of their need of assistance, insofar as such action may reasonably be expected of him;
(c) After a collision to render assistance to the other ship, her crew and her passengers and, where possible, to inform the other ship of the name of his own ship, her port of registry and the nearest port at which she will call.

2. Every coastal state shall promote the establishment and maintenance of an adequate and effective search and rescue service regarding safety on and over the sea and—where circumstances so require—by way of mutual regional arrangements co-operate with neighbouring states for this purpose.

ARTICLE 13

Every state shall adopt effective measures to prevent and punish the transport of slaves in ships authorized to fly its flag, and to prevent the unlawful use of its flag for that purpose. Any slave taking refuge on board any ship, whatever its flag, shall *ipso facto* be free.

ARTICLE 14

All states shall co-operate to the fullest possible extent in the repression of piracy on the high seas or in any other place outside the jurisdiction of any state.

ARTICLE 15

Piracy consists of any of the following acts:

(1) Any illegal acts of violence, detention or any act of depredation, committed for private ends by the crew or the passengers of a private ship or a private aircraft, and directed:
  (a) On the high seas, against another ship or aircraft, or against persons or property on board such ship or aircraft;
  (b) Against a ship, aircraft, persons or property in a place outside the jurisdiction of any state;
(2) Any act of voluntary participation in the operation of a ship or of an aircraft with knowledge of facts making it a pirate ship or aircraft;
(3) Any act of inciting or of intentionally facilitating an act described in sub-paragraph 1 or sub-paragraph 2 of this article.

Article 16

The acts of piracy, as defined in Article 15, committed by a warship, government ship or government aircraft whose crew has mutinied and taken control of the ship or aircraft are assimilated to acts committed by a private ship.

Article 17

A ship or aircraft is considered a pirate ship or aircraft if it is intended by the persons in dominant control to be used for the purpose of committing one of the acts referred to in Article 15. The same applies if the ship or aircraft has been used to commit any such act, so long as it remains under the control of the persons guilty of that act.

Article 18

A ship or aircraft may retain its nationality although it has become a pirate ship or aircraft. The retention or loss of nationality is determined by the law of the state from which such nationality was derived.

Article 19

On the high seas, or in any other place outside the jurisdiction of any state, every state may seize a pirate ship or aircraft, or a ship taken by piracy and under the control of pirates, and arrest the persons and seize the property on board. The courts of the state which carried out the seizure may decide upon the penalties to be imposed, and may also determine the action to be taken with regard to the ships, aircraft or property, subject to the rights of third parties acting in good faith.

Article 20

Where the seizure of a ship or aircraft on suspicion of piracy has been effected without adequate grounds, the state making the seizure shall be liable to the state the nationality of which is possessed by the ship or aircraft, for any loss or damage caused by the seizure.

Article 21

A seizure on account of piracy may only be carried out by warships or *military aircraft, or other ships or aircraft on government service authorized* to that effect.

Article 22

1. Except where acts of interference derive from powers conferred by treaty, a warship which encounters a foreign merchant ship on the high seas is not justified in boarding her unless there is reasonable ground for suspecting:

(a) That the ship is engaged in piracy; or
(b) That the ship is engaged in the slave trade; or
(c) That, though flying a foreign flag or refusing to show its flag, the ship is, in reality, of the same nationality as the warship.

2. In the cases provided for in sub-paragraphs (a), (b) and (c) above, the warship may proceed to verify the ship's right to fly its flag. To this end, it may send a boat under the command of an officer to the suspected ship. If suspicion remains after the documents have been checked, it may proceed to a further examination on board the ship, which must be carried out with all possible consideration.

3. If the suspicions prove to be unfounded, and provided that the ship boarded has not committed any act justifying them, it shall be compensated for any loss or damage that may have been sustained.

ARTICLE 23

1. The hot pursuit of a foreign ship may be undertaken when the competent authorities of the coastal state have good reason to believe that the ship has violated the laws and regulations of that state. Such pursuit must be commenced when the foreign ship or one of its boats is within the internal waters or the territorial sea or the contiguous zone of the pursuing state, and may only be continued outside the territorial sea or the contiguous zone if the pursuit has not been interrupted. It is not necessary that, at the time when the foreign ship within the territorial sea or the contiguous zone receives the order to stop, the ship giving the order should likewise be within the territorial sea or the contiguous zone. If the foreign ship is within a contiguous zone, as defined in Article 24 of the Convention on the Territorial Sea and the Contiguous Zone, the pursuit may only be undertaken if there has been a violation of the rights for the protection of which the zone was established.

2. The right of hot pursuit ceases as soon as the ship pursued enters the territorial sea of its own country or of a third state.

3. Hot pursuit is not deemed to have begun unless the pursuing ship has satisfied itself by such practicable means as may be available that the ship pursued or one of its boats or other craft working as a team and using the ship pursued as a mother ship are within the limits of the territorial sea, or as the case may be within the contiguous zone. The pursuit may only be commenced after a visual or auditory signal to stop has been given at a distance which enables it to be seen or heard by the foreign ship.

4. The right of hot pursuit may be exercised only by warships or military aircraft, or other ships or aircraft on government service specially authorized to that effect.

5. Where hot pursuit is effected by an aircraft:

(a) The provisions of paragraphs 1 to 3 of this article shall apply *mutatis mutandis;*

(b) The aircraft giving the order to stop must itself actively pursue the ship until a ship or aircraft of the coastal state, summoned by the aircraft, arrives to take over the pursuit, unless the aircraft is itself able to arrest the ship. It does not suffice to justify an arrest on the high seas that the ship was merely sighted by the aircraft as an offender or suspected offender, if it was not both ordered to stop and pursued by the aircraft itself or other aircraft or ships which continue the pursuit without interruption.

6. The release of a ship arrested within the jurisdiction of a state and escorted to a port of that state for the purposes of an enquiry before the competent authorities, may not be claimed solely on the ground that the ship, in the course of its voyage, was escorted across a portion of the high seas, if the circumstances rendered this necessary.
7. Where a ship has been stopped or arrested on the high seas in circumstances which do not justify the exercise of the right of hot pursuit, it shall be compensated for any loss or damage that may have been thereby sustained.

Article 24

Every state shall draw up regulations to prevent pollution of the seas by the discharge of oil from ships or pipelines or resulting from the exploitation and exploration of the seabed and its subsoil, taking account of existing treaty provisions on the subject.

Article 25

1. Every state shall take measures to prevent pollution of the seas from the dumping of radioactive waste, taking into account any standards and regulations which may be formulated by the competent international organizations.
2. All states shall co-operate with the competent international organizations in taking measures for the prevention of pollution of the seas or airspace above, resulting from any activities with radioactive materials or other harmful agents.

Article 26

1. All states shall be entitled to lay submarine cables and pipelines on the bed of the high seas.
2. Subject to its right to take reasonable measures for the exploration of the continental shelf and the exploitation of its natural resources, the coastal state may not impede the laying or maintenance of such cables or pipelines.
3. When laying such cables or pipelines the state in question shall pay due regard to cables or pipelines already in position on the seabed. In particular, possibilities of repairing existing cables or pipelines shall not be prejudiced.

Article 27

Every state shall take the necessary legislative measures to provide that the breaking or injury by a ship flying its flag or by a person subject to its jurisdiction of a submarine cable beneath the high seas done wilfully or through culpable negligence, in such a manner as to be liable to interrupt or obstruct telegraphic or telephonic communications, and similarly the breaking or injury of a submarine pipeline or high-voltage power cable shall be a punishable offence. This provision shall not apply to any break or injury caused by persons who acted merely with the legitimate object of saving their lives or their ships, after having taken all necessary precautions to avoid such break or injury.

ARTICLE 28

Every state shall take the necessary legislative measures to provide that, if persons subject to its jurisdiction who are the owners of a cable or pipeline beneath the high seas, in laying or repairing that cable or pipeline, cause a break in or injury to another cable or pipeline, they shall bear the cost of the repairs.

ARTICLE 29

Every state shall take the necessary legislative measures to ensure that the owners of ships who can prove that they have sacrificed an anchor, a net or any other fishing gear, in order to avoid injuring a submarine cable or pipeline, shall be indemnified by the owner of the cable or pipeline, provided that the owner of the ship has taken all reasonable precautionary measures beforehand.

ARTICLE 30

The provisions of this Convention shall not affect conventions or other international agreements already in force, as between states parties to them.

ARTICLE 31

This Convention shall, until 31 October 1958, be open for signature by all States Members of the United Nations or of any of the specialized agencies, and by any other state invited by the General Assembly to become a party to the Convention.

ARTICLE 32

This Convention is subject to ratification. The instruments of ratification shall be deposited with the Secretary-General of the United Nations.

ARTICLE 33

This Convention shall be open for accession by any states belonging to any of the categories mentioned in Article 31. The instruments of accession shall be deposited with the Secretary-General of the United Nations.

ARTICLE 34

1. This Convention shall come into force on the thirtieth day following the date of deposit of the twenty-second instrument of ratification or accession with the Secretary-General of the United Nations.

2. For each state ratifying or acceding to the Convention after the deposit of the twenty-second instrument of ratification or accession, the Convention shall enter into force on the thirtieth day after deposit by such state of its instrument of ratification or accession.

CONVENTION ON FISHING AND CONSERVATION OF THE LIVING RESOURCES OF THE HIGH SEAS[1]

Signed at Geneva, April 29, 1958

Article 1

1. All states have the right for their nationals to engage in fishing on the high seas, subject (a) to their treaty obligations, (b) to the interests and rights of coastal states as provided for in this Convention, and (c) to the provisions contained in the following articles concerning conservation of the living resources of the high seas.

2. All states have the duty to adopt, or to co-operate with other states in adopting, such measures for their respective nationals as may be necessary for the conservation of the living resources of the high seas.

Article 2

As employed in this Convention, the expression "conservation of the living resources of the high seas" means the aggregate of the measures rendering possible the optimum sustainable yield from those resources so as to secure a maximum supply of food and other marine products. Conservation programmes should be formulated with a view to securing in the first place a supply of food for human consumption.

Article 3

A state whose nationals are engaged in fishing any stock or stocks of fish or other living marine resources in any area of the high seas where the nationals of other states are not thus engaged shall adopt, for its own nationals, measures in that area when necessary for the purpose of the conservation of the living resources affected.

Article 4

1. If the nationals of two or more states are engaged in fishing the same stock or stocks of fish or other living marine resources in any area or areas of the high seas, these states shall, at the request of any of them, enter into negotiations with a view to prescribing by agreement for their nationals the necessary measures for the conservation of the living resources affected.

2. If the states concerned do not reach agreement within twelve months, any of the parties may initiate the procedure contemplated by Article 9.

Article 5

1. If, subsequent to the adoption of the measures referred to in Articles 3 and 4, nationals of other states engage in fishing the same stock or stocks of fish or other living marine resources in any area or areas of the high seas, the other states shall apply the measures, which shall not be discriminatory in form or in fact, to their own nationals not later than seven months after the date on which the measures shall have been notified to the Director-General of the Food and Agriculture Organization of the United Nations. The Director-General shall notify such measures to any state

[1] U.N. Doc. A/CONF. 13/L.54

which so requests and, in any case, to any state specified by the state initiating the measure.

2. If these other states do not accept the measures so adopted and if no agreement can be reached within twelve months, any of the interested parties may initiate the procedure contemplated by Article 9. Subject to paragraph 2 of Article 10, the measures adopted shall remain obligatory pending the decision of the special commission.

Article 6

1. A coastal state has a special interest in the maintenance of the productivity of the living resources in any area of the high seas adjacent to its territorial sea.

2. A coastal state is entitled to take part on an equal footing in any system of research and regulation for purposes of conservation of the living resources of the high seas in that area, even though its nationals do not carry on fishing there.

3. A state whose nationals are engaged in fishing in any area of the high seas adjacent to the territorial sea of a coastal state shall, at the request of that coastal state, enter into negotiations with a view to prescribing by agreement the measures necessary for the conservation of the living resources of the high seas in that area.

4. A state whose nationals are engaged in fishing in any area of the high seas adjacent to the territorial sea of a coastal state shall not enforce conservation measures in that area which are opposed to those which have been adopted by the coastal state, but may enter into negotiations with the coastal state with a view to prescribing by agreement the measures necessary for the conservation of the living resources of the high seas in that area.

5. If the states concerned do not reach agreement with respect to conservation measures within twelve months, any of the parties may initiate the procedure contemplated by Article 9.

Article 7

1. Having regard to the provisions of paragraph 1 of Article 6, any coastal state may, with a view to the maintenance of the productivity of the living resources of the sea, adopt unilateral measures of conservation appropriate to any stock of fish or other marine resources in any area of the high seas adjacent to its territorial sea, provided that negotiations to that effect with the other states concerned have not led to an agreement within six months.

2. The measures which the coastal state adopts under the previous paragraph shall be valid as to other states only if the following requirements are fulfilled:

(a) That there is a need for urgent application of conservation measures in the light of the existing knowledge of the fishery;

(b) That the measures adopted are based on appropriate scientific findings;

(c) That such measures do not discriminate in form or in fact against foreign fishermen.

3. These measures shall remain in force pending the settlement, in accordance with the relevant provisions of this Convention, of any disagreement as to their validity.

4. If the measures are not accepted by the other states concerned, any of the parties may initiate the procedure contemplated by Article 9. Subject to paragraph 2 of Article 10, the measures adopted shall remain obligatory pending the decision of the special commission.

5. The principles of geographical demarcation as defined in Article 12 of the Convention on the Territorial Sea and the Contiguous Zone shall be adopted when coasts of different states are involved.

Article 8

1. Any state which, even if its nationals are not engaged in fishing in an area of the high seas not adjacent to its coast, has a special interest in the conservation of the living resources of the high seas in that area, may request the state or states whose nationals are engaged in fishing there to take the necessary measures of conservation under Articles 3 and 4 respectively, at the same time mentioning the scientific reasons which in its opinion make such measures necessary, and indicating its special interest.

2. If no agreement is reached within twelve months, such state may initiate the procedure contemplated by Article 9.

Article 9

1. Any dispute which may arise between states under Articles 4, 5, 6, 7 and 8 shall, at the request of any of the parties, be submitted for settlement to a special commission of five members, unless the parties agree to seek a solution by another method of peaceful settlement, as provided for in Article 33 of the Charter of the United Nations.

2. The members of the commission, one of whom shall be designated as chairman, shall be named by agreement between the states in dispute within three months of the request for settlement in accordance with the provisions of this article. Failing agreement they shall, upon the request of any state party, be named by the Secretary-General of the United Nations, within a further three-month period, in consultation with the states in dispute and with the President of the International Court of Justice and the Director-General of the Food and Agriculture Organization of the United Nations, from amongst well-qualified persons being nationals of states not involved in the dispute and specializing in legal, administrative or scientific questions relating to fisheries, depending upon the nature of the dispute to be settled. Any vacancy arising after the original appointment shall be filled in the same manner as provided for the initial selection.

3. Any state party to proceedings under these articles shall have the right to name one of its nationals to the special commission, with the right to participate fully in the proceedings on the same footing as a member of the commission but without the right to vote or to take part in the writing of the commission's decision.

4. The commission shall determine its own procedure, assuring each party to the proceedings a full opportunity to be heard and to present its case. It shall also determine how the costs and expenses shall be divided between the parties to the dispute, failing agreement by the parties on this matter.

5. The special commission shall render its decision within a period of five months from the time it is appointed unless it decides, in case of necessity, to extend the time limit for a period not exceeding three months.

6. The special commission shall, in reaching its decisions, adhere to these articles and to any special agreements between the disputing parties regarding settlement of the dispute.

7. Decisions of the commission shall be by majority vote.

Article 10

1. The special commission shall, in disputes arising under Article 7, apply the criteria listed in paragraph 2 of that article. In disputes under Articles 4, 5, 6 and 8, the commission shall apply the following criteria, according to the issues involved in the dispute:

(a) Common to the determination of disputes arising under Articles 4, 5 and 6 are the requirements:

(i) That scientific findings demonstrate the necessity of conservation measures;
(ii) That the specific measures are based on scientific findings and are practicable; and
(iii) That the measures do not discriminate, in form or in fact, against fishermen of other states.

(b) Applicable to the determination of disputes arising under Article 8 is the requirement that scientific findings demonstrate the necessity for conservation measures, or that the conservation programme is adequate, as the case may be.

2. The special commission may decide that pending its award the measures in dispute shall not be applied, provided that, in the case of disputes under Article 7, the measures shall only be suspended when it is apparent to the commission on the basis of *prima facie* evidence that the need for the urgent application of such measures does not exist.

Article 11

The decisions of the special commission shall be binding on the states concerned and the provisions of paragraph 2 of Article 94 of the Charter of the United Nations shall be applicable to those decisions. If the decisions are accompanied by any recommendations, they shall receive the greatest possible consideration.

ARTICLE 12

1. If the factual basis of the award of the special commission is altered by substantial changes in the conditions of the stock or stocks of fish or other living marine resources or in methods of fishing, any of the states concerned may request the other states to enter into negotiations with a view to prescribing by agreement the necessary modifications in the measures of conservation.

2. If no agreement is reached within a reasonable period of time, any of the states concerned may again resort to the procedure contemplated by Article 9 provided that at least two years have elapsed from the original award.

ARTICLE 13

1. The regulation of fisheries conducted by means of equipment embedded in the floor of the sea in areas of the high seas adjacent to the territorial sea of a state may be undertaken by that state where such fisheries have long been maintained and conducted by its nationals, provided that non-nationals are permitted to participate in such activities on an equal footing with nationals except in areas where such fisheries have by long usage been exclusively enjoyed by such nationals. Such regulations will not, however, affect the general status of the areas as high seas.

2. In this article, the expression "fisheries conducted by means of equipment embedded in the floor of the sea" means those fisheries using gear with supporting members embedded in the sea floor, constructed on a site and left there to operate permanently, or if removed, restored each season on the same site.

ARTICLE 14

In Articles 1, 3, 4, 5, 6 and 8, the term "nationals" means fishing boats or craft of any size having the nationality of the state concerned, according to the law of that state, irrespective of the nationality of the members of their crews.

ARTICLE 15

This Convention shall, until 31 October 1958, be open for signature by all States Members of the United Nations or of any of the specialized agencies, and by any other state invited by the General Assembly to become a party to the Convention.

ARTICLE 16

This Convention is subject to ratification. The instruments of ratification shall be deposited with the Secretary-General of the United Nations.

Article 17

This Convention shall be open for accession by any states belonging to any of the categories mentioned in Article 15. The instruments of accession shall be deposited with the Secretary-General of the United Nations.

Article 18

1. This Convention shall come into force on the thirtieth day following the date of deposit of the twenty-second instrument of ratification or accession with the Secretary-General of the United Nations.

2. For each state ratifying or acceding to the Convention after the deposit of the twenty-second instrument of ratification or accession, the Convention shall enter into force on the thirtieth day after deposit by such state of its instrument of ratification or accession.

UNITED STATES v. CALIFORNIA

United States Supreme Court, 1965

381 U.S. 139

Mr. Justice Harlan delivered the opinion of the Court.

The United States contends that we must ignore the Convention of the Territorial Sea and the Contiguous Zone in performing our duty of giving content to "inland waters" as used in the Submerged Lands Act, and must restrict ourselves to determining what our decision would have been had the question been presented to us for decision on May 22, 1953, the passage date of the Act. At that time there was no international accord on any definition of inland waters, and the best evidence (although strenuously contested by California) of the position of the United States was the letters of the State Department which the Special Master refused to treat as conclusive.

We do not think that the Submerged Lands Act has so restricted us. Congress, in passing the Act, left the responsibility for defining inland waters to this Court. We think that it did not tie our hands at the same time. Had Congress wished us simply to rubber-stamp the statements of the State Department as to its policy in 1953, it could readily have done so itself. It is our opinion that we best fill our responsibility of giving content to the words which Congress employed by adopting the best and most workable definitions available. The Convention of the Territorial Sea and the Contiguous Zone, approved by the Senate and ratified by the President, provides such definitions. We adopt them for purposes of the Submerged Lands Act. This establishes a single coastline for both the administration of the Submerged Lands Act and the conduct of our future international relations (barring an unexpected change in the rules established by the Convention). Furthermore the comprehensiveness of the Convention provides answers to many of the lesser problems related to coastlines which, absent the Convention, would be most troublesome.

California argues, alternatively to its claim that "inland waters" embrace all ocean areas lying within a State's historic seaward boundaries, that if Congress intended "inland waters" to be judicially defined in accordance with international usage, such definition should possess an ambulatory quality so as to encompass future changes in international law or practice. Thus, if 10 years from now the definitions of the Convention were amended, California would say that the extent of the Submerged Lands Act grant would automatically shift, at least if the effect of such amendment were to enlarge the extent of submerged lands available to the States. We reject this open-ended view of the Act for several reasons. Before today's decision no one could say with assurance where lay the line of inland waters as contemplated by the Act; hence there could have been no tenable reliance on any particular line. After today that situation will have changed. Expectations will be established and reliance placed on the line we define. Allowing future shifts of international understanding respecting inland waters to alter the extent of the Submerged Lands Act grant would substantially undercut the definiteness of expectation which should attend it. Moreover, such a view might unduly inhibit the United States in the conduct of its foreign relations by making its ownership of submerged lands vis-à-vis with foreign nations. "Freezing" the meaning of "inland waters" in terms of the Convention definition largely avoids this, as well as serving to fulfill the requirements of definiteness and stability which should attend any congressional grant of property rights belonging to the United States.

Once it is decided that the definiteness of the Convention on the Contiguous Zone apply, many of the subsidiary issues before us fall into place.

1. Straight Base Lines.--California argues that because the Convention permits a nation to use the straight base line method for determining its seaward boundaries if its "coast line is deeply indented and cut into, or if there is a fringe of islands along the coast in its immediate vicinity," California is therefore free to use such boundary lines across the openings of its bays and around its islands. We agree with the United States that the Convention recognizes the validity of straight base lines used by other countries, Norway for instance, and would permit the United States to use such base lines if it chose, but that California may not **use such base lines to extend our international boundaries beyond their traditional international limits against the expressed opposition of the United States. The national responsibility for conducting our international relations obviously must be accommodated with the legitimate interests of the States in the territory over which they are sovereign. Thus a contraction of a State's recognized territory imposed by the Federal Government in the name of foreign policy would be highly questionable. But an extension of state sovereignty to an international area by claiming it as inland water would necessarily also extend national sovereignty, and unless the Federal Government's responsibility for questions of external sovereignty is hollow, it must have the power to prevent States from so enlarging themselves. We conclude that the choice under the Convention to use the straight base line**

method for determining inland waters claimed against other nations is one that rests with the Federal Government, and not with the individual States...

2. Twenty-four Mile Closing Rule.--The Convention recognizes, and it is the present United States position, that a 24-mile closing rule together with the semicircle test should be used for classifying bays in the United States. Applying these tests to the segments of California's coast here in dispute, it appears that Monterey Bay is inland water and that none of the other coastal segments in dispute fulfill these aspects of the Convention test. We so hold.

3. Historic Inland Waters.--By the terms of the Convention the 24-mile closing rule does not apply to so-called "historic" bays. Essentially these are bays over which a coastal nation has traditionally asserted and maintained dominion with the acquiescence of foreign nations. California claims that virtually all the waters here in dispute are historic inland waters as the the term is internationally understood. It relies primarily on an interpretation of its State Constitution to the effect that the State boundaries run three miles outside the islands and bays, plus several court decisions which so interpret it as applied to Monterey, Santa Monica, and San Pedro Bays. The United States counters that, as with straight base lines, California can maintain no claim to historic inland waters unless the claim is endorsed by the United States. The Special Master found it unnecessary to decide that question because, on the evidence before him, he concluded that California had not traditionally exercised dominion over any of the claimed waters.

Since the 24-mile rule includes Monterey Bay, we do not consider it here. As to Santa Monica Bay, San Pedro Bay, and the other water areas in dispute, we agree with the Special Master that they are not historic inland waters of the United States.

UNITED KINGDOM v. NORWAY

FISHERIES CASE

International Court of Justice, 1951

1951 I.C.J. Rep. 116

[The Government of the United Kingdom raised objection to the operation of a Norwegian decree law of 1935 delimiting Norwegian territorial waters on the basis of base lines drawn from point to point on islands lying off the northern Norwegian coast. No objection was taken to a four-mile breadth of territorial waters, however, in view of Norway's historic claim to this distance. The Court held in favor of Norway's use of straight base lines, rather than following all the sinuosities of the coast. In so doing it rejected Britain's arguments that the outer limits of territorial waters must not be more than four miles from some point on shore, and that with the exception of bays the base line must be the low-water mark. The Court considered the configurations of the coast which comprise some 120,000 rocks, reefs and islands, and accepted the principle that the territorial waters should "follow the general direction of the coast." It found that the "practice of States does not justify the formulation of any general rule of law" with respect to how wide the opening of a bay might be to warrant limiting a headland-to-headland base line to a ten-mile opening.]

The opinion of the Court follows in part:

... The coast of the mainland does not constitute, as it does in practically all other countries, a clear dividing line between land and sea. What matters, what really constitutes the Norwegian coast line, is the outer line of the "skjaergaard."...

The Court has no difficulty in finding that, for the purpose of measuring the breadth of the territorial sea, it is the low-water mark as opposed to the high-water mark, or the mean between the two tides, which has generally been adopted in the practice of States....

The Parties also agree that in the case of a low-tide elevation (drying rock) the outer edge at low water of this low-tide elevation may be taken into account as a base-point for calculating the breadth of the territorial sea....

It does not at all follow that, in the absence of rules having the technically precise character alleged by the United Kingdom Government, the delimitation undertaken by the Norwegian Government in 1935 is not subject to certain principles which make it possible to judge as to its validity under international law. The delimitation of sea areas has always an international aspect; it cannot be dependent merely upon the will of the coastal State as expressed in its municipal law. Although it is true that the act of delimitation is necessarily a unilateral act, because only the coastal State is competent to undertake it, the validity of the delimitation with regard to other States depends upon international law.

In this connection, certain basic considerations inherent in the nature of the territorial sea, bring to light certain criteria which, though not precise, can provide courts with an adequate basis for their decisions, which can be adapted to the diverse facts in question.

Among these considerations, some reference must be made to the close dependence of the territorial sea upon the land domain. It is the land which confers upon the coastal State a right to the waters off its coasts. It follows that while such a State must be allowed the latitude necessary in order to be able to adapt its delimitation to practical needs and local requirements, the drawing of base-lines must not depart to any appreciable extent from the general direction of the coast.

Another fundamental consideration, of particular importance in this case, is the more or less close relationship existing between certain sea areas and the land formations which divide or surround them. The real question raised in the choice of base-lines is in effect whether certain sea areas lying within these lines are sufficiently closely linked to the land domain to be subject to the regime of internal waters. This idea, which is at the basis of the determination of the rules relating to bays, should be liberally applied in the case of a coast, the geographical configuration of which is as unusual as that of Norway.

Finally, there is one consideration not to be overlooked, the scope of which extends beyond purely geographical factors: that of certain economic interests peculiar to a region, the reality and importance of which are clearly evidenced by a long usage....

Norway has been in a position to argue without any contradiction that neither the promulgation of her delimitation Decrees in 1869 and in 1889, nor their application, gave rise to any opposition on the part of foreign States. Since, moreover, these Decrees constitute, as has been shown above, the application of a well-defined and uniform system, it is indeed this system itself which would reap the benefit of general toleration, the basis of an historical consolidation which would make it enforceable as against all States.

The general toleration of foreign States with regard to the Norwegian practice is an unchallenged fact. For a period of more than sixty years the United Kingdom Government itself in no way contested it....

The United Kingdom Government has argued that the Norwegian system of delimitation was not known to it and that the system therefore lacked the notoreity necessary to provide the basis of an historic title enforceable against it. The Court is unable to accept this view. As a coastal State on the North Sea, greatly interested in the fisheries in this area, as a maritime Power traditionally concerned with the law of the sea and concerned particularly to defend the freedom of the seas, the United Kingdom could not have been ignorant of the Decree of 1869 which had at once provoked a request for explanations by the French Government. Nor, knowing of it, could it have been under any misapprehension as to the significance of its terms, which clearly described it as constituting the application of a system....

The Court notes that in respect of a situation which could only be strengthened with the passage of time, the United Kingdom Government refrained from formulating reservations.

The notoreity of the facts, the general toleration of the international community, Great Britain's position in the North Sea, her own interest in the question, and her prolonged abstention would in any case warrant Norway's enforcement of her system against the United Kingdom.

The Court is thus led to conclude that the method of straight lines, established in the Norwegian system, was imposed by the peculiar geography of the Norwegian coast; that even before the dispute arose, this method had been consolidated by a constant and sufficiently long practice, in the face of which the attitude of governments bears witness to the fact that they did not consider it to be contrary to international law....

[With respect to fishing in the Lopphavet basin, in particular, the Court referred to hunting and fishing practices prior to 1812 and grants of exclusive rights.]

These historical concessions tend to confirm the Norwegian Government's contention that the fisheries zone reserved before 1812 was in fact much more extensive than the one delimited in 1935. It is suggested that it included all fishing banks from which land was visible, the range of vision being, as is recognized by the United Kingdom Government, the principle of delimitation in force at that time. The Court considers that, although it is not always clear to what specific areas they apply, the historical data produced in support of this contention by the Norwegian Government lend some weight to the idea of the survival of traditional rights reserved to the inhabitants of the Kingdom over fishing grounds included in the 1935 delimitation, particularly in the case of Lopphavet. Such rights, founded on the vital needs of the population and attested by very ancient and peaceful usage, may legitimately be taken into account in drawing a line which, moreover, appears to the Court to have been kept within the bounds of what is moderate and reasonable.

[By a vote of ten to two the Court held that the method of delimitation was not contrary to international law. By eight to four it held that the base lines did not violate international law.]

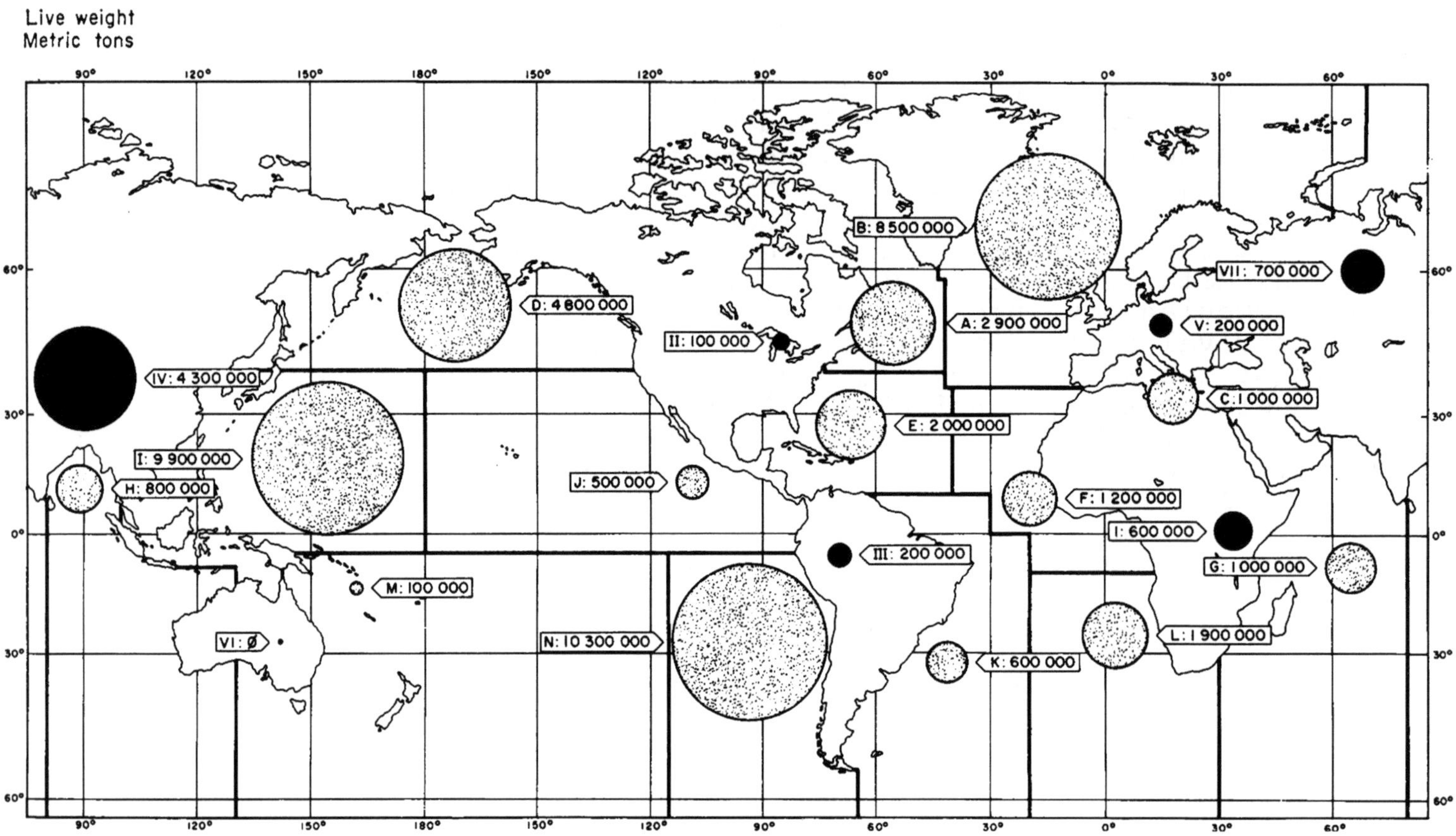

WORLD FISH CATCH BY REGIONS

Table 1. World Catch [1] of Fish, Shellfish, Etc. by Leading Countries, 1954–66

(In billions of pounds)

Country ranking by 1966 catch figures	1954	1955	1956	1957	1958	1959	1960	1961	1962	1963	1964	1965	1966 [2]
Peru	0.4	0.5	0.7	1.1	2.2	4.8	7.9	11.7	15.3	15.2	20.2	16.5	19.4
Japan	10.0	10.8	10.5	11.9	12.1	13.0	13.7	14.8	15.1	14.8	14.0	15.2	15.6
China	5.1	5.6	5.8	6.9	8.9	11.0	12.8	NA	NA	NA	NA	NA	NA
U.S.S.R.	5.0	5.5	5.8	5.6	5.8	6.1	6.7	7.2	8.0	8.3	9.9	11.0	11.8
Norway	4.5	4.0	4.8	3.9	3.2	3.5	3.4	3.4	2.9	3.1	3.5	5.0	6.3
United States	6.1	6.1	6.5	6.0	5.9	6.4	6.2	6.5	6.6	6.1	5.8	6.0	5.5
World	60.5	63.5	67.1	69.3	72.4	80.1	87.1	94.6	102.0	105.0	114.0	115.5	125.0

[1] Total commercial catches, including fresh water fish, on a live weight basis. Weights of shells of univalve and bivalve mollusks are included.
[2] Preliminary.
NA = Not available.

NOTE.—U.S. totals in table H-15 are smaller than those for comparable years in the above table since the weights of mollusk shells are not included.

Source: Yearbook of Fishery Statistics, Food and Agriculture Organization of the United Nations.

CHAPTER FIVE

LIVING RESOURCES OF THE SEA AND THEIR REGULATION

Introductory Note

Ambiguities are present in the policies of most states with respect to exploitation and use of the living resources of the oceans. The living marine resources include fish of many kinds, mollusks, crustaceans, and edible growths such as seaweeds of various kinds. Most national policies encourage commercial fisheries and the enjoyment of sport fishing, while at the same time seek to preserve the fisheries. This conflict of interest found within national marine policies must be recognized and accepted as a reality.

Frequently conservation at sea is interpreted to mean securing the optimal freedom for one's own nationals to take as much as they can catch, while placing restrictions upon the liberties of others. When the arguments supporting restrictive measures are stripped of their rationalizations, one realizes that each nation wants as much nutrient food from the oceans as possible, while curbing the activities of others, especially in waters close to one's own shores, or where fishermen have enjoyed an historical right to fish, or where there is a particularly prized fishery.

Numerous conservation techniques are employed in fisheries today. These take the form of: (1) excluding foreign fleets from fishing in territorial waters and contiguous zones; (2) negotiating agreements to limit fishing to particular stocks or to certain seasons or to specify the types of gear or sizes of mesh in trawling nets that may be used; (3) seeking arrangements to close designated fisheries for periods of time to allow stocks to replenish themselves; (4) setting standards for sizes of fish that may be taken, as for example lobsters weighing less than one pound or measuring less than five inches in body length must be thrown back into the water; (5) prohibiting, by mutual agreement, fishing in particular bays, estuaries, or within so many miles of certain islands, or in specified areas of the high seas as east of the Xth parallel of longitude and north of the Yth parallel of latitude; (6) limiting fishing in given locales, as in Chesapeake Bay, to fixed days of the month and to certain types of boats.

The annual world fish catch, according to the U.N. Food and Agriculture Organization (FAO), is currently estimated to be between 115-125 billion pounds. This gives some indication of the degree of fishing activity that is presently occurring. The catch, for the most part, is confined to a relatively few species, and,as the accompanying map shows, is fairly widely dispersed among regions.

The world catch has risen quite steadily since the 1950's as Table I indicates. This is partially due to the fact that countries are fürnishing more accurate records of fish caught. Moreover, during the past fifteen years fishermen from a greater number of countries are utilizing the fisheries. The increase in the number of independent countries has forced men to secure their own food supplies rather than relying heavily upon former controlling powers to satisfy their needs. Another reason for the growth of the world catch has been the intervention of larger, more highly mechanized fishing fleets with more efficient detection equipment, accompanied in some instances by factory ships for storing and freezing large quantities of fish thus greatly reducing the frequency of trips to home ports.

The trend toward greater employment of the fisheries seems destined to continue barring the introduction of restraining agreements among nations. With famine facing millions of people in Asia and parts of Africa, it is hardly likely that the inputs of effort will be voluntarily limited for the next ten to twenty-five years. What happens to the growth of world population during this time will also have important effects upon the intensity with which the fisheries are used. One area to which more attention will doubtless be given is the Indian Ocean which has been an under-fished area in modern times. Moreover, if the use of fish protein concentrate becomes generally accepted, many species of fish which are now rejected as trash will be kept, ground up into meal, and sold to the world's needy. Pilot plants are already being erected in the United States and India.

Can the world's fisheries withstand intensified applications of effort ? Already experts have noted declines in the catches of haddock, cod, mackerel, and other desired species of fish in the North Atlantic fishery. What will happen when operations are stepped up; when others introduce larger trawlers, better detection devices, and accompanying factory ships ? Will the specter of the Great Reaper of Death stalk the world's edible fishing grounds as it has in the whaling industry ?

FAO experts, as well as those in the Bureau of Commercial Fisheries in Washington, take a more optimistic view of the future. They speculate that if man will handle the fisheries with care the yield could amount to several times the present total catch and still sustain the fisheries. Unfortunately, such calculations depend upon maintenance of the ecological balance of the marine environment. Our knowledge as yet is extremely limited as to what various air pollutants such as gas fumes from automobiles, and soilage of the waters by oil and chemicals,will do to the living resources of the sea. We only know that pollution can affect to varying degrees virtually all forms of life. More biological research is needed to clarify the long-run effects of introducing polluting elements into sea water.

A factor which could have a positive effect upon the world reserves would be large-scale applications of aquaculture or fish farming. Today this is primarily confined to the countries of the Orient. There is no reason why aquaculture cannot be employed in many countries of the temperate zone. Furthermore, ocean scientists are beginning to think about "fencing in" limited portions of the seas with electronic or sonic beams and stimulating intensive production of fish in these areas through the use of special feeding. As world population rises this is one sector where large inputs of effort could perhaps yield significant results for the wellbeing of mankind.

Fishing agreements between states, like other international arrangements, may be bilateral, limited multilateral, regional, or general international agreements. They may be formally concluded, as treaties, or arranged in more flexible ways through executive agreements and understandings.

One of the earliest arrangements to be concluded modern times was the European Fisheries Convention of This was eventually superceded in 1959 and again in 1964 by conventions applying to the Northeast Atlantic and to

European fisheries respectively. These agreements, accepted by most Western European nations, provide for minimum size mesh in nets, standardization of vessel markings, inspection by national officials, and the establishment of certain closed areas. Each state is responsible to its own fishermen for enforcing the conventions' provisions. These arrangements have worked reasonably well, although with radio communications fishermen generally have information about the presence of inspectors and therefore are able to protect themselves.

The International Fur Seals Convention concluded in 1911 between the United States, Britain, Japan and Russia has regulated pelagic sealing in the Bering Sea area. Unregulated killing had threatened to exterminate the seal herds before the treaty was consumated. The agreement forbids the killing of seals in waters more than three miles from shore, places restrictions on the number that may be captured in any year, and specifies that catching shall be limited on shore to American and Russian sealers. Indemnities were paid to Britain and Japan in exchange for their refraining from sealing. Moreover, the United States and Russia agreed to share the annual catches, or proceeds therefrom, with the other contracting parties. Wesley Marx offers a testimony to the success of this agreement in his book <u>The Frail Sea</u> in saying "No other marine creature has been placed under such rewarding management, both biological and economic. This is being accomplished without resort to two-hundred mile sea boundaries, unilateral conservation, and technological races."

Since World War II numerous agreements have been concluded for regulating fishing in the Atlantic and Pacific. Among these one of the most significant is the International Convention for the Northwest Atlantic Fisheries, known as ICNAF. This is composed of twelve parties and thus represents all but two of the nations that engage in fishing off the Grand Banks. The functions of the ICNAF Commission include gathering and sifting of data, conducting investigations, holding hearings, publishing reports, and making recommendations to the governments for joint action. The Commission may also close specific areas for periods of time "in order to make possible the maintenance of a maximum sustained catch." However, the Commission depends upon the member states to approve its recommendations and to take any action against parties refusing to cooperate in conserving the fisheries. This situation obviously produces some serious drawbacks. The Soviet Union has been unwilling to accept the Commission's suggestion to limit the size of its catches. This is a matter of deep concern to others and may affect the future usefulness of the arrangement.

Various steps have been considered to try to obtain a greater measure of order in the North Atlantic fishery before irreparable damage is done to the fish stocks. One suggestion has been to extend Canadian jurisdiction beyond the Banks so as to exclude those who refuse to cooperate in limiting their catch. Such action would contradict the historic United States and Canadian positions. It would deride the stance the U.S. has taken in opposing the claims of the west coast South American states with respect to the tuna and anchovy fisheries. For the time being at least this is a suggestion which Washington could not agree to. Efforts to exclude the fishing vessels of a major power such as the Soviet Union would be likely to lead to serious disputes at the minimum, and to clashes on the sea at the other extreme. An alternate suggestion would be to subsidize the construction of much larger fishing vessels and gear with which to meet Soviet competition. Subsidies have already been made available in this country and Canada for this purpose, but construction has been proceeding slowly and the fishermen seem content to continue using modest size boats. Such a move would not basically improve the reserves of fish available. It would rather lead to an earlier decimation of the remaining schools of fish. Diplomacy must find a solution and policy makers must discover the means of applying sufficient inducements or pressure to persuade states to exercise self-limiting measures.

The Inter-American Tropical Tuna Commission (1949) is another example of a regional specialized arrangement. It is similar to ICNAF in that it depends upon the governments of its five member states, including the United States, to implement its recommendations and to bring violators to bar.

Although the Commission has assembled much useful information about the tuna fishery it is still in need of wider support and scope, for the tuna roams far beyond American waters. Either other regional arrangements -- as for the South Pacific -- or a wider international regime are needed to protect the stocks of tuna for future consumption.

Agreements have been concluded between the United States and Canada relating to salmon and halibut fishing, and between these countries, the Soviet Union and Japan, for the conservation of these fish in the Northeastern Pacific Ocean.

A Convention on the Regulation of Whaling was opened for signature at Geneva in 1931 and was followed some years later by an amendatory protocol. This instrument applied to whaling in "all waters of the world." It prohibited the taking of "right" whales and limited the capture of "baleen" whales to certain seasons and to waters south of 40 degrees south latitude. Factory ships were excluded from some areas, and the parties agreed to furnish data on their catches to an International Bureau on Whaling Statistics located at Sandefjord, Norway. Despite these steps the whale population underwent continued depletion as modern technology enabled whalers to improve the efficiency of their operations with motorized chasers, harpoon guns, and use of large factory vessels. In 1946 a new convention was negotiated in

Washington which called for inspectors to be stationed on board each factory ship to watch for violations. Unfortunately, the necessary number of ratifications to bring the Convention into force was not received until 1959. Various states refused to participate altogether. Some South American nations went to the extent of organizing their own commission and refused to recognize the rights of others to extend the jurisdiction of the ICW to their "sovereign waters." The result of such indecisive and uncooperative actions was the virtual disappearance of sperm whales from the seas by the time the Convention came into operation. As with the stripping of virgin forests from the land and the despoiling of country-sides by strip-mining, the shortsightedness of man led to the destruction of a valuable resource.

A *cause célèbre* in the whaling business was the capture in 1954 of the factory ship *Olympic Challenger*. This vessel had been registered in Panama, but was owned by A.S. Onassis, a Greek-born British shipowner. Units of the Peruvian Navy sighted the *Olympic Challenger* together with eleven other ships engaged in whaling 110 miles west of their shores. Four vessels were captured on site. The factory ship put to sea and after hot pursuit lasting twenty-four hours was captured beyond the 200 mile line. Between 2,500 and 3,000 whales were reported to have been taken by the expedition. The vessels and their masters were taken into the port of Paita where they were condemned and fined $3 million. Notwithstanding protests by Britain and the United States, the Peruvian Government refused to release the ships.

Inspection and enforcement of marine observance of conservation agreements are the most troublesome aspects of international regulatory arrangements. Many states do not look favorably upon inspection, boarding and seizure upon the high seas by others than their own national authorities. They are less willing to have their nationals and vessels taken before foreign courts over actions occurring outside of generally accepted territorial waters. Usually vessels caught in the act of violating conventions are turned over to their own state for trial and punishment. Differences in applying law to such persons often lead, however, to misunderstandings and ill feelings, but this is hardly avoidable under the present international system.

Fishery conventions usually function best when the participants are few in number and have compatible interests. Where there are strong rivalries or suspicions, difficulties almost inevitably occur in the implementation of conservation and regulatory arrangements. At the least these are limited to disputes among fishermen at sea arising from such actions as trawling over one another's lines, cutting marker buoys loose, and the like. In more extreme form they can lead to acrimonious conflicts among states themselves. Although there is considerable agreement as to the desirability of conservation, the practice of this principle has been another matter. In the background of most arrangements stand power factors; the balance of power between states. Under favorable circumstances the international arrangements work smoothly. Their functioning cannot be altogether detached from the general posture of relationships among countries.

Management of fisheries by international cooperation has been quite limited. Arrangements between Canada and the United States have on the whole worked quite satisfactorily. But in the more extensive fisheries of the North Atlantic and the North Pacific, where competition is keen and where there are numerous parties engaged in the fisheries, regulation has been limited and most arrangements have been confined to gathering data, publishing statistics and reports, and offering recommendations to governments.

Some scholars feel that an effort should be made to treat fisheries on a community-wide basis under an assumption that they comprise a commonwealth of global concern. It has been suggested, for instance, that the United Nations should declare its competence to supervise and license those who wish to engage in fishing beyond national limits and assume jurisdiction to conserve the resources of the high seas. Thus far, however, the powers have shown little willingness to do more than participate in a dialogue on the broad principles for peaceful use of the seas and conservation of marine resources. This may in time lead to the taking of additional steps if states become persuaded of the advantages of such measures. Meanwhile, promotion of commercial fishing, on the one hand, and trying to secure as much conservation as is compatible with this, on the other hand, remain the business of each state.

The readings that follow provide a cross-section illustration of some of the measures that are currently in force among states relating to the living resources of the oceans.

For further readings see Francis T. Christy,Jr. and Anthony Scott, The Common Wealth in Ocean Fisheries (Baltimore, Johns Hopkins Press,1965); Richard Cooley, Politics and Conservation: The Decline of the Alaskan Salmon (New York, Harper and Row,1963); Douglas Johnston, International Law of Fisheries (New Haven, Yale University Press, 1965); E.J. Slijper, Whales (New York, Basic Books, 1962); Marjorie M. Whiteman, Digest of International Law (Washington, Government Printing Office, 1965), Vol. 4, Chapter XII; Thomas H. Lineaweaver,III, "Our Catch-as-Catch Can Fisheries," The Reporter Magazine, September 7, 1967, pp. 38-40; J.E. Carros and A.G. Roche, "The Proposed International Commission for the Conservation of Atlantic Tuna," American Journal of International Law, Vol.61 (1967), pp.673-702; L.D. White, "A Code of Conduct on the Fishbry Grounds," U.S. Naval Institute Proceedings, Mardh 1965, pp. 76-82; Samuel W. Matthews, "Science Explores the Monsoon Sea," National Geographic Magazine, Vol. 132, No.4, October 1967, pp.554-575, with map of the Indian Ocean floor.

UNITED STATES FISH AND WILDLIFE ACT OF 1956

Public Law 1036
84th Congress
August 8, 1956
70 Stat. 1119
United States Code,
Title 16

Sec. 742 a. Declaration of Policy

The Congress declares that the fish, shellfish, and wildlife resources of the Nation make a material contribution to our national economy and food supply, as well as a material contribution to the health, recreation, and well-being of our citizens; that such resources are a living, renewable form of national wealth that is capable of being maintained and greatly increased with proper management, but equally capable of destruction if neglected or unwisely exploited; that such resources afford outdoor recreation throughout the Nation and provide employment, directly or indirectly, to a substantial number of citizens; that the fishing industries strengthen the defense of the United States through the provision of a trained seafaring citizenry and action-ready fleets of seaworthy vessels; that the training and sport afforded by fish and wildlife resources strengthen the national defense by contributing to the general health and physical fitness of millions of citizens; and that properly developed, such fish and wildlife resources are capable of steadily increasing these valuable contributions to the life of the Nation.

The Congress further declares that the fishing industry, in its several branches, can prosper and thus fulfill its proper function in national life only if certain fundamental needs are satisfied by means that are consistent with the public interest and in accord with constitutional functions of governments. Among these needs are:

(1) Freedom of enterprise - freedom to develop new areas, methods, products, and markets in accordance with sound economic principles, as well as freedom from unnecessary administrative or legal restrictions that unreasonably conflict with or ignore economic needs;

(2) Protection of opportunity - maintenance of an economic atmosphere in which domestic production and processing can prosper; protection from subsidized competing products; protection of opportunity to fish on the high seas in accordance with international law;

(3) Assistance - assistance consistent with that provided by the Government for industry generally ...

Sec. 742 f. Policies, Procedures and Recommendations

(a) The Secretary of the Interior ... shall consider and determine the policies and procedures that are necessary and desirable in carrying out effectively and in the public interest the laws relating to fish and wildlife. The Secretary ... shall -

(1) develop and recommend measures which are appropriate to assure the maximum sustainable production of fish and fishery products and to prevent unnecessary and excessive fluctuations in such production;

(2) study the economic condition of the industry, and whenever he determines that any segment of the domestic fisheries has been seriously disturbed either by wide fluctuations in the abundance of the resource supporting it, or by unstable market or fishing conditions or due to any other factors, he shall make such recommendations to the President and the Congress as he deems appropriate to aid in stabilizing the domestic fisheries ...

(4) take such steps as may be required for the development, advancement, management, conservation, and protection of the fishery [and wildlife] resources ...

Sec. 742 i. Effect on Rights of States and International Commissions

Nothing in ... this title shall be construed (1) to interfere in any manner with the rights of any State under the Submerged Lands Act or otherwise provided by law, or to supercede any regulatory authority over fisheries exercised by the States either individually or under interstate compacts; or (2) to interfere in any manner with the authority exercised by any International Commission established under any treaty or convention to which the United States is a party.

ACT TO PROMOTE COMMERCIAL FISHERIES

Public Law 88-309,
88th Congress, S. 627,
May 20, 1964

Be it enacted ... That this Act may be cited as the "Commercial Fisheries Research and Development Act of 1964".

Sec. 2. As used in this Act, the term

"Commercial fisheries" means any organization, individual, or group of organizations or individuals engaged in the harvesting, catching, processing, distribution, or sale of fish, shellfish, or fish products. ...

"Raw fish" means aquatic plants and animals. ...

Sec. 3. (a) The purpose of this Act is to authorize the Secretary of the Interior to cooperate with the States through their respective State agencies in carrying out projects designed for the research and development of the commercial fisheries resources of the Nation. Federal funds made available under this Act will be used to supplement, and, to the extent practicable, increase the amounts of State funds that would be made available for commercial fisheries research and development in the absence of these Federal funds.

(b) (1) Nothing in this Act prevents any two or more States from acting jointly in carrying out a project.

(2) The Congress consents to any compact or agreement between any two or more States for the purpose of carrying out a project. The right to alter, amend, or repeal this subsection or the consent granted under this subsection is expressly reserved.

Sec. 4. (a) There is authorized to be appropriated to the Secretary of the Interior for the next fiscal year beginning after the date of enactment of this Act, and for the four secceeding fiscal years, $5,000,000 in each year for apportionment to the States to carry out the purposes of this Act.

(b) In addition to the amounts authorized in subsection (a) of this section there is authorized to be appropriated for the next fiscal year beginning after the date of enactment of this Act, and for the succeeding fiscal year, $400,000 in each such year, and for the next three succeeding fiscal years, $650,000 in each such year, which shall be made available to the States in such amounts as the Secretary may determine appropriate for the purposes of this Act: Provided, That the Secretary shall give a preference to those States in which he determines there is a commercial fishery failure due to a resource disaster arising from natural or undetermined causes, and any sums made available under this subsection may be used either by the States or directly by the Secretary in cooperation with the States for any purpose that the Secretary determines is appropriate to restore the fishery affected by such failure or to prevent a similar failure in the future: Provided further, That the funds authorized to be appropriated under this subsection shall not be available to the Secretary for use as grants for chartering fishing vessels. Amounts appropriated pursuant to this subsection shall remain available until expended.

(c) In addition to the funds authorized in subsection (a) and (b), there is authorized to be appropriated $100,000 for the fiscal year beginning after the date of enactment of this act and for each succeeding fiscal year during the term of this Act, which shall be made available to the States in such amounts as the Secretary may determine for developing a new commercial fishery therein.

Sec. 5. (a) Funds appropriated pursuant to section 4 (a) shall be apportioned among the States, by the Secretary, on July 1 of each year or as soon as practicable thereafter, on a basis determined by the ratio which the average of the value of raw fish harvested by domestic commercial fishermen and received within the State (regardless where caught) for the three most recent calendar years for which data satisfactory to the Secretary are available plus the average of the value to the manufacturer of manufactured and processed fishery merchandise manufactured within each State for the three most recent calendar years for which data satisfactory to the Secretary are available, bears to the total average value of all raw fish harvested by domestic commercial fishermen and received within the States (regardless where caught) and fishery merchandise manufactured and processed within the States for the three most recent calendar years for which data satisfactory to the Secretary are available. However, no State may receive an apportionment for any fiscal year of less than one-half of 1 per centum of funds or more than 6 per centum of the funds. ...

ACT TO PROMOTE PRODUCTION OF FISH PROTEIN CONCENTRATE

Public Law 89-701,
89th Congress, S. 2720,
November 2, 1966

Be it enacted ... That the Secretary of the Interior is authorized to conduct, and through grants to and contracts with public and private agencies to promote studies, research, and experiments designed to develop the best and most economical processes and methods to reduce fish which are in abundant supply and which are not now widely sought after for human food to a nutritious, wholesome, and stable fish protein concentrate, as well as to conduct food technology and feasibility studies with respect to such products.

Sec. 2.(a) The Secretary is also authorized to construct not to exceed one experiment and demonstration plant for the production of a fish protein concentrate and to acquire by lease one additional plant for such purpose. ...

CONVENTION FOR THE PRESERVATION AND PROTECTION OF FUR SEALS

Signed at Washington July 7, 1911[1]

The United States of America, His Majesty the King of the United Kingdom of Great Britain and Ireland, and of the British Dominions beyond the Seas, Emperor of India, His Majesty the Emperor of Japan, and His Majesty the Emperor of all the Russias, being desirous of adopting effective means for the preservation and protection of the fur seals which frequent the waters of the North Pacific Ocean, have resolved to conclude a Convention for the purpose, and to that end have named as their Plenipotentiaries ...

Article I

The High Contracting Parties mutually and reciprocally agree that their citizens and subjects respectively, and all persons subject to their laws and treaties, and their vessels, shall be prohibited, while this Convention remains in force, from engaging in pelagic sealing in the waters of the North Pacific Ocean, north of the thirtieth parallel of north latitude and including the Seas of Bering, Kamchatka, Okhotsk and Japan, and that every such person and vessel offending against such prohibition may be seized, except within the territorial jurisdiction of one of the other Powers, and detained by the naval or other duly commissioned officers of any of the Parties to this Convention, to be delivered as soon as practicable to an authorized official of their own nation at the nearest point to the place of seizure, or elsewhere as may be mutually agreed upon; and that the authorities of the nation to which such person or vessel belongs alone shall have jurisdiction to try the offense and impose the penalties for the same; and that the witnesses and proofs necessary to establish the offense, as far as they are under the control of any of the Parties to this Convention, shall also be furnished with all reasonable promptitude to the proper authorities having jurisdiction to try the offense.

Article II

Each of the High Contracting Parties further agrees that no person or vessel shall be permitted to use any of its ports or harbors or any part of its territory for any purposes whatsoever connected with the operations of pelagic sealing in the waters within the protected area mentioned in Article I.

Article III

Each of the High Contracting Parties further agrees that no sealskins taken in the waters of the North Pacific Ocean within the protected area mentioned in Article I, and no sealskins identified as the species known as Callorhinus alascanus, Callorhinus ursinus, and Callorhinus kurilensis, and belonging to the American, Russian or Japanese herds, except such as are taken under the authority of the respective Powers to which the breeding grounds of such herds belong and have been oficially marked and certified as having been so taken, shall be permitted to be imported or brought into the territory of any of the Parties to this Convention.

Article IV

It is further agreed that the provisions of this Convention shall not apply to Indians, Ainos, Aleuts, or other aborigines dwelling on the coast of the waters mentioned in Article I, who carry on pelagic sealing in canoes not transported by or used in connection with other vessels, and propelled entirely by oars, paddles, or sails, and manned by not more than five persons each, in the way hitherto practiced and without the use of firearms; provided that such aborigines are not in the employment of other persons or under contract to deliver the skins to any person.

Article V

Each of the High Contracting Parties agrees that it will not permit its citizens or subjects or their vessels to kill, capture or pursue beyond the distance of three miles from the shore line of its territories sea otters in any part of the waters mentioned in Article I of this Convention.

Article VI

Each of the High Contracting Parties agrees to enact and enforce such legislation as may be necessary to make effective the foregoing provisions with appropriate penalties for violations thereof. [See 37 Stat.499]

Article VII

It is agreed on the part of the United States, Japan, and Russia that each respectively will maintain a guard or patrol in the waters frequented by the seal herd in the

protection of which it is especially interested, so far as may be necessary for the enforcement of the foregoing provisions.

Article VIII

All of the High Contracting Parties agree to cooperate with each other in taking such measures as may be appropriate and available for the purpose of preventing pelagic sealing in the prohibited area mentioned in Article I.

Article IX

The term pelagic sealing is hereby defined for the purposes of this Convention as meaning the killing, capturing or pursuing in any manner whatsoever of fur seals at sea.

Article X

The United States agrees that of the total number of sealskins taken annually under the authority of the United States upon the Pribilof Islands or any other islands or shores of the waters mentioned in Article I subject to the jurisdiction of the United States to which any seal herds hereafter resort, there shall be delivered at the Pribilof Islands at the end of each season fifteen per cent (15%) gross in number and value therof to an authorized agent of the Japanese Government; provided, however, that nothing herein contained shall restrict the right of the United States at any time and from time to time to suspend altogether the taking of sealskins on such islands or shores subject to its jurisdiction, and to impose such restrictions and regulations upon the total number of skins to be taken in any season and the manner and times and places of taking them as may seem necessary to protect and preserve the seal herd or to increase its number.

Article XI

The United States further agrees to pay the sum of two hundred thousand dollars ($200,000) to Great Britain and the sum of two hundred thousand dollars ($200,000) to Japan when this Convention goes into effect, as an advance payment in each case in lieu of such number of fur-seal skins to which Great Britain and Japan respectively would be entitled under the provisions of this Convention as would be equivalent in each case to two hundred thousand dollars ($200,000) reckoned at their market value at London at the date of their delivery before dressing and curing and less cost of transportation from the Pribilof Islands, such market value in case of dispute to be determined by an umpire to be agreed upon by the United States and Great

Britain, or by the United States and Japan, as the case may be, which skins shall be retained by the United States in satisfaction of such payments.

The United States further agrees that the British and Japanese shares respectively of the sealskins taken from the American herd under the terms of this Convention shall be not less than one thousand (1,000) each in any year even if such number is more than fifteen per cent (15%) of the number to which the authorized killing is restricted in such year, unless the killing of seals in such year or years shall have been absolutely prohibited by the United States for all purposes except to supply food, clothing, and boat skins for the natives on the islands, in which case the United States agrees to pay to Great Britain and to Japan each the sum of ten thousand dollars ($10,000) annually in lieu of any share of skins during the years when no killing is allowed; and Great Britain agrees, and Japan agrees, that after deducting the skins of their respective shares, which are to be retained by the United States as above provided to reimburse itself for the advance payment aforesaid, the United States shall be entitled to reimburse itself for any annual payments made as herein required, by retaining an additional number of sealskins from the British and Japanese shares respectively over and above the specified minimum allowance of one thousand (1,000) skins in any subsequent year or years when killing is again resumed, until the whole number of skins retained shall equal, reckoned at their market value determined as above provided for, the entire amount so paid, with interest at the rate of four percent (4%) per annum.

If, however, the total number of seals frequenting the United States islands in any year falls below one hundred thousand (100,000), enumerated by official account, then all killing, excepting the inconsiderable supply necessary for the support of the natives as above noted, may be suspended without allowance of skins or payment of money equivalent until the number of such seals again exceeds one hundred thousand (100,000), enumerated in like manner.

Article XII

It is agreed on the part of Russia that of the total number of sealskins taken annually upon the Commander Islands, or any other island or shores of the waters defined in Article I subject to the jurisdiction of Russia to which any seal herds hereafter resort, there shall be delivered at the Commander Islands at the end of each season fifteen per cent (15%) gross in number and value thereof to an authorized agent of the Canadian Government, and fifteen per cent (15%) gross in number and value therof to an authorized agent of the Japanese Government; provided, however, that nothing herein contained shall restrict the right of Russia at any time and from time to time during the first five years of the term of this Convention to suspend altogether the taking of sealskins on such islands or shores subject to its jurisdiction, and to impose during the term of this Convention such restrictions and regulations upon the total number of skins to be taken in any season, and the manner and times and places of taking them as may seem necessary to preserve and protect the Russian seal herd, or to increase its number; but it is agreed, nevertheless, on the part of Russia that during the last ten years of the term of this Convention not less than five per cent (5%) of the total number of seals on the Russian rookeries and hauling grounds will be killed annually, provided that said five per cent (5%) does not exceed eighty-five per cent (85%) of the three-year-old make seals hauling in such year.

If, however, the total number of seals frequenting the Russian islands in any year falls below eighteen thousand (18,000) enumerated by official count, then the allowance of skins mentioned above and all killing of seals except such as may be necessary for the support of the natives on the islands may be suspended until the number of such seals again exceeds eighteen thousand (18,000) enumerated in like manner.

Article XIII

It is agreed on the part of Japan that of the total number of sealskins taken annually upon Robben Island, or any other islands or shores of the waters defined in Article I subject to the jurisdiction of Japan to which any seal herd hereafter may resort, there shall be delivered at Robben Island at the end of each season ten per cent (10%) gross in nunber and value thereof to an authorized agent of the United States Government, ten per cent (10%) gross in number and value thereof to an authorized agent of the Canadian Government, and ten per cent (10%) gross in number and value thereof to an authorized agent of the Russian Government; provided, however, that nothing herein contained shall restrict the right of Japan at any time and from time to time during the first five years of the term of this Convention to suspend altogether the taking of sealskins on such islands or shores subject to its jurisdiction, and to impose during the term of this Convention such restrictions and regulations upon the total number of skins to be taken in any season, and the manner and times and places of taking them as may seem necessary to preserve and protect the Japanese herd, or to increase its number; but it is agreed, nevertheless, on the part of Japan that during the last ten years of the term of this Convention not less than five per cent (5%) of the total number of seals on the Japanese rookeries and hauling grounds will be killed, provided that said five per cent (5%) does not exceed eighty-five per cent (85%) of the three-year-old male seals hauling in such year.

If, however, the total number of seals frequenting the Japanese islands in any year falls below six thousand five hundred (6,500) enumerated by official count, then the allowance of skins mentioned above and all killing of seals except such as may be necessary for the support of the natives on the islands may be suspended until the number of such seals again exceeds six thousand five hundred (6,500) enumerated in like manner.

Article XIV

It is agreed on the part of Great Britain that in case any seal herd hereafter resorts to any islands or shores of the waters defined in Article I subject to the jurisdiction of Great Britain, there shall be delivered at the end of each season during the term of this Convention ten per cent (10%) gross in number and value of the total number of sealskins annually taken from such herd to an authorized agent of the United States Government, ten per cent (10%) gross in number and value of the total number of sealskins annually taken from such herd to an authorized agent of the Japanese Government, and ten per cent (10%) gross in number and value of the total number of sealskins annually taken from such herd to an authorized agent of the Russian Government.

Article XV

It is further agreed between the United States and Great Britain that the provisions of this Convention shall supersede, in so far as they are inconsistent therewith or in duplication thereof, the provisions of the treaty relating to the fur seals, entered into between the United States and Great Britain on the 7th day of February, 1911.

Article XVI

This Convention shall go into effect upon the 15th day of December,1911, and shall continue in force for a period of fifteen (15) years from that date, and thereafter until terminated by twelve (12) months' written notice given by one or more of the Parties to all of the others, which notice may be given at the expiration of fourteen years or at any time afterwards, and it is agreed that at any time prior to the termination of this Convention, upon the request of any one of the High Contracting Parties, a conference shall be held forthwith between representatives of all the Parties hereto, to consider and if possible agree upon a further extension of this Convention with such additions and modifications, if any, as may be found desirable.

Article XVII

This Convention shall be ratified....

1. United States Treaty Series, No. 564; 37 Statutes at Large,1542.

INTERNATIONAL CONVENTION FOR THE NORTHWEST ATLANTIC FISHERIES[1]

Signed at Washington, February 8, 1949; in force July 3, 1950

The Governments whose duly authorized representatives have subscribed hereto, sharing a substantial interest in the conservation of the fishery resources of the Northwest Atlantic Ocean, have resolved to conclude a convention for the investigation, protection and conservation of the fisheries of the Northwest Atlantic Ocean, in order to make possible the maintenance of a maximum sustained catch from those fisheries and to that end have, through their duly authorized representatives, agreed as follows:

Article I

1. The area to which this Convention applies, hereinafter referred to as "the Convention area," shall be all waters, except territorial waters, bounded by a line beginning at a point on the coast of Rhode Island in 71°40′ west longitud thence due south to 39°00′ north latitude; thence due east to 42°00′ west longitude; thence due north to 59°00′ north latitude; thence due west to 44°00′ west longitude; thence due north to the coast of Greenland; thence along the west coast of Greenland to 78°10′ north latitude; thence southward to a point in 75°00′ north latitude and 73°30′ west longitude; thence along a rhumb line to a point in 69°00′ north latitude and 59°00′ west longitude; thence due south to 61°00′ north latitude; thence due west to 64°30′ west longitude; thence due south to the coast of Labrador; thence in a southerly direction along the coast of Labrador to the southern terminus of its boundary with Quebec; thence in a westerly direction along the coast of Quebec, and in an easterly and southerly direction along the coasts of New Brunswick, Nova Scotia, and Cape Breton Island to Cabot Strait; thence along the coasts of Cape Breton Island, Nova Scotia, New Brunswick, Maine, New Hampshire, Massachusetts, and Rhode Island to the point of beginning.

2. Nothing in this Convention shall be deemed to affect adversely (prejudice) the claims of any Contracting Government in regard to the limits of territorial waters or to the jurisdiction of a coastal state over fisheries.

[1] Department of State, Treaties and Other International Acts Series, No. 2089 (Pub. 3941). Ratifications have been deposited by the following signatories: Canada (including Newfoundland), Denmark, Iceland, United Kingdom, United States. The instrument of ratification by Canada was deposited with the following observation: "That ratification by Canada of the Convention extends to Newfoundland, and that any claims Canada may have in regard to the limits of territorial waters or to the jurisdiction over fisheries, particularly as a result of the entry of Newfoundland into Confederation, will not be prejudiced."

3. The Convention area shall be divided into five sub-areas, the boundaries of which shall be those defined in the Annex to this Convention, subject to such alterations as may be made in accordance with the provisions of paragraph 2 of Article VI.

ARTICLE II

1. The Contracting Governments shall establish and maintain a Commission for the purposes of this Convention. The Commission shall be known as the International Commission for the Northwest Atlantic Fisheries, hereinafter referred to as "the Commission."

2. Each of the Contracting Governments may appoint not more than three Commissioners and one or more experts or advisers to assist its Commissioner or Commissioners.

3. The Commission shall elect from its members a Chairman and a Vice Chairman, each of whom shall serve for a term of two years and shall be eligible for re-election but not to a succeeding term. The Chairman and Vice Chairman must be Commissioners from different Contracting Governments.

4. The seat of the Commission shall be in North America at a place to be chosen by the Commission.

5. The Commission shall hold a regular annual meeting at its seat or at such place in North America as may be agreed upon by the Commission.

6. Any other meeting of the Commission may be called by the Chairman at such time and place as he may determine, upon the request of the Commissioner of a Contracting Government and subject to the concurrence of the Commissioners of two other Contracting Governments, including the Commissioner of a Government in North America.

7. Each Contracting Government shall have one vote which may be cast by any Commissioner from that Government. Decisions of the Commission shall be taken by a two-thirds majority of the votes of all the Contracting Governments.

8. The Commission shall adopt, and amend as occasion may require, financial regulations and rules and by-laws for the conduct of its meetings and for the exercise of its functions and duties.

ARTICLE III

1. The Commission shall appoint an Executive Secretary according to such procedure and on such terms as it may determine.

2. The staff of the Commission shall be appointed by the Executive Secretary in accordance with such rules and procedures as may be determined and authorized by the Commission.

3. The Executive Secretary shall, subject to the general supervision of the Commission, have full power and authority over the staff and shall perform such other functions as the Commission shall prescribe.

Article IV

1. The Contracting Governments shall establish and maintain a Panel for each of the sub-areas provided for by Article I, in order to carry out the objectives of this Convention. Each Contracting Government participating in any Panel shall be represented on such Panel by its Commissioner or Commissioners, who may be assisted by experts or advisers. Each Panel shall elect from its members a Chairman who shall serve for a period of two years and shall be eligible for re-election but not to a succeeding term.

2. After this Convention has been in force for two years, but not before that time, Panel representation shall be reviewed annually by the Commission, which shall have the power, subject to consultation with the Panel concerned, to determine representation on each Panel on the basis of current substantial exploitation in the sub-area concerned of fishes of the cod group (Gadiformes), of flat-fishes (Pleuronectiformes), and of rosefish (genus Sebastes), except that each Contracting Government with coastline adjacent to a sub-area shall have the right of representation on the Panel for the sub-area.

3. Each Panel may adopt, and amend as occasion may require, rules of procedure and by-laws for the conduct of its meetings and for the exercise of its functions and duties.

4. Each Government participating in a Panel shall have one vote, which shall be cast by a Commissioner representing that Government. Decisions of the Panel shall be taken by a two-thirds majority of the votes of all the Governments participating in that Panel.

5. Commissioners of Contracting Governments not participating in a particular Panel shall have the right to attend the meetings of such Panel as observers, and may be accompanied by experts and advisers.

6. The Panel shall, in the exercise of their functions and duties, use the services of the Executive Secretary and the staff of the Commission.

Article V

1. Each Contracting Government may set up an Advisory Committee composed of persons, including fishermen, vessel owners and others, well informed concerning the problems of the fisheries of the Northwest Atlantic Ocean. With the assent of the Contracting Government concerned, a representative or representativs of an Advisory Committee may attend as observers all non-executive meetings of the Commission or of any Panel in which their Government participates.

2. The Commissioners of each Contracting Government may hold public hearings within the territories they represent.

Article VI

1. The Commission shall be responsible in the field of scientific investigation for obtaining and collating the information necessary for maintaining those stocks of fish which support international fisheries in the Convention area and the Commission may, through or in collaboration with agencies of the Contracting Governments or other public or private agencies and organizations or, when necessary, independently:

(a) make such investigations as it finds necessary into the abundance, life history and ecology of any species of aquatic life in any part of the Northwest Atlantic Ocean;

(b) collect and analyze statistical information relating to the current conditions and trends of the fishery resources of the Northwest Atlantic Ocean;

(c) study and appraise information concerning the methods for maintaining and increasing stocks of fish in the Northwest Atlantic Ocean;

(d) hold or arrange such hearings as may be useful or essential in connection with the development of complete factual information necessary to carry out the provisions of this Convention;

(e) conduct fishing operations in the Convention area at any time for purposes of scientific investigation;

(f) publish and otherwise disseminate reports of its findings and statistical, scientific and other information relating to the fisheries of the Northwest Atlantic Ocean as well as such other reports as fall within the scope of this Convention.

2. Upon the unanimous recommendation of each Panel affected, the Commission may alter the boundaries of the sub-areas set out in the Annex. Any such alteration shall forthwith be reported to the Depositary Government which shall inform the Contracting Governments, and the sub-areas defined in the Annex shall be altered accordingly.

3. The Contracting Governments shall furnish to the Commission, at such time and in such form as may be required by the Commission, the statistical information referred to in paragraph 1 (b) of this Article.

Article VII

1. Each Panel established under Article IV shall be responsible for keeping under review the fisheries of its sub-area and the scientific and other information relating thereto.

2. Each Panel, upon the basis of scientific investigations, may make recommendations to the Commission for joint action by the Contracting Governments on the matters specified in paragraph 1 of Article VIII.

3. Each Panel may recommend to the Commission studies and investigations within the scope of this Convention which are deemed necessary in the development of factual information relating to its particular sub-area.

4. Any Panel may make recommendations to the Commission for the alteration of the boundaries of the sub-areas defined in the Annex.

5. Each Panel shall investigate and report to the Commission upon any matter referred to it by the Commission.

6. A Panel shall not incur any expenditure except in accordance with directions given by the Commission.

ARTICLE VIII

1. The Commission may, on the recommendations of one or more Panels, and on the basis of scientific investigations, transmit to the Depositary Government proposals, for joint action by the Contracting Governments, designed to keep the stocks of those species of fish which support international fisheries in the Convention area at a level permitting the maximum sustained catch by the application, with respect to such species of fish, of one or more of the following measures:

(a) establishing open and closed seasons;
(b) closing to fishing such portions of a sub-area as the Panel concerned finds to be a spawning area or to be populated by small or immature fish;
(c) establishing size limits for any species;
(d) prescribing the fishing gear and appliances the use of which is prohibited;
(e) prescribing an over-all catch limit for any species of fish.

2. Each recommendation shall be studied by the Commission and thereafter the Commission shall either

(a) transmit the recommendation as a proposal to the Depositary Government with such modifications or suggestions as the Commission may consider desirable, or
(b) refer the recommendation back to the Panel with comments for its reconsideration.

3. The Panel may, after reconsidering the recommendation returned to it by the Commission, reaffirm that recommendation, with or without modification.

4. If, after a recommendation is reaffirmed, the Commission is unable to adopt the recommendation as a proposal, it shall send a copy of the recommendation to the Depositary Government with a report of the Commission's decision. The Depositary Government shall transmit copies of the recommendation and of the Commission's report to the Contracting Governments.

5. The Commission may, after consultation with all the Panels, transmit proposals to the Depositary Government within the scope of paragraph 1 of this Article affecting the Convention area as a whole.

6. The Depositary Government shall transmit any proposal received by it to the Contracting Governments for their consideration and may make such suggestions as will facilitate acceptance of the proposal.

7. The Contracting Governments shall notify the Depositary Government of their acceptance of the proposal, and the Depositary Government shall notify the Contracting Governments of each acceptance communicated to it, including the date of receipt thereof.

8. The proposal shall become effective for all Contracting Governments four months after the date on which notifications of acceptance shall have been received by the Depositary Government from all the Contracting Governments participating in the Panel or Panels for the sub-area or sub-areas to which the proposal applies.

9. At any time after the expiration of one year from the date on which a proposal becomes effective, any Panel Government for the sub-area to which the proposal applies may give to the Depositary Government notice of the termination of its acceptance of the proposal and, if that notice is not withdrawn, the proposal shall cease to be effective for that Panel Government at the end of one year from the date of receipt of the notice by the Deposi-

tary Government. At any time after a proposal has ceased to be effective for a Panel Government under this paragraph, the proposal shall cease to be effective for any other Contracting Government upon the date a notice of withdrawal by such Government is received by the Depositary Government. The Depositary Government shall notify all Contracting Governments of every notice under this paragraph immediately upon receipt thereof.

Article IX

The Commission may invite the attention of any or all Contracting Governments to any matters which relate to the objectives and purposes of this Convention.

Article X

1. The Commission shall seek to establish and maintain working arrangements with other public international organizations which have related objectives, particularly the Food and Agriculture Organization of the United Nations and the International Council for the Exploration of the Sea, to ensure effective collaboration and coordination with respect to their work and, in the case of the International Council for the Exploration of the Sea, the avoidance of duplication of scientific investigations.

2. The Commission shall consider, at the expiration of two years from the date of entry into force of this Convention, whether or not it should recommend to the Contracting Governments that the Commission be brought within the framework of a specialized agency of the United Nations.

Article XI

1. Each Contracting Government shall pay the expenses of the Commissioners, experts and advisers appointed by it.

2. The Commission shall prepare an annual administrative budget of the proposed necessary administrative expenditures of the Commission and an annual special projects budget of proposed expenditures on special studies and investigations to be undertaken by or on behalf of the Commission pursuant to Article VI or by or on behalf of any Panel pursuant to Article VII.

3. The Commission shall calculate the payments due from each Contracting Government under the annual administrative budget according to the following formula:

(a) from the administrative budget there shall be deducted a sum of 500 United States dollars for each Contracting Government;

(b) the remainder shall be divided into such number of equal shares as corresponds to the total number of Panel memberships;

(c) the payment due from any Contracting Government shall be the equivalent of 500 United States dollars plus the number of shares equal to the number of Panels in which that Government participates.

4. The Commission shall notify each Contracting Government the sum due from that Government as calculated under paragraph 3 of this Article and as soon as possible thereafter each Contracting Government shall pay to the Commission the sum so notified.

5. The annual special projects budget shall be allocated to the Contracting Governments according to a scale to be determined by agreement among the Contracting Governments, and the sums so allocated to any Contracting Government shall be paid to the Commission by that Government.

6. Contributions shall be payable in the currency of the country in which the seat of the Commission is located, except that the Commission may accept payment in the currencies in which it may be anticipated that expenditures of the Commission will be made from time to time, up to an amount established each year by the Commission in connection with the preparation of the annual budgets.

7. At its first meeting the Commission shall approve an administrative budget for the balance of the first financial year in which the Commission functions and shall transmit to the Contracting Governments copies of that budget together with notices of their respective allocations.

8. In subsequent financial years, the Commission shall submit to each Contracting Government drafts of the annual budgets together with a schedule of allocations, not less than six weeks before the annual meeting of the Commission at which the budgets are to be considered.

Article XII

The Contracting Governments agree to take such action as may be necessary to make effective the provisions of this Convention and to implement any proposals which become effective under paragraph 8 of Article VIII. Each Contracting Government shall transmit to the Commission a statement of the action taken by it for these purposes.

Article XIII

The Contracting Governments agree to invite the attention of any Government not a party to this Convention to any matter relating to the fishing activities in the Convention area of the nationals or vessels of that Government which appear to affect adversely the operations of the Commission or the carrying out of the objectives of this Convention.

Article XIV

The Annex, as attached to this Convention and as modified from time to time, forms an integral part of this Convention.

Article XV

1. This Convention shall be ratified by the signatory Governments and the instruments of ratification shall be deposited with the Government of the United States of America, referred to in this Convention as the "Depositary Government."

2. This Convention shall enter into force upon the deposit of instruments of ratification by four signatory Governments, and shall enter into force with respect to each Government which subsequently ratifies on the date of the deposit of its instrument of ratification.

3. Any Government which has not signed this Convention may adhere thereto by a notification in writing to the Depositary Government. Adherences received by the Depositary Government prior to the date of entry into force of this Convention shall become effective on the date this Convention enters into force. Adherences received by the Depositary Government after the date of entry into force of this Convention shall become effective on the date of receipt by the Depositary Government.

4. The Depositary Government shall inform all signatory Governments and all adhering Governments of all ratifications deposited and adherences received.

5. The Depositary Government shall inform all Governments concerned of the date this Convention enters into force.

Article XVI

1. At any time after the expiration of ten years from the date of entry into force of this Convention, any Contracting Government may withdraw from the Convention on December thirty-first of any year by giving notice on or before the preceding June thirtieth to the Depositary Government which shall communicate copies of such notice to the other Contracting Governments.

2. Any other Contracting Government may thereupon withdraw from this Convention on the same December thirty-first by giving notice to the Depositary Government within one month of the receipt of a copy of a notice of withdrawal given pursuant to paragraph 1 of this Article.

JAPAN-UNION OF SOVIET SOCIALIST REPUBLICS

CONVENTION CONCERNING THE HIGH SEAS FISHERIES OF THE NORTHWEST PACIFIC OCEAN

Signed at Moscow, May 14, 1956; in force, December 12, 1956 *

(Unofficial Translation)

The Governments of Japan and the Union of Soviet Socialist Republics,

Considering the common interest of the Contracting Parties with respect to the development, on a rational basis, of the fisheries in the Northwest Pacific Ocean, and their mutual responsibility with respect to the condition of the fish and other marine living resources, as well as to the effective utilization of those resources,

Recognizing that it will serve the common interest of mankind, as well as the interests of the Contracting Parties to maintain the maximum sustained productivity of fisheries in the Northwest Pacific Ocean,

Considering that each of the Contracting Parties should assume an obligation, on a free and equal footing, to conserve and increase the above mentioned resources,

Recognizing that it is highly desirable to promote and co-ordinate the scientific studies of the Contracting Parties, the purpose of which is to maintain the maximum sustained productivity of fisheries of interest to the two Contracting Parties,

Have, therefore, decided to conclude this Convention, and for this purpose have appointed their respective representatives who have agreed as follows:

Article I

1. The area to which this Convention applies, hereinafter referred to as "the Convention area," shall be all waters, other than territorial waters, of the Northwest Pacific Ocean, including the Japan Sea, the Okhotsk Sea and the Bering Sea.

2. Nothing in this Convention shall be deemed to affect in any way the position of the Contracting Parties in regard to the limits of territorial sea or to the jurisdiction over fisheries.

Article II

1. The Contracting Parties in order to conserve and develop the fish and other marine living resources, hereinafter referred to as the "fishery

* Reprinted from Japanese Annual of International Law, No. 1 (1957), pp. 119–124.

resources,'' agree to carry out in the Convention area, the co-ordinated measures specified in the Annex to this Convention.

2. The Annex attached hereto shall form an integral part of this Convention. All references to the ''Convention'' shall be understood as including the said Annex either in its present terms or as revised in accordance with the provisions of paragraph (a) of Article IV.

Article III

1. In order to realize the objectives of this Convention, the Contracting Parties shall establish the Japan-Soviet Northwest Pacific Fisheries Commission, hereinafter referred to as ''the Commission.''

2. The Commission shall be composed of two national sections, each consisting of three members appointed by the governments of the respective Contracting Parties.

3. All resolutions, recommendations and other decisions of the Commission shall be made only by agreement between the national sections.

4. The Commission may decide upon and revise, as occasion may require, the rules for the conduct of its meetings.

5. The Commission shall meet at least once each year and at such other times as may be requested by one of the national sections. The date and place of the first meeting shall be determined by agreement between the Contracting Parties.

6. At its first meeting the Commission shall select a Chairman and Vice-Chairman from different national sections. The Chairman and Vice-Chairman shall hold office for a period of one year. The selection of a Chairman and Vice-Chairman from the national sections shall be made in such a manner as will yearly provide each Contracting Party in turn with representation in those offices.

7. The official languages of the Commission shall be Japanese and Russian.

8. The expenses incurred by a member of the Commission in connection with participation in the meetings of the Commission shall be paid by the appointing government. Joint expenses incurred by the Commission shall be paid by the Commission through contributions made by the Contracting Parties in the form and proportion recommended by the Commission and approved by the Contracting Parties.

Article IV

The Commission shall perform the following functions:

(a) At the regular annual meeting, consider the appropriateness of co-ordinated measures being enforced at the time, and if necessary revise the Annex to this Convention. Such revision shall be determined on the basis of scientific findings.

(b) When it is required by the Annex to fix the total annual catch of a stock of fish, determine the total annual catch of such stock by the Contracting Parties and notify the said Parties.

(c) Determine the kind and scope of statistics and other reports to be submitted to the Commission by each of the Contracting Parties for carrying out the provisions of this Convention.

(d) For the purpose of studying the fishery resources, prepare and adjust co-ordinated scientific research programs and recommend them to the Contracting Parties.

(e) Submit annually to the Contracting Parties a report on the operations of the Commission.

(f) In addition to the functions stipulated above, make recommendations to the Contracting Parties with respect to the matter of conservation and increase of fishery resources in the Convention area.

Article V

The Contracting Parties agree, for the purpose of mutually exchanging experiences concerning the study and conservation of fishery resources and regulation of fisheries, to exchange men of learning and experience in fisheries. The exchange of such men shall be conducted by agreement from time to time between the two Parties.

Article VI

1. The Contracting Parties shall take appropriate and effective measures in order to carry out the provisions of this Convention.

2. When in receipt of the notification from the Commission concerning the total annual catch fixed for each of the Contracting Parties in accordance with paragraph (b) of Article IV, the Contracting Parties shall issue licenses or certificates to their fishing vessels and inform each other of all such licenses and certificates issued.

3. The licenses and certificates issued by the Contracting Parties shall be in both the Japanese and Russian languages, and the fishing vessels, when engaged in fishing operations, shall have on board their license or certificate without fail.

4. The Contracting Parties agree, for the purpose of rendering effective the provisions of this Convention, to enact and enforce necessary laws and regulations, with regard to their nationals, organizations and fishing vessels, with appropriate penalties against violations thereof and to submit to the Commission a report on any action taken by them with regard thereto.

Article VII

1. When authorized officials of either of the Contracting Parties have reasonable ground to believe that a fishing vessel of the other Party is actually violating the provisions of this Convention, such officials may board and search the vessel to ascertain whether the said provisions are being observed.

Such officials shall present credentials issued by their Government and written in both the Japanese and Russian languages, if requested by the master of the vessel.

2. If it becomes clear as a result of the search conducted by such officials that there is vidence that the fishing vessel or any person on board such vessel is violating the Convention, the said officials may seize such vessel or arrest such person.

In that case, the Contracting Party to which the officials belong shall notify as soon as possible the other Contracting Party to which such fishing vessel or person belongs of the arrest or seizure, and shall deliver such vessel or person as promptly as practicable to the authorized officials of the Contracting Party to which the vessel or person belongs at the place of arrest or seizure unless another place is agreed upon by the Contracting Parties. Provided, however, that when the Contracting Party which receives such notification cannot immediately accept delivery and requests of the other Contracting Party, the latter Party receiving the request may keep such vessel or person under surveillance within its own territory, under the conditions agreed upon by the Contracting Parties.

3. Only the authorities of the Party to which the above-mentioned fishing vessel or person belongs have jurisdiction to try cases arising in connection with this article and impose penalties therefor. Written evidence and proof establishing the offense shall be furnished as promptly as possible to the Contracting Party having jurisdiction to try the case.

Article VIII

1. This Convention shall become effective from the date of entry into force of the Peace Treaty between Japan and the Union of Soviet Socialist Republics or from the date of restoration of diplomatic relations between the said countries.

2. After this Convention has remained in force for a period of ten years, either Contracting Party may give notice to the other Contracting Party of an intention to abrogate the said Convention, and it shall terminate one year after the date of receipt of the said notification by the latter Party.

IN WITNESS WHEREOF, the undersigned representatives have signed this Treaty.

CONVENTION BETWEEN THE UNITED STATES OF AMERICA AND CANADA FOR THE PRESERVATION OF THE HALIBUT FISHERY OF THE NORTHERN PACIFIC OCEAN AND BERING SEA[1]

March 2, 1953

The Government of the United States of America and the Government of Canada, desiring to provide more effectively for the preservation of the halibut fishery of the Northern Pacific Ocean and Bering Sea, have resolved to conclude a Convention... [as follows]:

ARTICLE I

1. The nationals and inhabitants and fishing vessels and boats of the United States of America and Canada, respectively, are hereby prohibited from fishing for halibut (Hippoglossus) in Convention waters as herein defined, except as provided by the International Pacific Halibut Commission in regulations designed to develop the stocks of halibut in the Convention waters to those levels which will permit the maximum sustained yield and to maintain the stocks at those levels pursuant to Article III of this Convention.

2. "Convention waters" means the territorial waters and the high seas off the western coasts of the United States of America and of Canada, including the southern as well as the western coasts of Alaska.

3. It is understood that nothing contained in this Convention shall prohibit the nationals or inhabitants or the fishing vessels or boats of the United States of America or of Canada from fishing in the Convention waters for other species of fish during any season when fishing for halibut in the Convention waters is prohibited by this Convention or any regulations adopted pursuant to this Convention. It is further understood that nothing contained in this Convention shall prohibit the International Pacific Halibut Commission from conducting or authorizing fishing operations for investigation purposes at any time.

ARTICLE II

1. Every national or inhabitant, vessel or boat of the United States of America or of Canada engaged in fishing on the high seas in violation of this Convention or of any regulation adopted pursuant thereto may be seized by duly authorized officers of either Contracting Party and detained by

the officers making such seizure and delivered as soon as practicable to an authorized official of the country to which such person, vessel or boat belongs, at the nearest point to the place of seizure or elsewhere as may be agreed upon. The authorities of the country to which such person, vessel or boat belongs alone shall have jurisdiction to conduct prosecutions for the violation of the provisions of this Convention or any regulations which may be adopted in pursuance thereof and to impose penalties for such violation, and the witnesses and proof necessary for such prosecutions, so far as any witnesses or proofs are under the control of the other Contracting Party, shall be furnished with all reasonable promptitude to the authorities having jurisdiction to conduct the prosecutions.

2. Each Contracting Party shall be responsible for the proper observance of this Convention and of any regulations adopted under the provisions thereof in the portion of its waters covered thereby.

ARTICLE III

1. The Contracting Parties agree to continue under this Convention the Commission known as the International Fisheries Commission established by the Convention for the Preservation of the Halibut Fishery, signed at Washington, March 2, 1923, continued by the Convention signed at Ottawa, May 9,1930, and further continued by the Convention, signed at Ottawa, January 29,1937, except that after the date of entry into force of this Convention it shall consist of six members, three appointed by each Contracting Party, and shall be known as the International Pacific Halibut Commission. This Commission shall make investigations as are necessary into the life history of the halibut in the Convention waters and shall publish a report of its activities and investigations from time to time. Each Contracting Party shall have power to fill, and shall fill from time to time, vacancies which may occur in its representation on the Commission. Each Contracting Party shall pay the salaries and expenses of its own members. Joint expenses incurred by the Commission shall be paid by the two Contracting Parties in equal moieties. All decisions of the Commission shall be made by a concurring vote of at least two of the Commissioners of each Contracting Party.

2. The Contracting Parties agree that for the purpose of developing the stocks of halibut of the Northern Pacific Ocean and Bering Sea to levels which will permit the maximum sustained yield from that fishery and for maintaining the stocks at those levels, the International Pacific Halibut Commission, with the approval of the President of the United States of America and of the Governor General in Council of Canada, may, after investigation has indicated such action to be necessary, in respect of the nationals and inhabitants and fishing vessels

and boats of the United States of America and of Canada, and in respect of halibut:

(a) divide the Convention waters into areas;

(b) establish one or more open or closed seasons, as to each area;

(c) limit the size of the fish and the quantity of the catch to be taken from each area within any season during which fishing is allowed;

(d) during both open and closed seasons, permit, limit, regulate or prohibit, the incidental catch of halibut that may be taken, retained, possessed, or landed from each area or portion of an area, by vessels fishing for other species of fish;

(e)prohibit departure of vessels from any port or place, or from any receiving vessel or station, to any area for halibut fishing,after any date when in the judgment of the International Pacific Halibut Commission the vessels which have departed for that area prior to that date or which are known to be fishing in that area shall suffice to catch the limit which shall have been set for that area under section (c) of this paragraph;

(f) fix the size and character of halibut fishing appliances to be used in any area;

(g) make such regulations for the licencing and departure of vessels and for the collection of statistics of the catch of halibut as it shall find necessary to determine the condition and trend of the halibut fishery and to carry out the other provisions of this Convention;

(h) close to all taking of halibut such portion or portions of an area or areas as the International Halibut Commission finds to be populated by small, immature halibut and designates as nursery grounds.

ARTICLE IV

The Contracting Parties agree to enact and enforce such legislation as may be necessary to make effective the provisions of this Convention and any regulations adopted thereunder, with appropriate penalties for violations thereof.

ARTICLE V

1. This Convention shall be ratified....

1. Text from Treaties and Other International Acts Series, Department of State, No. 2900. This Convention entered into force on October 28, 1953.

AGREEMENT BETWEEN THE GOVERNMENT OF THE UNITED STATES AND THE UNION OF SOVIET SOCIALIST REPUBLICS ON FISHERIES IN THE NORTHEASTERN PART OF THE PACIFIC OCEAN OFF THE COAST OF THE UNITED STATES OF AMERICA.

Signed at Washington, February 13,1967;[1]
in force on same date

The Government of the United States of America and the Government of the Union of Soviet Socialist Republics, being mutually interested in having the fisheries in the northeastern part of the Pacific Ocean off the coast of the United States conducted with due attention to their respective interests,

Considering it desirable that the fisheries in the said area be conducted with due regard to the conservation of fish stocks, and that measures be taken to prevent damage to the fishing gear used by fishermen of the two countries, and

Considering it desirable also to expand scientific research in the field of fisheries and the exchange of scientific data,

Have agreed on the following:

1. Fishing vessels of the Soviet Union may fish and conduct loading operations in the nine mile zone contiguous to the territorial sea of the United States in the following areas:

a. In the gulf of Alaska between $140^\circ 30'$ west longitude and $142^\circ 30'$ west longitude, and

b. In the Aleutian Islands between 169° west longitude and 173° west longitude and west of $178^\circ 30'$ west longitude.

Fishing in these areas will not exceed the present level.

2. In addition, fishing vessels of the Soviet Union may conduct loading operations in the following areas in the nine mile zone contiguous to the territorial sea of the United States:

a. Near Cape Lookout in the State of Oregon between $45^\circ 18'$ north latitude and $45^\circ 23'$ north latitude;

b. Near Destruction Island in the State of Washington between 47° 36' north latitude and 47° 45' north latitude;

c. Near the mouth of the Rogue River in the State of Oregon between 42° 21' north latitude and 42° 33' north latitude;

d. Near Forrester Island in the State of Alaska in the waters bounded on the north by 54° 54' north latitude, on the east by 133° 16' west longitude, and on the south by 54° 44' north latitude;

e. On the east side of Kayak Island in the State of Alaska between 59° 52' north latitude and 59° 56' north latitude west of 143° 53' west longitude and on the west side of Kayak Island between 59° 56' north latitude and 60° 00' north latitude;

f. On the west side of Sanak Island in the State of Alaska in the waters bounded on the north by 54° 36' north latitude, and on the south by 54° 26' north latitude, on the west by 163° 05' west longitude, and on the east by 162° 40' west longitude; and in the following alternate areas:

g. Near Cape Blanco in the State of Oregon, between 42° 51' north latitude and 42° 56' north latitude; and

h. Near Cape Elizabeth in the State of Washington between 47° 20' north latitude and 47° 23' north latitude.

3. The Government of the Soviet Union will adopt the measures necessary to ensure that citizens and vessels of the Soviet Union:

a. Refrain from fishing in the waters of the Pacific coast of the United States between 46° 14' north latitude and 46° 56' north latitude landward of the isobath of 110° meters and in the waters bounded by an arc with a radius of 15 nautical miles with its center at the mouth of Alsea Bay in the State of Oregon;

b. Refrain from concentrating fishing vessels during the period from June 15th through September 15th between 47° 54' north latitude and 48° 28' north latitude east of 125° 10' west longitude;

c. During the period from May 9th to May 23rd, refrain from fishing in the following areas: ...

[a list of areas enclosed by lines connecting the coordinates 56° 30' north latitude and 156° 07' west longitude, and between 58° 00' north latitude and 150° 49' west longitude]

4. It is agreed that nationals and vessels of the respective countries shall not engage in trawl fishing in the following areas of high concentrations of ocean perch for the period of this agreement: ...

[a series of areas enclosed by lines connecting the coordinates ranging from 45°35' north latitude and 124°26' west longitude, to 44°48'30" north latitude and 124°32' west longitude]

This paragraph shall not apply to vessels under 110 feet in length.

5. The Government of the United States will adopt the measures necessary to ensure that nationals and vessels under its control engaged in the ocean perch fishery in waters off the coasts of the States of Oregon and Washington will use trawl gear having a mesh size of no less than three inches (76mm.) in the cod end.

6. Each Government will take appropriate measures with regard to areas of heavy concentration of fishing operations of both countries directed at prevention of damage to fishing gear, including:

a. Measures leading to improvement of the means for marking fixed fishing gear and for reciprocal notification of areas in which fixed gear is concentrated;

b. Measures to ensure that fixed gear is set with due regard for the operation of mobile gear;

c. Measures to ensure that vessels operating with mobile gear will pass clearly marked fixed gear at a distance of not less than 400 meters from the nearest marker.

7. Both Governments will take appropriate measures to ensure that, to the extent practicable, waste materials are discharged at sea only in waters deeper than 1000 meters.

8. Both Governments consider it useful to arrange, when appropriate, for visits of representatives of fishermens' organizations of the two countries to each other's fishing fleets operating in the northeastern part of the Pacific Ocean. Such visits may be arranged on mutually agreeable terms determined in each particular case by the Chief of the Joint-Expedition in the Soviet fleet, DALRYBA, and the Regional Director of the United States Bureau of Commercial Fisheries in Seattle, Washington or Juneau, Alaska, as may be appropriate.

9. Both Governments consider it desirable to expand fishery research in the northeastern part of the Pacific Ocean

on species of common interest, both on a national basis and in the form of joint investigations. The competent agencies of the two Governments will arrange for the exchange of scientific data and results of research on the fisheries, for meetings of scientists and, when appropriate, for participation by scientists of each Government in investigations carried out on board research vessels of the other Government.
Each Government will, within the scope of its domestic laws and regulations, facilitate entry into appropriate ports for research vessels of the other Government engaged in such joint research.

10. Nothing in this agreement shall be interpreted as prejudicing the views of either Government with regard to freedom of fishing on the high seas or to traditional fisheries.

11. This agreement shall remain in force for the period of one year. Representatives of the two Governments will meet at a mutually convenient time prior to the expiration of the period of validity of this agreement to review the operation of this agreement and to decide on future arrangements.

In witness whereof the undersigned, being duly authorized for this purpose, have signed this agreement and have affixed their seals thereto...

For the United States of America: Donald L.McKernan

For the Government of the Union of Soviet Socialist Republics: M.N. Sukhoruchenko.

1. Department of State, Treaties and Other International Acts Series 6218.

CONVENTION ESTABLISHING INTER-AMERICAN TROPICAL TUNA COMMISSION

Signed May 31,1949;in force March 3,1950 [1]

The United States of America and the Republic of Costa Rica considering their mutual interest in maintaining the populations of yellowfin and skipjack tuna and of other kinds of fish taken by tuna fishing vessels in the eastern Pacific Ocean which by reason of continued use have come to be of common concern, and desiring to cooperate in the gathering and interpretation of factual information to facilitate maintaining the populations of these fishes at a level which will permit maximum sustained catches year after year, have agreed to conclude a Convention for these purposes and to that end have named as their plenipotentiaries...

Article 1

1. The High Contracting Parties agree to establish and operate a joint Commission, to be known as the Inter-American Tropical Tuna Commission, hereinafter referred to as the Commission, which shall carry out the objectives of this Convention. The Commission shall be composed of national sections, each consisting of from one to four members, appointed by the Governments of the respective High Contracting Parties.

2. The Commission shall submit annually to the Government of each High Contracting Party a report of its investigations and findings, with appropriate recommendations, and shall also inform such Governments, whenever it is deemed advisable, on any matter relating to the objectives of this Convention.

3. Each High Contracting Party shall determine and pay the expenses incurred by its section. Joint expenses incurred by the Commission shall be paid by the High Contracting Parties through contributions in the form and proportion recommended by the Commission and approved by the High Contracting Parties. The proportion of joint expenses to be paid by each High Contracting Party shall be related to the proportion of the total catch from the fisheries covered by this Convention utilized by that High Contracting Party.

4. Both the general annual program of activities and the budget of joint expenses shall be recommended by the Commission and submitted for approval to the High Contracting Parties.

5. The Commission shall decide on the most convenient place or places for its headquarters.

6. The Commission shall meet at least once each year, and at such other times as may be requested by a national section.

The date and place of the first meeting shall be determined by agreement between the High Contracting Parties.

7. At its first meeting the Commission shall select a chairman and a secretary from different national sections. The chairman and the secretary shall hold office for a period of one year. During succeeding years, selection of the chairman and the secretary from the national sections shall be in such a manner that the chairman and the secretary will be of different nationalities, and as will provide each High Contracting Party, in turn, with an opportunity to be represented in those offices.

8. Each national section shall have one vote. Decisions, resolutions, recommendations, and publications of the Commission shall be made only by a unanimous vote.

9. The Commission shall be entitled to adopt and to amend subsequently, as occasion may require, by-laws or rules for the conduct of its meetings.

10. The Commission shall be entitled to employ necessary personnel for the performance of its functions and duties.

11. Each High Contracting Party shall be entitled to establish an Advisory Committee for its section, to be composed of persons who shall be well informed concerning tuna fishery problems of common concern. Each such Advisory Committee shall be invited to attend the non-executive sessions of the Commission.

12. The Commission may hold public hearings. Each national section also may hold public hearings within its own country.

13. The Commission shall designate a Director of Investigations who shall be technically competent and who shall be responsible to the Commission and may be freely removed by it. Subject to the instruction of the Commission and with its approval, the Director of Investigations shall have charge of:

(a) the drafting of programs of investigations, and the preparation of budget estimates for the Commission;

(b) authorizing the disbursement of the funds for the joint expenses of the Commission;

(c) the accounting of the funds for the joint expenses of the Commission;

(d) the appointment and immediate direction of technical and other personnel required for the functions of the Commission;

(e) arrangements for the cooperation with other organizations or individuals in accordance with paragraph 16 of this Article;

(f) the coordination of the work of the Commission with that of organizations and individuals whose cooperation has been arranged for;

(g) the drafting of administrative, scientific and other reports for the Commission;

(h) the performance of such other duties as the Commission may require.

14. The official languages of the Commission shall be English and Spanish, and members of the Commission may use either language during meetings. When requested, translation shall be made to the other language. The minutes, official documents, and publications of the Commission shall be in both languages, but official correspondence of the Commission may be written, at the discretion of the secretary, in either language.

15. Each national section shall be entitled to obtain certified copies of any documents pertaining to the Commission except that the Commission will adopt and may amend subsequently rules to ensure the confidential character of records of statistics of individual catches and individual company operations.

16. In the performance of its duties and functions the Commission may request the technical and scientific services of, and information from, official agencies of the High Contracting Parties, and any international, public, or private institution or organization, or any private individual.

Article II

The Commission shall perform the following functions and duties:

1. Make investigations concerning the abundance, biology, biometry, and ecology of yellowfin (Neothunnus) and skipjack (Katsuwonus) tuna in the waters of the eastern Pacific Ocean fished by the nationals of the High Contracting Parties, and the kinds of fishes commonly used as bait in the tuna fisheries, especially the anchovetta, and of other kinds of fish taken by tuna fishing vessels; and the effects of natural factors and human activities on the abundance of the populations of fishes supporting all these fisheries.

2. Collect and analyze information relating to current and past conditions and trends of the populations of fishes covered by this Convention.

3. Study and appraise information concerning methods and procedures for maintaining and increasing the populations of fishes covered by this Convention.

4. Conduct such fishing and other activities, on the high seas and in waters which may be under the jurisdiction of the High Contracting Parties, as may be necessary to attain the ends referred to in subparagraphs 1,2, and 3 of this Article.

5. Recommend from time to time, on the basis of scientific investigations, proposals for joint action by the High Contracting Parties designed to keep the populations of fishes covered by this Convention at those levels of abundance which will permit the maximum sustained catch.

6. Collect statistics and all kinds of reports concerning catches and the operations of fishing boats, and other information concerning the fishing for fishes covered by this Convention, from vessels or persons engaged in these fisheries.

7. Publish or otherwise disseminate reports relative to the results of its findings and such other reports as fall within the scope of this Convention, as well as scientific, statistical, and other data relating to the fisheries maintained by the nationals of the High Contracting Parties for the fishes covered by this Convention.

Article III

The High Contracting Parties agree to enact such legislation as may be necessary to carry out the purposes of this Convention.

Article IV

Nothing in this Convention shall be construed to modify any existing treaty or convention with regard to the fisheries of the eastern Pacific Ocean previously concluded by a High Contracting Party, nor to preclude a High Contracting Party from entering into treaties or conventions with other States regarding these fisheries, the terms of which are not incompatible with the present Convention.

Article V

1. The present Convention shall be ratified....

3. Any government, whose nationals participate in the fisheries covered by this Convention, desiring to adhere to the present Convention, shall address a communication to that effect to each of the High Contracting Parties. Upon receiving the unanimous consent of the High Contracting Parties to adherence, such Government shall deposit with the Government

of the United States of America an instrument of adherence which shall stipulate the effective date thereof. The Government of the United States of America shall furnish a certified copy of the Convention to each government desiring to adhere thereto. Each adhering government shall have all the rights and obligations under the Convention as if it had been an original signatory thereof.

4. At any time after the expiration of ten years from the date of entry into force of this Convention any High Contracting Party may give notice of its intention of denouncing the Convention. Such notification shall become effective with respect to such notifying government one year after its receipt by the Government of the United States of America. After the expiration of the said one year period the Convention shall be effective only with respect to the remaining High Contracting Parties.

5. The Government of the United States of America shall inform the other High Contracting Parties of all instruments of adherence and of notifications of denunciation received.

In Witness Whereof....

1. United Nations Treaty Series, Vol. 80 (1951), pp.4-12. In force between the United States, Costa Rica, Ecuador, Panama, and Mexico.

CHAPTER SIX

MINERAL RESOURCES AND THEIR EXPLOITATION

Introductory Note

Government experts have estimated that the demand for ores, minerals and fossil fuels by the year 2,000 will approximate three and one-half times present consumption. Of course the accuracy of this prediction depends upon such variables as population trends, public health, economic development, stability of international relations, and the supply, demand and price triangle.

The need for additional reserves of some minerals is likely to be only moderate, whereas for others, like manganese and petroleum, the growth rate may be exponential. It would be rash to suggest that land resources have been depleted. The vast discoveries of late years in Alaska, the Canadian northlands, and in the wilderness of South America disprove fears that the world's riches are about to be exhausted. Undoubtedly, there are enormous stores of untapped resources, yet one cannot deny that mining involves entropy -- a reduction of capital created over millions of years through natural processes which once used are gone.

Discoveries of mineral and fossil fuels on the ocean floor and in the subsoil of the continental shelves suggest that significant amounts of these commodities lie on or within the appendages to the land. At present most of these areas have been only imperfectly surveyed. But research has revealed that the shelves contain such properties as bromine, salt, potash and sulphur, as well as large masses of usable gravels. Supplies of phosphorus, manganese, nickel and cobalt nodules have also been found. Notable quantities of diamonds have already been gathered off the coast of Southwest Africa, while tin has been dredged from the shallow waters off Thailand and Indonesia. Coal has been mined from shafts extending out under the seas from Great Britain, and copper sulphides have recently been detected in hot water pockets within the Red Sea by a Woods Hole surveying expedition.

More exciting still have been the petroleum and gas findings along the continental shelf off Louisiana, Texas, California and Alaska, as well as in the Persian Gulf, the North Sea, and off the southern coast of Australia. The search for oil and gas has become so competitive that various national, international and wild cat oil companies have taken out leases for exploration rights to much of the coast of Canada, many sections of Africa, and large parts of the Australian litoral. In places such as the Santa Barbara Channel in Southern California bids have extended to the 1,800 foot depth line and run over $61 million for a 5,400 acre tract. Still only about one per cent of the known area of the continental shelves has been leased.

Geological surveys suggest it is unlikely that the basaltic rock of the submarine abyss will yield mineral riches comparable to the strata of the continental shelves. However, so little is known of what lies in the abyss that at this stage prognostications are mainly speculation. Minerals associated with igenous rock may be present where volvanic action has occurred or is presently taking place, as off the shores of Iceland, the Azores, Hawaii, the Philippines and Indonesia. It is chiefly in the sedimentary overlays along the continental shelves, in the outreaches of old stream beds along sunken coasts, and possibly in some of the mid-ocean ridges -- as in the Atlantic and Indian Oceans --, but primarily in the continent-dominated areas, that extensive mineral and fossil fuel findings will be most significant for the next few years.

Manganese nodules have been seen and photographed in vast quantities on the floor of the Atlantic and Pacific Oceans. There is no question of their existence and extent. They constitute an enormously abundant reserve for mankind. Some have an assay value exceeding supplies of manganese ore found on the land, but the costs of extracting and transporting them ashore are currently more than their worth. Nevertheless, it may be expected that technology will eventually render the recovery and conversion of these nodules economically feasible.

Offshore mining operations are subject to a number of factors that need not be considered when the resources are extracted from the land. These include such elements as : (1) difficult technological requirements in terms of equipment and operational techniques; (2) exposure of rigs and other equipment to storm damage; (3) hazards from navigation; (4) problems of waste disposal and its effect upon the ecological balance of the sea thereby exposing mining operators to complaints from fishermen and others. It has been speculated that capital investment on the order of $100-300 million is currently necessary for deep water mining.

Gradually difficulties are sure to be overcome as the need for minerals increases, as technology advances, and as engineering capabilities improve.

The number of minerals now known to exist on the sea-beds falls below the 136 used in the United States. However, as we increase our knowledge of the marine environment we may discover that the continental shelf will yield extensive contributions to the world economy.

It has been stated that the United States petroleum industry already has invested approximately $7 billion in current operations along the American coasts. The capital investment in the first six months of 1968 is reported to have been in excess of $1 billion. Yet this has hardly scratched the Atlantic margin, and drilling from surface platforms has not extended beyond the 300 foot depth line. Within a short time, however, the industry will have equipment to drill in 600 and 1,000 foot water and to sub-floor depths of 1,200 feet. As drilling continues to move farther from shore, geological studies suggest that the prospects of finding productive pools of oil and gas will improve, particularly in such places as Georges Bank in the Gulf of Maine, the Grand Banks, and off of Cape Cod and New Jersey.

Among the unresolved questions two are of utmost concern: (1) what effects will underwater oil operations have upon valuable fisheries; and (2) under whose jurisdiction do the areas in which the resources are situated fall? Both domestic and international political and legal problems are associated with opening these areas up to mining activity.

The readings that follow in the chapter deal with some of

the issues of policy and law relating to mining in the seas. In Chapter Nine will be found materials bearing upon the current debate concerning the United Nations and the issue of deep ocean resources.

For further readings see Victor Basiuk, "Marine Resources Development, Foreign Policy and the Spectrum of Choice," Orbis, Spring 1968, pp. 39-72; David B. Brooks, Low Grade and Non-Conventional Sources of Manganese (Washington, Resources for the Future, Inc., 1966); John P. Craven, "Sea Power and the Sea Bed," U.S. Naval Institute Proceedings, April 1966, pp. 48-49; W.J. Cromie, "Who Will Own the Ocean's Wealth?", ibid., January 1965, pp. 52-61; Ely Northcutt, "American Policy Options in the Development of Undersea Mineral Resources," The International Lawyer, January 1968, pp. 215-223; Louis Henkin, Law for the Sea's Mineral Resources, Columbia University, Institute for the Study of Science in Human Affairs, Monograph No. 1, May 1968; Marine Technology Society, Exploiting the Ocean, Transactions of the 2nd MTS Conference, June 1966; John Mero. The Mineral Resources of the Sea (New York, American Elsevier, 1964); U.S. House of Representatives, The United Nations and the Issue of Deep Ocean Resources, Interim Report, together with Hearings before Subcommittee on International Organizations and Movements, Committee on Foreign Affairs, 90th Congress, 1st Session, December 1967; U.S. Senate, Governing the Use of Ocean Space, Hearings before the Committee on Foreign Relations, 90th Congress, 1st Session, November 1967.

MARINE OIL DRILL PLATFORM

Courtesy Standard Oil Co. (N.J.)

"The ocean is the earth's greatest storehouse of minerals. . . . Our search for mineral wealth often leads us back to the seas." —RACHEL L. CARSON

ENCOURAGING DEVELOPMENT OF NON-LIVING RESOURCES [1]

ORES, minerals, and fossil fuels are basic sources of the energy, construction materials, metals, chemicals, and fertilizers required by any advanced industrial economy. The United States thus needs continuous access to an adequate, dependable, and economic supply of raw materials to meet demands of an expanding population with a rising standard of living.

Federal policies on mineral resources are designed to contribute to economic development and national security by assisting the Nation in:

—developing adequate and dependable supplies of needed mineral raw materials;

—acquiring mineral supplies at lowest costs consistent with the satisfaction of other national objectives;

—emphasizing domestic supplies of mineral resources to assist in maintaining a favorable balance of payments;

—providing a climate for American industry to produce efficiently, under competitive conditions, the minerals required for the domestic economy and foreign trade;

—conserving the Nation's mineral resources by using them wisely and efficiently;

—preserving the quality of the environment while obtaining needed minerals.

By 1980, the U.S. consumption of non-fuel minerals is expected to double, and that of petroleum products is expected to increase by about 50 percent from today's base. The United States currently imports 21 percent of its minerals and 13.5 percent of its petroleum; the percentage is considerably higher for certain strategic metals such as manganese. The world-wide demand for minerals also will increase because of industrialization and rising levels of consumption. Such projections create incentives for geological exploration for new reserves and for technological advances to permit use of lower grade sources or substitute materials.

Significance of Offshore Production

Federal policies on solid mineral resources and fossil fuels have traditionally been based on the assumption that the supply would come very largely from land sources. In recent years, however, the grade of minerals from land sources has decreased and production costs have risen. These trends have motivated industry, with the aid of new technology, to turn to the sea for oil, gas, and sulfur, and to begin to look seaward for new sources of aggregates and other materials. This quest, for the time being, is largely pursued in the relatively shallow waters of the Continental Shelf, which approximates 860,000 square miles, one-third of our present land area.

Although little of the U.S. Continental Shelf has been systematically surveyed to determine the presence, distribution, and richness of seabed deposits, this Nation's economy is already benefitting significantly from its resources; this new frontier now provides almost 9 percent of the dollar value of U.S. petroleum production, significant amounts of sulfur, and contributes to national production of other minerals as well. Table IV.1 shows the value of U.S. offshore mineral production. Table IV.2 summarizes recent marine mining activities. Figure IV.1 shows some of the current exploratory drilling around the world.

The value of all minerals produced from Federal and State off-shore waters in the past seven years exceeds $6 billion. The value of petroleum production through 1967 from the Outer Continental Shelf lands (under Federal jurisdiction) has totalled about $4 billion, and if State lands are included, over $5 billion. Since the first Federal off-shore lease sale in 1954, 1,276 oil and gas leases have been sold resulting in a total bonus income of almost $2 billion. Federal royalties from production of oil, gas, and sulfur from the Outer Continental Shelf have totalled more than $700 million through 1967, and the Federal Government now receives more than $12 million per month in royalties.[1]

[1] The Outer Continental Shelf is that portion of the Shelf beyond three miles from the coast, except along the Gulf coasts of Florida and Texas, where it is defined as beyond three marine leagues.

Table IV.1—Value of Mineral Production from Oceans Bordering the United States, 1960–66

[Millions of dollars]

MARINE MINERAL PRODUCTION BY SOURCE

Year	Magnesium metal and compounds, salt and bromine [1]	From wells: Petroleum, natural gas, and sulfur [2]	Sand and gravel, zircon, feldspar, cement rock and limestone [3]	Combined
1960	$69.0	$423.6	$46.8	$539.4
1961	73.0	496.6	46.2	615.8
1962	89.1	620.7	44.3	754.1
1963	84.6	730.8	42.5	857.9
1964	94.5	820.3	43.6	958.4
1965	102.6	933.3	51.4	1,087.3
1966	117.0	1,177.7	49.2	1,343.9
7-year total	629.8	5,203.0	324.0	6,156.8

[1] Sea water.
[2] Ocean subfloors.
[3] Beaches and seafloors.
Source: Bureau of Mines, Department of the Interior.

The petroleum industry's continued confidence in the potential of off-shore production was demonstrated in the June 1967 Federal lease sale off Louisiana which resulted in $510 million in bonuses bid for 150 tracts. Many tracts were in water depths of more than 300 feet; thus the active bidding indicates that industry expects to have technology for operations in deeper water relatively soon.

The Shelf is thus a logical focus for a new era of systematic surveys. The growing world-wide demand for resources, the unexplored areas of the Continental Shelf with geological continuity from adjacent land areas which have yielded great mineral wealth, and scattered positive indications that resources are there, all direct attention to learning more about non-living resources under the sea, as on the Continent itself. See Figure IV.1. Delineation of the distribution and quantity of resources, together with advances in technology to reduce the disparity in costs between on-shore and off-shore extraction operations, will in large measure determine the pace of developing the Shelf. Other factors—legal, economic, and political—will also influence its development in competition with other sources of minerals or their substitutes.

Mineral and fuel resources from land sources are developed almost entirely through private investment and initiative. Private industry is expected to continue to take a similar role on the Continental Shelf.

A major issue thus is presented: How should Federal policies and activities appropriately evolve to enhance and accelerate sound development by private industry of marine resources on public off-shore lands? Should

Table IV.2—Recent Marine Mining Activities

Location	Activity [1]	Depth (feet) [2]	Interest
AFRICA			
Red Sea	Exploration	6,000±	Sulfide muds.
Southwest Africa	Dredging	600−	Diamonds.
Union of South Africa	Exploration	(?)	Phosphate.
ASIA			
Borneo	Exploration	600−	Tin.
India	Exploration	(?)	Phosphate.
Indonesia	Dredging	150−	Tin.
Japan	Dredging	30−	Iron sands.
Malaysia	Exploration	600−	Tin.
Papua and New Guinea	Exploration	600−	Iron sands.
Philippines	Exploration	600−	Iron; gold; titanium.
Thailand	Dredging	150−	Tin.
EUROPE			
Iceland	Dredging	150±	Shell sands.
Great Britain	Exploration	600−	Tin.
NORTH AMERICA			
Bahamas	Dredging	150?	Aragonite.
Canada (B.C.)	Exploration	12,000±	Manganese nodules.
Caribbean Sea	Exploration	200−	(?).
Mexico	Exploration	600−	Phosphate sands.
Pacific Ocean	Exploration	12,000+	Manganese nodules.
U.S.A.:			
Alaska	Exploration	200−	Gold.
Blake Plateau	Exploration	600–2,400	Manganese; phosphate.
California	Dredging	30±	Shells.
California	Exploration (inactive)	600±	Phosphate.
Louisiana	Mining (Frasch)	60±	Sulfur.
New England	Dredging	300−	Sand.
North Carolina	Exploration	600−	Phosphate sands.
OCEANIA			
Australia	Exploration	600−	Phosphate; heavy metals.
New Zealand	Exploration	600−	Heavy metals.
Solomon Islands	Exploration	600−	Tin.
Tasmania	Exploration	600−	Heavy metals.

[1] Dredging operations generally include exploration activity. Does not include mines originating on land and drifted out under the sea floor.
[2] Less than is represented by −; more than is represented by +; approximately is represented by ±.

Source: Department of the Interior.

Figure IV-1— Worldwide Drilling Activity in Offshore Areas (as of June 1967)

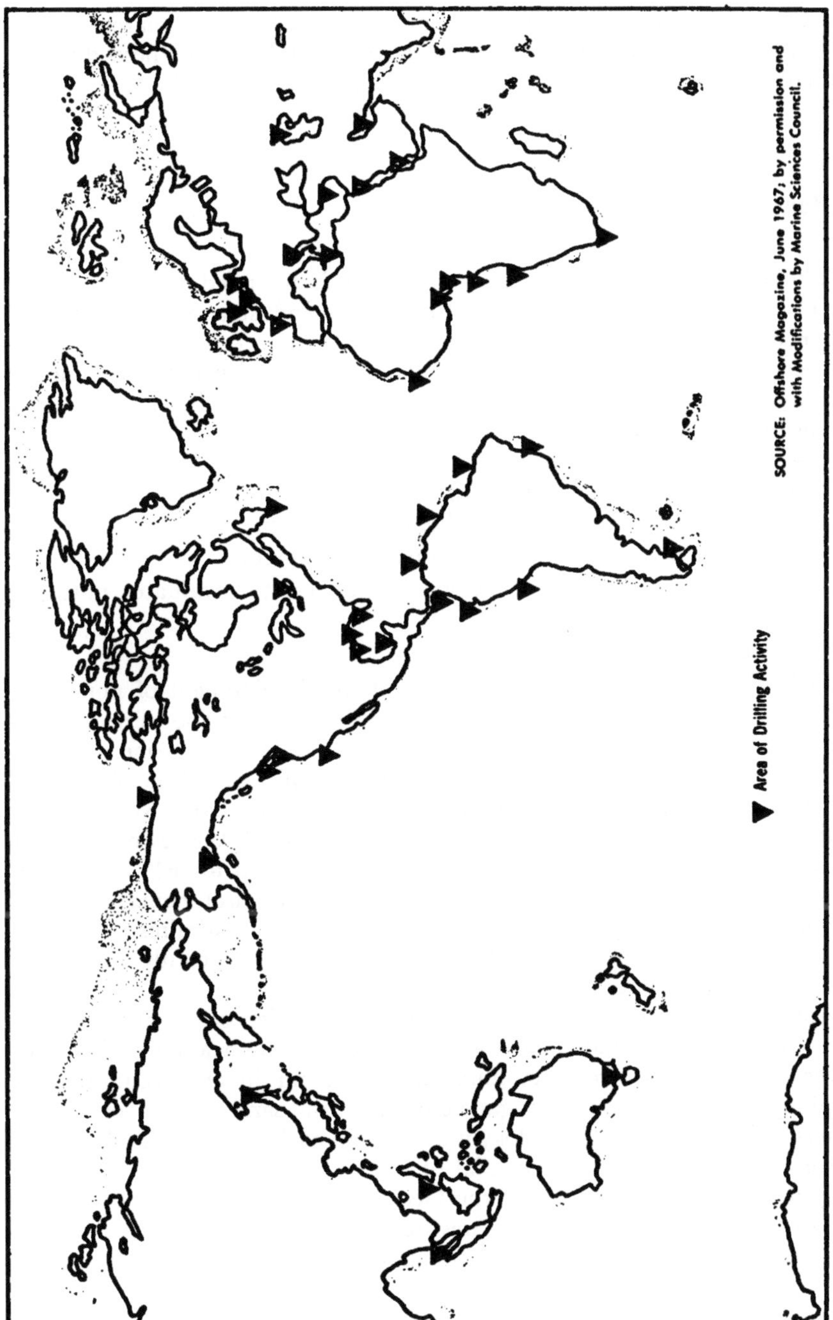

SOURCE: Offshore Magazine, June 1967; by permission and with Modifications by Marine Sciences Council.

the Federal Government support reconnaissance mapping, research and development, and other forms of assistance? What levels of these different activities will, in the next few years, be in the national interest?

Federal Marine Minerals Programs

The Federal program in marine minerals is intended to promote the development of a domestic mineral extraction industry, and to that end the Federal Government plays several distinct roles: It serves as mediator between public and private interests, and it is a source of incentives, economic assistance, and services to industry, as outlined in Chapter XIII.

Facilitating services include:

—mapping and charting;

—weather and ocean prediction;

—measures to protect safety of life and property;

—geological surveys to identify potential resources;

—mining research to develop techniques to evaluate potential resources;

—instrumentation development.

Federal programs specifically directed at the development of non-living resources from the marine environment include the marine minerals programs of the Geological Survey and the Bureau of Mines, marine water resource studies of the Geological Survey and the Office of Saline Water, and the resource management functions of the Bureau of Land Management with technical assistance from the Geological Survey.[2] As shown in Figure IV.2, these programs amount to $9.8 million requested for FY 1969, compared with $8.1 million appropriated for FY 1968. Environmental measurements and charting by Environmental Science Services Administration and Navy described in Chapter VIII also contribute significantly to marine minerals development.

Apart from oil, gas, and sulfur, marine mineral deposits of possible economic importance include placer accumulations of the heavy metals (gold, silver, and platinum), iron, titanium, chromium, and tin, and accumulations of phosphorite, glauconite, manganese nodules, and sand and gravel, among others. Marine mineral technology is at such an early stage of development, however, that the resource potential of the seabed has yet to be meaningfully defined. Current efforts of the Geological Survey and the Bureau of Mines are thus directed primarily toward identifying the minerals available from the marine environment, in economic as well as geologic terms.

[2] The Office of Saline Water programs of development and demonstration of desalting methods are not included herein.

Figure IV-2— Federal Investment in Marine Science for Development of Non-Living Resources

1. *The Geological Survey's* marine program is directed to an analysis of the seabed and underlying material on the Continental Shelf and Slope for the purposes of:

(1) appraising the undeveloped mineral, water, and energy resources potential on and beneath the seafloor;

(2) studying marine geological processes to develop new insights about the natural occurrence of resources both on land and on the ocean floor;

(3) evaluating geological and engineering hazards related to seafloor and slope stability;

(4) supplying geological data essential to the management of marine mineral resources and wise land-use planning;

(5) contributing fundamental data on the history and origin of the continental margins and the deep ocean basins.

To accomplish those objectives, the Survey has planned a scientific program for:

(a) providing maps of the Continental Shelf area at a reconnaissance scale (1:1,000,000), utilizing information from all cooperating agencies, from private institutions, and from private industry as available;

(b) providing maps of significant areas of the Continental Shelf at an intermediate scale (1:250,000), incorporating measurements made by all cooperating agencies;

(c) preparation of detailed maps (1:62,500) and analysis of selected areas of high economic potential to be explored in the future on the basis of findings from (a) and (b).

Data from many sources will be analyzed for geological implications. In addition, plans are being drawn to work in deep sea areas, initially for measurements and mapping of areas off Hawaii and island territories, after priority needs under (a) and (b) are met.

The Geological Survey currently supports research in-house, at universities, and at oceanographic institutions, through service contracts with industry, and by cooperative programs with other Federal agencies. Among recent accomplishments of these programs are:

—Reconnaissance investigations of the submerged Atlantic Continental Margin from Nova Scotia to Florida indicated oil deposits on the Continental Shelf and Slope, manganese and phosphate deposits on the Blake Plateau, and sand and gravel off New Jersey and New York.

—On the Continental Shelf of the Bering Sea, the petroleum potential was found to be greater than previously thought, with the discovery there of several large basins.

—In southern Alaska, a study was completed on the effects of submarine slides and of their locally generated waves resulting from the Alaskan earthquake in 1964.

—On the Continental Shelf of northern California and southern Oregon, acoustical, sub-bottom profiling delineated major faults and late Tertiary sediments. Systematic magnetometer surveys have located concentrations of heavy minerals (some of gold) and of nearshore ancient sedimentary rocks (a common locale of petroleum accumulations).

—In the Gulf of Mexico, the dynamics of formation and sedimentary healing rates of numerous washover scars inflicted on the Padre Island National Seashore by hurricane Beulah were determined.

—Acoustical profiling in San Francisco Bay defined the geometry of the sediments in the central part of the Bay and located several hitherto unknown faults, increasing knowledge of the earthquake hazards to urban development of the Bay area.

2. *The Bureau of Mines* conducts continuing studies of the United States position with respect to consumption, domestic production, and reserves of more than 80 mineral commodities. The Bureau of Mines also examines the economics of minerals production and acquisition from marine and alternative sources. The marine program of the Bureau is designed to assist in the development of technology for the extraction and beneficiation of marine minerals; and the development of equipment and techniques for sampling and delineation of marine mineral deposits. The Bureau is also concerned with identifying the new technology required for economic recovery of materials from the sea. The program, finally, is intended to develop the basis for sound advice on Federal policy concerning ocean mineral leasing and regulation of ocean mining operations.

The Bureau of Mines works in cooperation with private, educational, and Government organizations to improve economic marine mineral production. The cooperative program is designed to provide an opportunity for companies to develop experience in the marine minerals field, crystallize their interests, and determine probable opportunities for their own commercial ventures in the sea through:

—collecting, assembling, and analyzing oceanographic data pertinent to marine mining;

—evaluating and improving techniques for marine mineral sampling and deposit delineation, including participation in research cruises on the Pacific Coast;

—collecting, assembling, and analyzing performance and cost data on dredging and other technology applicable to marine mining.

3. The heavy metals program of the *Bureau of Mines* and the *Geological Survey,* with supporting survey operations provided by the Environmental Science Services Administration and Navy, is directed to stimulating the

domestic production of heavy metals that are in short supply, including gold, silver, platinum metals, mercury, tin, bismuth, antimony, and tantalum. The initial emphasis is on gold, a resource for which the demand is unusually acute. Apart from Government purchases, industrial demand for gold in 1966 in the United States was over three times the domestic output. Projected requirements over the next few decades, considering industrial uses only, indicate a widening gap between demand and domestic supply.

The area off the southern Seward Peninsula near Nome, Alaska, was sampled for undersea placer deposits during the summer of 1967. The test samples contained low but repeated finds of gold in every drill hole, but due to unknown costs of mining offshore in this area, the commercial significance is uncertain.

4. Development of water resources is a major activity of *the Geological Survey.* It investigates offshore fresh water sources and interaction of fresh and salt water in estuaries. Particular attention has been given to the Atlantic Continental Shelf, off Florida, where fresh water was identified in offshore drill holes. Although desalting technology has not been included within the scope of the marine science program, the oceans are an increasingly attractive source of fresh water in some coastal areas. Also, corrosion-reduction technologies developed for desalting programs have broad applications to marine engineering.

Resource Management

The Federal program for exploration, leasing, and development of oil, gas, sulfur, and other minerals of the submerged lands of the Outer Continental Shelf was first authorized by the Outer Continental Shelf Lands Act of August 7, 1953. The Act authorizes the Secretary of the Interior to approve geological and geophysical explorations in the OCS and to grant oil and gas and other mineral leases for further exploration and development of these deposits. Regulation of leasing is administered by the Bureau of Land Management, and the supervision of drilling and production is a function of the Geological Survey.

The Bureau of Land Management prepares leasing maps, recommends lease sales, holds lease sales, issues leases, and approves assignments of lease interests. The Bureau also issues rights-of-way for pipelines and other needed facilities and furnishes technical information for securing final determinations of boundaries between Federal and State jurisdictions. The Bureau's leases contain standard provisions for conservation practices and for protection of aquatic and environmental resources, and any special stipulations that may be necessary for particular situations in consideration of all resource values.

The possible need for improved licensing procedures for minerals other than oil, gas, and sulfur which will protect the heavy exploratory investments required to delineate such minerals is under consideration. This project, together with increased emphasis on evaluation of OCS resources to guide the timing and extent of offerings of tracts for lease bids, will be undertaken by an expanded analytical staff in the Bureau of Land Management.

The Geological Survey's program related to leasing policies includes consideration of: (1) the conservation of mineral resources, (2) the protection of aquatic life and other natural resources of the marine environment, (3) the safety of life and property, and (4) the protection of the public interest by adequate royalty accounting to insure against potential losses in rental and royalty revenues.

The Bureau of Land Management, Geological Survey, and Bureau of Commercial Fisheries recently entered into a Memorandum of Agreement outlining procedures to insure that mineral exploration and development under Department of Interior licenses or permits will be compatible with preservation of marine living resources.

Possible coastal pollution from off-shore industrial activity and safety of these operations are discussed in chapters V and XIII.

Future Development of the Continental Shelf

Despite severe shortages of particular mineral commodities from time to time, supply has historically kept pace with demand. Except for short-term fluctuations, the price of mineral commodities relative to the general price level has not changed. This significant achievement is the result of industrial enterprise and continued advances in the techniques of mineral exploration, production, processing, and utilization.

On land, the lead time from inception of exploration through discovery and development to the beginning of commercial production averages about 15 years. This assumes the existence of regional geological knowledge which generally is lacking offshore. To assist in evaluation of marine mineral resources, the Marine Sciences Council sponsored a contract study of the economic potential of material resources of the U.S. Continental Shelf and Slope. The report is scheduled for completion in early 1968. On the basis of existing data about markets and extraction practices, it was found that at least two decades—perhaps more, depending on the rate of exploration and the development of off-shore technology—probably will elapse before the United States can expect significant production of materials other than oil, gas, and sulfur from the Continental Shelf.

As to oil and gas, there is almost universal agreement that exploration and production offshore will continue to increase to the extent that, by the year 2000, perhaps 25 percent of the world-wide demand will be met by marine sources.

Further, it has been predicted that, over the course of the next 10 years, the oil industry will invest more than $25 billion in off-shore exploration, in 100 different countries. If to this were added the expenditures for off-shore leases and production facilities, annual outlays could well double. This compares with an annual investment now of some $1 billion, on the shelves of all continents. Another $1 billion is invested in off-shore drilling equipment at work around the world. Just 11 years ago the count of off-shore mobile rigs was only 25; last year it had reached 150. We can look forward to comparable growth in the rig fleet in the years ahead.

These projections emphasize the importance of prompt reconnaissance surveys of the Shelf—as a guide to both resource development and to policy formulation. Knowing what is there is a necessary prerequisite to other decisions, public and private, national and international. The Marine Sciences Council has to this end identified as an important next step the completion of geological, geophysical, and bathymetric mapping of the Continental Shelves of the United States at reconnaissance scale.

During FY 1969, resource appraisal activities of the Geological Survey are budgeted at $2.4 million. Bathymetric mapping and other studies of ESSA, which contribute to resource mapping, are budgeted at nearly $13.6 million, and substantial contributions will be made by the Navy. The program also will include participation by universities, research institutions, and industry as well as the Federal Government. The activity has four major aspects:

—production of bathymetric maps of selected areas on a scale of 1:250,000 as a basis for all engineering activity on the Shelf;

—completion of geological and geophysical reconnaissance of the Shelf and Slopes, analysis, and publication of technical studies;

—delineation of the seaward extension of state and national boundaries;

—reduction of time and cost of Shelf surveys through new technology, including automation.

Other marine science needs for eventual development of mineral resources from the marine environment include:

—studies on physical, chemical, and biological oceanography of the water-seafloor system of sedimentation;

—engineering studies of off-shore mining systems;

—chemical understanding of the form of ores recovered from the marine environment and chemical and mechanical engineering of beneficiation processes.

Increased emphasis is being placed by Bureau of Mines on analyses of the demand for and supply of individual minerals and the techno-economics of production from different sources. The experience and judgment of the petroleum and mining industries are being utilized through consultations with policy and technical representatives.

The discussion of non-living resources has concentrated almost exclusively on their extraction from the Continental Shelf in relatively shallow water. How about the deep sea? Any off-shore development, as an extension of land-based activities, depends critically on relative costs. Marine sources will be exploited when the costs are comparable to those on land. Thus, the richness and distribution of the resources and the costs of technology for their exploration and extraction will pace such development. Geological information about the deep ocean seabed is relatively sparse and, in general, the industrial cost for operations in deep water is high. It seems likely, therefore, that the seaward extension of marine mineral development will be a gradual movement from shallow coastal waters to deep waters. Industry might be quickly attracted to the deep sea, however, if rich deposits of a mineral in high demand such as nickel and copper are discovered in the deep sea, or if there are technological breakthroughs.

Coupled to the economic considerations is the importance of a legal framework to encourage large capital investments for which returns may be long deferred. The promise of return from the deep seabed will thus depend significantly on identification and assessment of seabed resources, ready availability of technology from all possible sources including the military, and a stable international code of law.

Many of these objectives can be achieved only by cooperative activities with other nations, as discussed earlier.

1. Marine Science Affairs - A Year of Plans and Progress. Second Report of the President to the Congress on Marine Resources and Engineering Development, March 1968, Chapter IV.

CHAPTER SEVEN

POLLUTION OF WATERS

Introductory Note

With the current practice of dumping industrial wastes, sewage and chemicals into rivers, harbors and seas, major bodies of water are being polluted at an alarming rate.

Shellfish operations have had to be suspended in places due to pollution rendering these foods unsafe for human consumption. Pollution in Lake Erie has been so extensive that supplies of oxygen and marine growth which are essential for survival of the fish population have been choked off with the result that large quantities of fish have either died or disappeared from the Lake. And so polluted have become some rivers of the United States that salmon, trout and other game fish are no longer found in these waterways.

Instances of poisonous effects caused by careless use of the sea as a dumping ground are not unknown. In 1965 the people of Noordwijk, Netherlands, were plagued by large numbers of dead fish being washed up on their shores. To determine the reason for this costly destruction of marine life the Netherlands Institute for Fisheries Investigation conducted a series of tests which revealed an abundance of copper sulphate crystals in the water. This led to the discovery that quantities of a copper compound, which was being disposed of as a waste into the North Sea, were responsible for the damage. Another since 1950 in cleaning up the atmosphere and river waters of this city are proof that major alterations can be achieved when industry, municipal authorities, capital and labor work together in a constructive endeavor.

Use of the sea as an inexpensive dumping ground for human and industrial wastes must be progressively curbed by municipal authorities, industry and shipping if the oceans and shorelands are to be preserved as healthy sites for recreation and for raising increased supplies of foodstuffs through intensive fish farming methods. One need only see or smell the murkey waste-laden waters which flow past some of the world's principal cities such as Tokyo, Osaka, London and New York to become aware of the magnitude of the pollution problem some states have on their front doorsteps. With rising world populations and the delicate ecological balance that exists between health and livelihood on the one hand and disease and starvation on the other, these situations can hardly be left to take care of themselves. Remedial measures cannot be postponed indefinitely. Notwithstanding the strides public health has made in preventive and curative medicine, these floating cesspools are a constant hazard to health. Only by removing the sources of pollution and clearing up the shores and river bottoms can the dangers be abated. Fortunately, campaigns to reduce pollution and to beautify countrysides have begun to catch public imagination with resultant support for new legislation, executive decrees and administrative enforcement measures. There is still a long way to go, however, and continual vigilance will be needed to insure lasting progress.

limited to the oceans and other bodies of water. Pollution of the atmosphere has likewise become a critical matter. One of the major sources of air pollution is lead fallout from automobile exhausts. What the ultimate effects of this will be as the number of cars multiply has not yet been established. Scientists at the California Institute of Technology have estimated that the fallout may amount to nearly five hundred thousand tons a year from United States vehicles alone. Will lead poisoning eventually confront mankind through the cyclical route of sea life absorbing minute particles, concentrating it as shellfish have mercuric and DDT compounds, and then passing it on to man via his digestive tract? The situation has become sufficiently critical to have spurred pressure from the Government to require placement of improved carburetors and exhaust manifolds on cars beginning in 1969. Whether this will be sufficient to abate the hazard remains to be seen. Eventually some form of power for propulsion other than the gasoline engine must be found if widescale pollution of the air is to be avoided.

Other harmful forms of air pollution stem from the fumes emitted by oil refineries and lead processing plants, from leakages of radio-active by-products of nuclear operations, and from the discharge of heavily laden smokes from blast furnaces and ore smelters. How to improve the industrial processes that give off these hazardous residues without occasioning prohibitive costs are among the urgent problems confronting the scientist, engineer and management in rectifying the use of air and water. The extrodinary changes wrought in Pittsburgh serious incident occurred in Minimata, Kyushu, Japan, where cases of paralytic insanity were traced by the National Institute of Health to the consumption of contaminated shellfish, which had absorbed minute quantities of mercuric chloride -- a waste discharged into a nearby bay by a chemical plant manufacturing plastic products.

Notwithstanding the ability of the oceans to dilute harmful substances, shellfish have demonstrated ability to concentrate quantities of poisonous effluents to a point where they become toxic to man. Oysters, for instance, are known to concentrate DDT at seventy thousand times the rate that exists in the surrounding waters. DDT used on Florida beaches to destroy dogflies and mosquitoes has found its way into minnows, oysters, shrimp and sea birds with devastating effects. Residues of DDT have even been detected in penguins of the Antarctic, presumably carried there by winds or by ocean currents.

Heavy oil substances pumped from the bilges of tankers and other vessels are a peril to marine fowl. Floating on the surface, these coat the feathers of ducks and other sea birds to the point where they cannot fly from the water and thus die from exhaustion or starvation. National laws and international conventions have made it unlawful for vessels to pump their bilges in the vicinity of coastal waters. And technology now enables vessels to clean their bilges without expelling harmful wastes into the sea. Nevertheless, recurrent reports of sizeable oil slicks sighted off various states lead to suspicions that bilge pumping is continuing to be practised.

Damage to the natural environment has by no means been

An unforeseen complication resulting from the construction of the super-tankers now being employed for carraige of fuel oils is the damage that can be done if marine accidents beset these carriers. This was graphically illustrated by the grounding and subsequent break-up of the Liberian tanker Torrey Canyon off the Scilly Isles in 1967 when harbors and miles of beaches in Southern England were fouled by heavy crude oil from the stricken tanker. Thousands of birds, fish, as well as other forms of animal and plant life suffered from this accident, while valuable shore properties were coated with a thick disgusting slick. Because of the extensive damages done by the thousands of tons of oil that poured from the wrecked tanker, and the complicated legal questions relating to her conduct, as well as that of those who sought to destroy the vessel once she was impaled upon the ledge, we have reconstructed in the following pages the story of her sinking. The issues that surround this case are likely to be a *cause célèbre* for a considerable time to come.

More subtle, and of possibly even greater danger, may be radiation leakage from containers of atomic wastes which have been sunk in the high seas. Sufficient knowledge of the lasting effects of radioactive material upon marine and human life is not yet available. Enough is known, however, of the genetic effects of exposure to harmful doses of radiation to cause mounting concern over this method of waste disposal.

Roger Revelle, Director of the Harvard University Center of Population Studies, has warned that the "most serious potential hazards to human beings from the introduction of radioactive products into the marine environment are those that may arise through the uptake of the radio-isotopes by organisms used for human food."

Although containers of atomic wastes have been sunk in deep water far from shore, nature and man have conspired to move them. Ocean currents, little understood by disposal parties, have cast up containers on remote beaches. And trawlers have reported hauling up drums labelled "Atomic Energy Commission - DANGER - Radioactive Materials." What actually happens to the containers as they are tossed about among ledges on the ocean floor and at the foot of the continental shelfs no one knows. Conceivably they can be weakened enough to allow radioactivity to escape and begin its perilous journey back to man. Because of the uncertainties further dumping has been stopped by the United States. Only time can tell what the consequences of past disposal, and that of other states, may prove to be.

Stirred by the hazards and damages already being caused by pollutants, states have begun to take measures to require correction of the most serious conditions. Tangled legal issues surround many of these situations, however. States, individuals, industry and property owners are still groping for footings of rights, obligations and liabilities. Law and justice have lagged in dealing with these questions. Meanwhile, debate points to a slowly emerging consensus that the welfare of the community must take priority over the freedom of the individual. Such is the attitude which lies behind many of the constraints and requirements now being applied to forestall the spread of dangerous communicable diseases.

There is need for more intensive research to improve ways of handling wastes as populations mount and as economic development and industrial growth spread throughout the world. At a time when the needs for edible food and potable water are increasing, mankind can hardly afford to jeopardize sources of these essential commodities by ill-advised methods of waste disposal.

The materials in this chapter illustrate various steps being taken by public policy to deal with some of the problems of pollution.

For further readings see Robert Cowen, Frontiers of the Sea (New York, Doubleday, 1960); Wesley Marx, The Frail Ocean (New York, Coward-McCann, 1967); Crispin Gill, Frank Booker & Tony Soper, The Wreck of the Torrey Canyon (Newton Abbot, David & Charles, 1967); "Keeping Oil Out of the Sea," Ocean Industry, November 1967, pp. 10-16; J.J. Hanks and H.D. Kube, "Industry Action to Combat Pollution," Harvard Business Review, September-October, 1966, pp. 49-62; E.E. Pyatt, "Water Pollution and Public Policy," Business and Economic Dimensions, February 1967, pp. 1-8; "Fouling of the American Environment: Symposium," Saturday Review, May 22, 1965, pp. 31-48; "Man and His Habitat: Problems of Water Pollution," Bulletin of Atomic Scientists, March 1965, pp. 18-20; ibid., April 1965, pp. 16-26; J. Walsh, "Pollution: PSAC Panel Takes a Panoramic View," Science, November 19, 1965, pp. 1006-1008; J. Walsh, "Pollution: NAS Report Examines Dual Aspect of the Problem," ibid., April 15, 1966, 328-331; Claude Zo Bell, "The Occurrence, Effects, and Fate of Oil Polluting the Sea," Proceedings, International Conference on Water Pollution

Research, 1962 (London, Pergamon Press, 1963); U.S. Department of Interior, Bureau of Commercial Fisheries, "Symposium on Red Tide," Special Scientific Report - Fisheries No. 521, Fish and Wildlife Service (Washington, Government Printing Office, 1965); Roger Revelle and Milner Schaefer, "General Considerations Concerning the Ocean as a Receptacle for Artifically Radioactive Materials," Contribution from the Scripps Institution of Oceanography, New Series, No. 901, 1957; Stanley Cain, "Desalination and Water Pollution Control", Journal of Undersea Technology, January 1967, pp. 36-40.

OIL POLLUTION ACT, 1924

United States Code
Title 33
Sections 431-437

Section 1 Short Title

This Act may be cited as the "Oil Pollution Act, 1924"

Section 2 Definitions

When used in this Act, unless the context otherwise requires--

(1) "oil" means oil of any kind or in any form, including fuel oil, sludge, and oil refuse;

(2) "person" means an individual, company, partnership, corporation, or association; any owner, operator, master, officer, or employee of a vessel; and any officer, agent or employee of the United States;

(3) "discharge" means any grossly negligent, or willful spilling, leaking, pumping, pouring, emitting, or emptying of oil;

(4) "navigable waters of the United States" means all portions of the sea within the territorial jurisdiction of the United States, and all inland waters navigable in fact; and

(5) "Secretary" means the Secretary of the Interior.

Section 3 Prohibitions

(a) Except in case of emergency imperiling life or property, or unavoidable accident, collision, or stranding, and except as otherwise permitted by regulations prescribed by the Secretary as hereinafter authorized, it is unlawful for any person to discharge or permit the discharge from any boat or vessel of oil by any method, means, or manner into or upon the navigable waters of the United States, and adjoining shorelines of the United States.

(b) Any person discharging or permitting the discharge of oil from any boat or vessel, into or upon the navigable waters of the United States shall remove the same from the navigable waters of the United States, and adjoining shorelines immediately. If such person fails to do so, the Secretary may remove the oil or may arrange for its removal, and such person shall be liable to the United States, in addition to the penalties prescribed in section 4of this Act, for all costs and expenses reasonably incurred by the Secretary in removing the oil from the navigable waters of the United States, and adjoining shorelines of the United States. These costs and expenses shall constitute a lien on such boat or vessel which may be recovered in proceedings by libel in rem.

(c) The Secretary may prescribe regulations which--

(1) permit the discharge of oil from boats or vessels in such quantities under such conditions, and at such times and places as in his opinion will not be deleterious to health or marine life or a menace to navigation, or dangerous to persons or property engaged in commerce on navigable waters of the United States; and

(2) relate to the removal or cost of removal or both, of oil from the navigable waters of the United States, and adjoining shorelines of the United States.

Section 4 Penalties

(a) Any person who violates section 3(a) of this Act shall, upon conviction thereof, be punished by a fine not exceeding $2,500, or by imprisonment not exceeding one year, or by both such fine and imprisonment for each offense.

(b) Any boat or vessel other than a boat or vessel owned and operated by the United States from which oil is discharged in violation of section 3(a) of this Act shall be liable for a penalty of not more than $10,000. Clearance of a boat or vessel liable for this penalty from a port of the United States may be withheld until the penalty is paid. The penalty shall constitute a lien on such boat or vessel which may be recovered in proceedings by libel in rem in the district court of the United States for any district within which such boat or vessel may be.

Section 5 Revocation or Suspension of License

The Commandant of the Coast Guard may, subject to the provisions of section 4450 of the Revised Statutes, as amended (46 U.S.C. 239), suspend or revoke a license issued to the master or other licensed officer of any boat or vessel found violating the provisions of section 3 of this Act.

Section 5 Enforcement

In the administration of this Act the Secretary may, with the consent of the Commandant of the Coast Guard or the Secretary of the Army, make use of the organization, equipment, and agencies, including engineering, clerical, and other personnel, employed by the Coast Guard or the Department of the Army, respectively, for the preservation and protection of navigable waters of the United States. For the better enforcement of the provisions of this Act, the officers and agents of the United States in charge of river and harbor improvements and persons employed under them by authority of the Secretary of the Army, and persons employed by the Secretary, and officers of the Customs and and Coast Guard of the United States shall have the power and authority and it shall be their duty to swear out process and to arrest and take into custody, with or without process, any person who may violate any of such provisions, except that no person shall be arrested without process for a violation not committed in the presence of some one of the aforesaid persons. Whenever any arrest is made under the Provisions of this Act the person so arrested shall be brought forthwith before a commissioner, judge, or court of the United States for examination of the offenses alleged against him, and such commissioner, judge or court shall proceed in respect thereto as authorized by law in cases of crimes against the United States.

Section 7 Other Authority Not Affected

This Act shall be in addition to other laws for the preservation and protection of navigable waters of the United States and shall not be construed as repealing, modifying, or in any manner affecting the provisions of such laws.

WRECKED TANKER TORREY CANYON SPILLS OIL ON SEA

Courtesy Wide World Photos

FEDERAL WATER POLLUTION CONTROL ACT, AS AMENDED, 1966 (EXTRACTS)

United States Code
Title 33
Section 466

DECLARATION OF POLICY

Section 1. (a) The purpose of this Act is to enhance the quality and value of our water resources and to establish a national policy for the prevention, control, and abatement of water pollution.

(b) In connection with the exercise of jurisdiction over the waterways of the Nation and in consequence of the benefits resulting to the public health and welfare by the prevention and control of water pollution, it is hereby declared to be the policy of Congress to recognize, preserve, and protect the primary responsibilities and rights of the States in preventing and controlling water pollution, to support and aid technical research relating to the prevention and control of water pollution, and to provide Federal technical services and financial aid to State and interstate agencies and to municipalities in connection with the prevention and control of water pollution. The Secretary of the Interior (hereinafter in this Act called "Secretary") shall administer this Act through the Administration created by section 2 of this Act, and with the assistance of an Assistant Secretary of the Interior designated by him, shall supervise and direct the head of such Administration in administering this Act. Such Assistant Secretary shall perform such additional functions as the Secretary may prescribe.

(c) Nothing in this Act shall be construed as impairing or in any manner affecting any right or jurisdiction of the States with respect to the waters (including boundary waters) of such States.

FEDERAL WATER POLLUTION CONTROL ADMINISTRATION

Sec. 2. Effective ninety days after the date of enactment of this section there is created within the Department of Interior a Federal Water Pollution Control Administration (hereinafter in this Act referred to as the "Administration").

COMPREHENSIVE PROGRAMS FOR WATER POLLUTION CONTROL

Sec. 3. (a) The Secretary shall, after careful investigation, and in cooperation with other Federal agencies, with State water pollution control agencies and interstate agencies, and with the municipalities and industries involved, prepare or develop comprehensive programs for eliminating or reducing the pollution of interstate waters and tributaries thereof and improving the sanitary condition of surface and underground waters. In the development of such comprehensive programs due regard shall be given to the improvements which are necessary to conserve such waters fc public water supplies, propagation of fish and aquatic life and wildlife, recreational purposes, and agricultural, industrial, and other legitimate uses. For the purpose of this section, the Secretary is authorized to make joint investigations with any such agencies of the condition of any waters in any State or States, and of the discharges of any sewage, industrial wastes, or substance which may adversely affect such waters...

(2) Each planning agency receiving a grant under this subsection shall develop a comprehensive pollution control and abatement plan for the basin which--

(A) is consistent with any applicable water quality standards established pursuant to current law within the basin;

(B) recommends such treatment works and sewer systems as will provide the most effective and economical means of collection, storage, treatment, and purification of wastes and recommends means to encourage both municipal and industrial use of such works and systems; and

(C) recommends maintenance and improvement of water quality standards within the basin or portion thereof and recommends methods of adequately financing those facilities as may be necessary to implement the plan.

(3) For the purposes of this subsection the term "basin" includes, but is not limited to, rivers and their tributaries, streams, coastal waters, sounds, estuaries, bays, lakes, and portions thereof, as well as the lands drained thereby.

INTERSTATE COOPERATION AND UNIFORM LAWS

Sec. 4. (a) The Secretary shall encourage cooperative activities by the States for the prevention and control of water pollution; encourage the enactment of improved and, so far as practicable, uniform State laws relating to the prevention and control of water pollution; and encourage compacts between States for the prevention and control of water pollution.

(b) The consent of the Congress is hereby given to two or more States to negotiate and enter into agreements or compacts, not in conflict with any law or treaty of the United States, for (1) cooperative effort and mutual assistance for the prevention and control of water pollution and the enforcement of their respective laws relating thereto, and (2) the establishment of such agencies, joint or otherwise, as they may deem desirable for making effective such agreements and compacts. No such agreement or compact shall be binding or obligatory upon any State a party thereto unless and until it has been approved by the Congress.

RESEARCH, INVESTIGATIONS, TRAINING, AND INFORMATION

Sec. 5. (a) The Secretary shall conduct in the Department of the Interior and encourage, cooperate with, and render assistance to other appropriate public (whether Federal, State, interstate, or local) authorities, agencies, and institutions, private agencies and institutions, and individuals in the conduct of, and promote the coordination of, research, investigations, experiments, demonstrations, and studies relating to the causes, control, and prevention of water pollution. In carrying out the foregoing, the Secretary is authorized to--

(1) collect and make available, through publications and other appropriate means, the results of and other information as to research, investigations, and demonstrations relating to the prevention and control of water pollution, including appropriate recommendations in connection therewith;

(2) make grants-in-aid to public or private agencies and institutions and to individuals for research or training projects and for demonstrations, and provide for the conduct of research, training, and demonstrations by contract with public or private agencies and institutions and with individuals without regard to sections 3648 and 3709 of the Revised Statutes;

(3) secure, from time to time and for such periods as he deems advisable, the assistance and advice of experts, scholars, and consultants as authorized by section 15 of the Administrative Expenses Act of 1946 (5 U.S.C. 55a);

(4) establish and maintain research fellowships in the Department of the Interior with such stipends and allowances, including traveling and subsistence expenses, as he may deem necessary to procure the assistance of the most promising research fellowships:...

(g)(1) The Secretary shall, in cooperation with the Secretary of the Army, the Secretary of Agriculture, the Water Resources Council, and with other appropriate Federal, State, interstate, or local public bodies and private organizations, institutions, and individuals, conduct and promote, and encourage contributions to, a comprehensive study of the effects of pollution, including sedimentation, in the estuaries and estuarine zones of the United States on fish and wildlife, on sport and commercial fishing, on recreation, on water supply and water power, and on other beneficial purposes. Such study shall also consider the effect of demographic trends, the exploitation of mineral resources and fossil fuels, land and industrial development, navigation, flood and erosion control, and other uses of estuaries and estuarine zones upon the pollution of the waters therein.

(2) In conducting the above study, the Secretary shall assemble, coordinate, and organize all existing pertinent information on the Nation's estuaries and estuarine zones: carry out a program of investigations and surveys to supplement existing information in representative estuaries and estuarine zones; and identify the problems and areas where further research and study are required.

(3) The Secretary shall submit to the Congress a final report of the study authorized by this subsection not later than three years after the date of enactment of this subsection... The report shall include, but not limited to--

(A) an analysis of the importance of estuaries to the economic and social well-being of the people of the United States and of the effects of pollution upon the use and enjoyment of such estuaries;

(B) a discussion of the major economic, social and ecological trends occurring in the estuarine zones of the Nation;

(C) recommendations for a comprehensive national program for the preservation, study, use, and development of estuaries of the Nation, and the respective responsibilities which should be assumed by Federal, State, and local governments and by public and private interests...

(5) For the purpose of this subsection, the term "estuarine zones" means an environmental system consisting of any estuary and those transitional areas which are consistently influenced or affected by water from an estuary such as, but not limited to, salt marshes, coastal and intertidal areas, bays, harbors, lagoons, inshore waters, and channels, and the term "estuary" means all or part of the mouth of a navigable or interstate river or stream or other body of water having unimpaired natural connection with open sea and within which the sea water is measurably diluted with fresh water derived from land drainage...

GRANTS FOR RESEARCH AND DEVELOPMENT

Sec. 6. (a) The Secretary is authorized to make grants to any State, municipality, or intermunicipal or interstate agency for the purpose of--

(1) assisting in the development of any project which will demonstrate a new or improved method of controlling the discharge into any waters of untreated or inadequately treated sewage or other wastes from sewers which carry storm water or both storm water and sewage or other wastes, or

(2) assisting in the development of any project which will demonstrate advanced waste treatment and water purification methods (including the temporary use of new or improved chemical additives which provide substantial immediate improvement to existing treatment processes) or new or improved methods of joint treatment systems for municipal and industrial wastes, and for the purpose of reports, plans, and specifications in connection therewith...

ENFORCEMENT MEASURES AGAINST POLLUTION OF INTERSTATE OR NAVIGABLE WATERS

Sec. 10. (a) The pollution of interstate or navigable waters in or adjacent to any State or States (whether the matter causing or contributing to such pollution is discharged directly into such waters or reaches such waters after discharge into a tributary of such waters), which endangers the health or welfare of any persons, shall be subject to abatement as provided in this Act.

(b) Consistent with the policy declaration of this Act, State and interstate action to abate pollution of interstate or navigable waters shall be encouraged and shall not, except as otherwise provided by or pursuant to court order under subsection (h), be displaced by Federal enforcement action.

(c)(1) If the Governor of a State or a State water pollution control agency files, within one year after the date of enactment of this subsection, a letter of intent that such State, after public hearings, will before June 30, 1967, adopt (A) water quality criteria applicable to interstate waters or portions thereof within such State, and (B) a plan for the implementation and enforcement of the water quality criteria adopted, and if such criteria and plan are established in accordance with the letter of intent, and if the Secretary determines that such State criteria and plan are consistent with paragraph (3) of this subsection, such State criteria and plan shall thereafter be the water quality standards applicable to such interstate waters or portions thereof.

(2) If a State does not (A) file a letter of intent or (B) establish water quality standards in accordance with paragraph (1) of this subsection, or if the Secretary or the Governor of any State affected by water quality standards established pursuant to this subsection desires a revision in such standards, the Secretary may, after reasonable notice and a conference of representatives of appropriate Federal departments and agencies, interstate agencies, States, municipalities and industries involved, prepare regulations setting forth standards of water quality to be applicable to interstate waters or portions thereof. If, within six months from the date the Secretary publishes such regulations, the State has not adopted water quality standards found by the Secretary to be consistent with paragraph (3) of this subsection, or a petition for public hearing has not been filed under paragraph (4) of this subsection, the Secretary shall promulgate such standards.

(3) Standards of quality established pursuant to this subsection shall be such as to protect the public health or welfare, enhance the quality of water and serve the purposes of this Act. In establishing such standards the Secretary, the Hearing Board, or the appropriate State authority shall take into consideration their use and value for public water supplies, propagation of fish and wildlife, recreational purposes, and agricultural, industrial, and other legitimate uses.

(4) If at any time prior to 30 days after standards have been promulgated under paragraph (2) of this subsection, the Governor of any State affected by such standards petitions the Secretary for a hearing, the Secretary shall call a public hearing, to be held in or near one or more of the places where the water quality standards will take effect, before a Hearing Board of five or more persons appointed by the Secretary. Each State which would be affected by such standards shall be given an opportunity to select one member of the Hearing Board. The Department of Commerce and other affected Federal departments and agencies shall each be given an opportunity to select a member of the Hearing Board and not less than a majority of the Hearing Board shall be persons other than officers or employees of the Department of the Interior... If the Hearing Board approves the standards as published or promulgated by the Secretary, the standards shall take effect on receipt by the Secretary of the Hearing Board's recommendations. If the Hearing Board recommends modifications in the standards as published or promulgated by the Secretary, the Secretary shall promulgate revised regulations setting forth standards of water quality in accordance with the Hearing Board's recommendations which will become effective immediately upon promulgation.

(5) The discharge of matter into such interstate waters or portions thereof, which reduces the quality of such waters below

the water quality standards established under this subsection (whether the matter causing or contributing to such reduction is discharged directly into such waters or reaches such waters after discharge into tributaries of such waters), is subject to abatement in accordance with the provisions of paragraph (1) or (2) of subsection (g) of this section, except that at least 180 days before any abatement action is initiated under either paragraph (1) or (2) of subsection (g) as authorized by this subsection, the Secretary shall notify the violators and other interested parties of the violation of such standards. In any suit brought under the provisions of this subsection the court shall receive in evidence a transcript of the proceedings of the conference and hearing provided for in this subsection, together with the recommendations of the conference and Hearing Board and the recommendations and standards promulgated by the Secretary, and such additional evidence, including that relating to the alleged violation of the standards, as it deems necessary to a complete review of the standards and to a determination of all other issues relating to the alleged violation. The court, giving due consideration to the practicability and to the physical and economic feasibility of complying with such standards, shall have jurisdiction to enter such judgment and orders enforcing such judgment as the public interest and the equities of the case may require...

(2) Whenever the Secretary, upon receipt of reports, surveys, or studies from any duly constituted international agency, has reason to believe that any pollution referred to in subsection (a) of this section which endangers the health or welfare of persons in a foreign country is occurring, and the Secretary of State requests him to abate such pollution, he shall give formal notification thereof to the State water pollution control agency of the State in which such discharge or discharges originate and to the interstate water pollution control agency, if any, and shall call promptly a conference of such agency or agencies, if he believes that such pollution is occurring in sufficient quantity to warrant such action. The Secretary, through the Secretary of State, shall invite the foreign country which may be adversely affected by the pollution to attend and participate in the conference, and the representative of such country shall, for the purpose of the conference and any further proceeding resulting from such conference, have all the rights of a State water pollution control agency. This paragraph shall apply only to foreign country which the Secretary determines has given the United States essentially the same rights with respect to the prevention and control of water pollution occurring in that country as is given that country by this paragraph. Nothing in this paragraph shall be construed to modify, amend, repeal, or otherwise affect the provisions of the 1909 Boundary Waters Treaty between Canada and the United States or the Water Utilization Treaty of 1944 between Mexico and the United States (59 Stat. 1219), relative to the control and abatement of water pollution in waters covered by those treaties...

DEFINITIONS

Sec. 13. When used in this Act--

(a) The term "State water pollution control agency" means the

State health authority, except that, in the case of any State in which there is a single State agency, other than the State health authority, charged with responsibility for enforcing State laws relating to the abatement of water pollution, it means such other State agency.

(b) The term "interstate agency" means an agency of two or more States established by or pursuant to an agreement or compact approved by the Congress, or any other agency of two or more States, having substantial powers or duties pertaining to the control of pollution of waters.

(c) The term "treatment works" means the various devices used in the treatment of sewage or industrial wastes of a liquid nature, including the necessary intercepting of sewers, outfall sewers, pumping, power, and other equipment, and their appurtenances, and includes any extensions, improvements, remodeling, additions, and alterations thereof.

(d) The term "State" means a State, the District of Columbia, the Commonwealth of Puerto Rico, the Virgin Islands, and Guam.

(e) The term "interstate waters" means all rivers, lakes, and other waters that flow across or form a part of State boundaries, including coastal waters.

(f) The term "municipality" means a city, town, borough, county, parish, district, or other public body created by or pursuant to State law and having jurisdiction over disposal of sewage, industrial wastes, or other wastes, and an Indian tribe or an authorized Indian tribal organization...

INTERNATIONAL CONVENTION FOR THE PREVENTION OF POLLUTION OF THE SEA BY OIL, 1954, AS AMENDED

Signed at London, May 12, 1954
Amended at Conference of Contracting Governments
London, April 4-11, 1962

In Force

The Governments represented at the International Conference on Pollution of the Sea by Oil held in London from 26th April, 1954 to 12th May, 1954,

Desiring to take action by common agreement to prevent pollution of the sea by oil discharged from ships, ... have agreed as follows: ...

Article I

(1) For the purposes of the present Convention, the following expressions shall (unless the context otherwise requires) have the meanings hereby respectively assigned to them, that is to say: ...

'Discharge' in relation to oil or to oily mixture means any discharge or escape howsoever caused; ...

'Oil' means crude oil, fuel oil, heavy diesel oil and lubricating oil, and 'oily' shall be construed accordingly;

'Oily mixture' means a mixture with an oil content of 100 parts or more in 1,000,000 parts of the mixture; ...

2. The existing text of Article II of the Convention is replaced by the following:

Article II

(1) The present Convention shall apply to ships registered in any of the territories of a Contracting Government and to unregistered ships having the nationality of a Contracting Party, except:

(a) tankers of under 150 tons gross tonnage and other ships of under 500 tons gross tonnage, provided that each Contracting Government will take the necessary steps, so far as is reasonable and practicable, to apply the requirements of the Convention to such ships also, having regard to their size, service and the type of fuel used for their propulsion;

(b) ships for the time being engaged in the whaling industry when actually employed on whaling operations;

(c) ships for the time being navigating the Great Lakes of North America and their connecting and tributary waters as far east as the lower exit of St. Lambert Lock at Montreal in the Province of Quebec, Canada;

(d) naval ships and ships for the time being used as naval auxiliaries;

(2) Each Contracting Government undertakes to adopt appropriate measures ensuring that requirements equivalent to those of the present Convention are, so far as is reasonable and practicable, applied to the ships referred to in sub-paragraph (d) of paragraph (1) of this Article.

3. The existing text of Article III of the Convention is replaced by the following:

Article III

Subject to the provisions of Articles IV and V:

(a) the discharge from a tanker to which the present Convention applies, within any of the prohibited zones referred to in Annex A to the Convention, of oil or oily mixture shall be prohibited;

(b) the discharge from a ship to which the present Convention applies, other than a tanker, of oil or oily mixture shall be made as far as practicable from land. As from a date three years after that on which the Convention comes into force for the relevant territory in respect of the ship in accordance with paragraph (1) of Article II, sub-paragraph (a) of this Article shall apply to a ship other than a tanker, except that the discharge of oil or of oily mixture from such a ship shall not be prohibited when the ship is proceeding to a port not provided with such facilities for ships other than tankers as are referred to in Article VIII;

(c) the discharge from a ship of 20,000 tons gross tonnage or more, to which the present Convention applies and for which the building contract is placed on or after the date on which this provision comes into force, of oil or oily mixture shall be prohibited. However, if in the opinion of the master, special circumstances make it neither reasonable nor practicable to retain the oil or oily mixture on board, it may be discharged outside the prohibited zones referred to in Annex A to the Convention. The reasons for such discharge shall be reported to the Contracting Government of the relevant territory in respect of the ship in accordance with paragraph (1) of Article II. Full details of such discharges shall be reported to the Organization at least every twelve months by Contracting Governments.

4. The existing text of Article IV of the Convention is replaced by the following:

Article IV

Article III shall not apply to:

(a) the discharge of oil or of oily mixture from a ship for the purpose of securing the safety of a ship, preventing damage to a ship or cargo, or saving life at sea;

(b) the escape of oil or of oily mixture resulting from damage to a ship or unavoidable leakage, if all reasonable precautions have been taken after the occurrence of the damage or discovery of the leakage for the purpose of preventing or minimizing the escape;

(c) the discharge of residue arising from the purification or clarification of fuel oil or lubricating oil, provided that such discharge is made as far from land as is practicable.

5. The existing text of Article V of the Convention is replaced by the following:

Article V

Article III shall not apply to the discharge from the bilges of a ship:

(a) during the period of twelve months following the date on which the present Convention comes into force for the relevant territory in respect of the ship in accordance with paragraph (1) of Article II, of oily mixture;

(b) after the expiration of such period, of oily mixture containing no oil other than lubricating oil which has drained or leaked from machinery spaces.

6. The existing text of Article VI of the Convention is replaced by the following:

Article VI

(1) Any contravention of Articles III and IX shall be an offence punishable under the law of the relevant territory in respect of the ship in accordance with paragraph (1) of Article II.

(2) The penalties which may be imposed under the law of any of the territories of a Contracting Government in respect of the unlawful discharge from a ship of oil or oily mixture outside

the territorial sea of that territory shall be adequate in severity to discourage any such unlawful discharge and shall not be less than the penalties which may be imposed under the law of that territory in respect of the same infringements within the territorial sea.

(3) Each Contracting Government shall report to the Organization the penalties actually imposed for each infringement.

7. The existing text of Article VII of the Convention is replaced by the following:

Article VII

(1) As from a date twelve months after the present Convention comes into force for the relevant territory in respect of a ship in accordance with paragraph (1) of Article II, such a ship shall be required to be so fitted as to prevent, so far as reasonable and practicable, the escape of fuel oil or heavy diesel oil into bilges, unless effective means are provided to ensure that the oil in the bilges is not discharged in contravention of this Convention.

(2) Carrying water ballast in oil fuel tanks shall be avoided if possible.

8. The existing text of Article VIII of the Convention is replaced by the following:

Article VIII

(1) Each Contracting Government shall take all appropriate steps to promote the provision of facilities as follows:

(a) according to the needs of ships using them, ports shall be provided with facilities adequate for the reception, without causing undue delay to ships, of such residues and oily mixtures as would remain for disposal from ships other than tankers if the bulk of the water had been separated from the mixture;

(b) oil loading terminals shall be provided with facilities adequate for the reception of such residues and oily mixtures as would similarly remain for disposal by tankers;

(c) ship repair ports shall be provided with facilities adequate for the reception of such residues and oily mixtures as would similarly remain for disposal by all ships entering for repairs.

(2) Each Contracting Government shall determine which are the ports and oil loading terminals in its territories suitable for the purposes of sub-paragraphs (a), (b) and (c) of paragraph (1) of this Article.

(3) As regards paragraph (1) of this Article, each Contracting

Government shall report to the Organization, for transmission to the Contracting Government concerned, all cases where the facilities are alleged to be inadequate.

9. The existing text of Article IX of the Convention is replaced by the following:

Article IX

(1) Of the ships to which the present Convention applies, every ship which uses oil fuel and every tanker shall be provided with an oil record book, whether as part of the ship's official log book or otherwise, in the form specified in Annex B to the Convention.

(2) The oil record book shall be completed on each occasion, whenever any of the following operations takes place in the ship:

(a) ballasting of and discharge of ballast from cargo tanks of tankers;

(b) cleaning of cargo tanks of tankers;

(c) settling in slop tanks and discharge of water from tankers;

(d) disposal from tankers of oily residues from slop tanks or other sources;

(e) ballasting, or cleaning during voyage, of bunker fuel tanks of ships other than tankers;

(f) disposal from ships other than tankers of oily residues from bunker fuel tanks or other sources;

(g) accidental or other exceptional discharges or escapes of oil from tankers or ships other than tankers.

In the event of such discharge or escape of oil or oily mixture as is referred to in sub-paragraph (c) of Article III or in Article IV, a statement shall be made in the oil record book of the circumstances of, and reason for, the discharge or escape.

(3) Each operation described in paragraph (2) of this Article shall be fully recorded without delay in the oil record book so that all the entries in the book appropriate to that operation are completed. Each page of the book shall be signed by the officer or officers in charge of the operations concerned and, when the ship is manned, by the master of the ship. The written entries in the oil record book shall be in an official language of the relevant territory in respect of the ship in accordance with paragraph (1) of Article II, or in English or French.

(4) Oil record books shall be kept in such a place as to be readily available for inspection at all reasonable times, and,

except in the case of unmanned ships under tow, shall be kept on board the ship. They shall be preserved for a period of two years after the last entry has been made.

(5) The competent authorities of any of the territories of a Contracting Government may inspect on board any ship to which the present Convention applies, while within a port in that territory, the oil record book required to be carried in the ship in compliance with the provisions of this Article, and may make a true copy of any entry in that book and may require the master of the ship to certify that the copy is a true copy of such entry. Any copy so made which purports to have been certified by the master of the ship as a true copy of an entry in the ship's oil record book shall be made admissible in any judicial proceedings as evidence of the facts stated in the entry. Any action by the competent authorities under this paragraph shall be taken as expeditiously as possible and the ship shall not be delayed.

10. The existing text of Article X of the Convention is replaced by the following:

Article X

(1) Any Contracting Government may furnish to the Government of the relevant territory in respect of the ship in accordance with paragraph (1) of Article II particulars in writing of evidence that any provision of the present Convention has been contravened in respect of that ship, wheresoever the alleged contravention may have taken place. If it is practicable to do so, the competent authorities of the former Government shall notify the master of the ship of the alleged contravention.

(2) Upon receiving such particulars, the Government so informed shall investigate the matter, and may request the other Government to furnish further or better particulars of the alleged contravention. If the Government so informed is satisfied that sufficient evidence is available in the form required by its law to enable proceedings against the owner or master of the ship to be taken in respect of the alleged contravention, it shall cause such proceedings to be taken as soon as possible, and shall inform the other Government and the Organization of the result of such proceedings.

Article XI

Nothing in the present Convention shall be construed as derogating from the powers of any Contracting Government to take measures within its jurisdiction in respect of any matter to which the Convention relates or as extending the jurisdiction of any Contracting Government.

Article XII

Each Contracting Government shall send to the Bureau and to

the appropriate organ of the United Nations: -

(a) the text of laws, decrees, orders and regulations in force in its territories which give effect to the present Convention;

(b) all official reports or summaries of official reports in so far as they show the results of the application of the provisions of the Convention...

Article XIII

Any dispute between Contracting Governments relating to the interposition or application of the present Convention which cannot be settled by negotiation shall be referred at the request of either party to the International Court of Justice for decision unless the parties in dispute agree to submit it to arbitration.

11. The existing text of Article XIV of the Convention is replaced by the following:

Article XIV

(1) The present Convention shall remain open for signature for three months from this day's date and shall thereafter remain open for signature.

(2) Subject to Article XV, the Governments of States Members of the United Nations or of any of the Specialized Agencies or parties to the Statute of the International Court of Justice may become parties to the present Convention by:

(a) signature without reservation as to acceptance;

(b) signature subject to acceptance followed by acceptance, or

(c) acceptance.

(3) Acceptance shall be effected by the deposit of an instrument of acceptance with the Bureau, which shall inform all Governments that have already signed or accepted the present Convention of each signature and deposit of an acceptance and of the date of such signature or deposit.

Article XV

(1) The present Convention shall come into force twelve months after the date on which not less than ten Governments have become parties to the Convention, including five Governments of countries each with not less than 500,000 gross tons of tanker tonnage... (in force)

12. The existing text of Article XVI of the Convention is replaced by the following:

Article XVI

(1) (a) The present Convention may be amended by unanimous agreement between the Contracting Governments.

(b) Upon request of any Contracting Government a proposed amendment shall be communicated by the Organization to all Contracting Governments for consideration and acceptance under this paragraph.

(2) (a) An amendment to the present Convention may be proposed to the Organization at any time by any Contracting Government, and such proposal if adopted by a two-thirds majority of the Assembly of the Organization upon recommendation adopted by a two-thirds majority of the Maritime Safety Committee of the Organization shall be communicated by the Organization to all Contracting Governments for their acceptance.

(b) Any such recommendation by the Maritime Safety Committee shall be communicated by the Organization to all Contracting Governments for their consideration at least six months before it is considered by the Assembly.

(3) (a) A conference of Governments to consider amendments to the present Convention proposed by any Contracting Government shall at any time be convened by the Organization upon the request of one-third of the Contracting Governments.

(b) Every amendment adopted by such conference by a two-thirds majority of the Contracting Governments shall be communicated by the Organization to all Contracting Governments for their acceptance.

(4) Any amendment communicated to Contracting Governments for their acceptance under paragraph (2) or (3) of this Article shall come into force for all Contracting Governments, except those which before it comes into force make a declaration that they do not accept the amendment, twelve months after the date on which the amendment is accepted by two-thirds of the Contracting Governments.

(5) The Assembly, by a two-thirds majority vote, including two-thirds of the Governments represented on the Maritime Safety Committee, and subject to the concurrence of two-thirds of the Contracting Governments to the present Convention, or a conference convened under paragraph (3) of this Article by a two-thirds majority vote, may determine at the time of its adoption that the amendment is of such an important nature that any Contracting Government which makes a declaration under paragraph (4) of this Article and which does not accept the amendment within a period of twelve months after the amendment comes into force, shall, upon the expiry of this period, cease to be a party to the present Convention.

(6) The Organization shall inform all Contracting Governments of any amendments which come into force under this Article, together with the date on which such amendments shall come into force.

(7) Any acceptance or declaration under this Article shall be made by a notification in writing to the Organization which shall notify all Contracting Governments of the receipt of the acceptance or declaration.

Article XVII

(1) The present Convention may be denounced by any Contracting Government at any time after the expiration of a period of five years from the date on which the Convention comes into force for that Government.

(2) Denunciation shall be effected by a notification in writing addressed to the Bureau, which shall notify all the Contracting Governments of any denunciation received and of the date of its receipt.

(3) A denunciation shall take effect twelve months, or such longer period as may be specified in the notification, after its receipt by the Bureau.

13. The existing text of Article XVIII of the Convention is replaced by the following:

Article XVIII

(1)(a) The United Nations in cases where they are the administering authority for a territory or any Contracting Government responsible for the international relations of a territory shall as soon as possible consult with such territory in an endeavour to extend the present Convention to that territory and may at any time by notification in writing given to the Bureau declare that the Convention shall extend to such territory.

(b) The present Convention shall from the date of the receipt of the notification or from such other date as may be specified in the notification extend to the territory named therein.

(2)(a) The United Nations in cases where they are the administering authority for a territory or any Contracting Government which has made a declaration under paragraph (1) of this Article, at any time after the expiry of a period of five years from the date on which the present Convention has been so extended to any territory, may by a notification in writing given to the Bureau after consultation with such territory declare that the Convention shall cease to extend to any such territory named in the notification.

(b) The Present Convention shall cease to extend to any territory mentioned in such notification one year, or such longer period as may be specified therein, after the date of receipt of the notification by the Bureau.

(3) The Bureau shall inform all the Contracting Governments of the extension of the present Convention to any territory under

paragraph (1) of this Article, and of the termination of any such extension under the provisions of paragraph (2) stating in each case the date from which the Convention has been or will cease to be so extended.

1. Department of State, Treaties and Other International Acts Series, Nos. 4900 & 6109.

CONTAINER PORT, ELIZABETH, NEW JERSEY

Courtesy New York Port Authority

CHAPTER EIGHT

SAFETY OF LIFE AT SEA

Introductory Note

Public concern for the improvement of safety precautions at sea is gradually modifying merchant marine policy.

Unfortunately, tragedy has often been a prelude to advancing safety measures. For countless generations man has been aware of the hazards posed by large icebergs floating in the track of trans-Atlantic shipping. Yet it was not until after the sinking of the Titanic, with its great loss of life and property values, that nations were moved to establish an Iceberg Patrol in the North Atlantic. Similarly, the shock of the loss of hundreds of lives in the burning of the liner Morro Castle off Atlantic City prompted the passage of legislation requiring shipbuilders to eliminate wood and other combustible materials from the construction of American-flagged passenger vessels. Notwithstanding modernized construction, disasters can yet strike. This was evidenced by the burning of the S.S. Yarmouth Castle in the Bahamas in 1966. Likewise, the sinking of the Italian luxury liner Andrea Doria following the fog-bound collision with the S.S. Stockholm off Nantucket lightship a decade earlier, shows how fallible still navigators can be despite the presence of guidance and warning equipment.

It is to the credit of the United States Congress that after 1936 it required shipyards to eliminate wood paneling and other combustible material from the construction of passenger vessels registered in this country. Under pressure from this same source the United States Government took leadership during the postwar period to conclude with the principal maritime nations the International Convention for Safety of Life at Sea, which laid down minimum standards for reducing the dangers of fire, collision and loss of life at sea. As a result of these efforts modern vessels have been made more fireproof. Lifeboats are now more durable and may be more readily launched. Inspections and drills are enforced to prepare passengers and crews for emergencies. And periodic replacement of life jackets further insures the possibility of persons remaining afloat for rescue if a ship itself goes down.

Other conventions, notably the Geneva Convention on the High Seas, require that masters of vessels on the high seas proceed with all possible speed to the rescue of those in distress, and render such assistance as they are able in the event of collisions or other marine disasters.

Besides dealing with the problem of safety on the seas, maritime policy is also turning attention to meeting the competition of air travel and air cargo. Time honored methods of shipping ocean freight have become too slow and expensive for rapidly-paced modern business. Adoption of containerized packing, roll-on and roll-off freight conveyance methods, and construction of much faster shipping have helped to stay the drift toward international air freight carraige. This has meant redesigning cargo handling equipment, providing easier access to holds and offering more levels for stowing different types of containers including entire van loads. Likewise, expeditious handling of such freight requires new and separate port facilities. This in turn has raised issues regarding longshore labor and with this fresh disputes between management, labor and port authorities. A revolution, nevertheless, is underway.

A third area of public concern relating to merchant marine policy focuses on subsidies for underwriting parts of the costs of building and operating seagoing merchant vessels. Nearly every country, through one device or another, now provides some form of subsidy to insure that its flag remains upon the high seas. Different motives lie behind these policies, but all are occasioned by the fact that labor, fuel and other operating expenses more than offset profits. Some subsidy policies are frankly mercantilistic in their objectives; to gain income from ocean freight business. Some are chiefly nationalistic in their aims; to make certain there are ample vessels to carry the nation's exports and imports. In other instances countries resort to subsidization to insure the maintenance of an auxiliary fleet for the transport of men, food, vehicles, munitions and war equipment in times of national emergency.

A combination of motives underlies the various measures which have been passed by the United States Congress to keep an up-to-date merchant fleet operating upon the high seas. The need for such an arm has been vividly dramatized in two World Wars when the nation found its supply of suitable vessels dangerously low. The involvement of national interests in such areas as Southeast Asia and the Near East has further demonstrated the need for maintaining a large tonnage for use on short notice.

Although air transport is now able to deliver impressive quantities of freight to remote places rapidly, the bulk of international cargo is still moved by the less expensive means of ocean transportation. However, the rate at which vessels are capable of traveling must be greatly increased to offset mounting threats from submarine and air attacks in times of war. A challenge lies before the naval architect and ocean engineer to design and build faster and more versatile sea transport. Perhaps consideration of the principles underlying air and hovercraft may lead to the creation of a new oceanic vessel that can compete with other modes of transportation.

Nations destined to play a major role in world affairs must maintain a merchant marine adequate to the magnitude of their interests overseas and geared to the requirement and technology of the times.

For additional readings see John J. Clark and N.T. Norton, "Merchant Marine: Subsidies and Competition," U.S. Naval Institute Proceedings, January 1967, pp. 71-80; L.W. Garden, "IMCO: An Assistance to the American Merchant Marine," ibid., December 1966, pp. 71-83; S. Nakeyama, "Japan's Phenomenal Shipbuilders," ibid., August 1966, pp. 28-39; E.A. McDonald, "Our Icebreakers Are Not Good Enough," ibid., February 1966, pp. 60-69.

PROVISIONS OF UNITED STATES LAW AFFECTING SAFETY OF VESSELS

United States Code, Title 46

Chapters 1-2 Registration

Sec. 1. [The Commandant of the Coast Guard shall have general superintendence of the commercial marine and merchant seamen of the United States. The Commissioner of Customs shall have the power of decisions relating to registrations, enrollments and licenses of vessels.]

Sec. 11.All vessels built within the United States or belonging wholly to citizens thereof shall be registered in the United States.

[The registry certificate to specify the size, characteristics, measurements, tonnage, etc. of the vessel].

Chapter 2 A. Load Lines

Sec. 85. Load lines are established for the following vessels:

(a) Merchant vessels of one hundred and fifty gross tons or over, loading at or proceeding to sea from any port or place within the United States or its possessions for a foreign voyage by sea, or arriving within the jurisdiction of the United States or its possessions from a foreign voyage by sea....

Sec. 85 a. The Commandant of the Coast Guard is authorized and directed ... to establish by regulations from time to time the load water lines and marks thereof indicating the maximum depth to which such vessels may safely load....

[Subsequent sections direct the Commandant of the Coast Guard to take the provisions of the International Load Line Convention of May 1, 1931 into account, and provide penalties for vessels exceeding the load line marks].

Chapter 14. Inspection of Steam Vessels

Sec. 362. All steam vessels navigating any waters of the United States which are common highways of commerce or open to general or competitive navigation, excepting public vessels of the United States,... shall be subject to the provisions of Title 52 of the Revised Statutes....

Sec.369 (b). No passenger vessel of the United States of one hundred gross tons and over, propelled by machinery, the construction or material alterations of which shall be begun subsequent to May 27,1936, shall be granted a certificate of inspection by the Coast Guard unless the said general construction plans and specifications therefor shall have been submitted at least in triplicate to and approvdd by the aforesaid Commandant of the Coast Guard before the construction of such vessel or alteration thereof shall have been commenced; nor shall any such vessel, the said plans or specifications for which have been materially altered subsequent to such approval be granted a certificate, as aforesaid, unless such altered plans and specifications shall have been submitted in triplicate to and approved by the said Commandant, prior to such change in construction having been made. No such certificate shall be granted to any such vessel which has not been constructed in accordance with said plans and specifications approved as aforesaid....

(d) The words "plans and specifications" wherever used in this section shall be held to include prints of all general contract plans and copies of the specifications and other matters of a similar nature, as necessary to the purposes of this section for any vessel to which this section applies. The said plans and specifications of all passenger ships of one hundred gross tons and over shall specify for fire-retardant material in the construction so far as reasonable and practicable.

Chapter 15. Transportation of Passengers

Sec. 451. The Coast Guard officials shall state in every certificate of inspection granted to vessels carrying passengers, other than ferryboats, the number of passengers of each class that any such vessel has accomodations for and can carry with prudence and safety....

[Subsequent sections provide penalties for vessels carrying more passengers than are authorized.]

Chapter 16. **Regulation of Vessels Subject to Coast Guard**

Sec. 481. In order to provide against hazard to life and property, the Secretary of the Department in which the Coast Guard is operating shall prescribe such rules and regulations as may be necessary for vessels subject to inspection and certification by the United States Coast Guard with respect to the following matters:

(1) [Life-saving equipment ...]

(2) Fire fighting equipment and precautionary measures guarding against fire, including, but not limited to, the number, type, size, capacity, details of construction, methods of operation, storage, maintenance, manning, use, testing, and inspection of such equipment, and drills and exercises necessary to assure proper functioning and use of such equipment.

(3) [Muster lists ...] ...

Chapter 27. Merchant Marine Act of June 29, 1936

Sec. 1101. Declaration of Policy.

It is necessary for the national defense and development of its foreign and domestic commerce that the United States shall have a merchant marine (a) sufficient to carry its domestic water-borne commerce and a substantial portion of the water-borne export and import foreign commerce of the United States and to provide shipping service on all routes essential for maintaining the flow of such domestic and foreign water-borne commerce at all times, (b) capable of serving as a naval and military auxiliary in time of war or national emergency, (c) owned and operated under the United States flag by citizens of the United States in so far as may be practicable, and (d) composed of the best-equipped, safest, and most suitable types of vessels, constructed in the United States and manned with a trained and efficient citizen personnel. It is declared to be the policy of the United States to foster the development and encourage the maintenance of such a merchant marine.

Sec. 1120. Survey for Creation of Adequate American-Owned Fleet.

It shall be the duty of the Secretary of Commerce to make a survey of the American merchant marine ... to determine what additions and replacements are required to carry forward the national policy declared in section 1101 of this title, and the Secretary is directed to study, perfect, and adopt a long-range program for replacements and additions ... so that as soon as practicable the following objectives may be accomplished:

First, the creation of an adequate and well-balanced merchant fleet, including vessels of all types, to provide shipping service on all routes essential for maintaining the flow of the foreign commerce of the United States, the vessels in such fleet to be so designed as to be readily and quickly convertible into transport and supply vessels in time of national emergency. In planning the development of such a fleet the Secretary is directed to cooperate closely with the Navy Department as to national defense needs and the possible speedy adaptation of the merchant fleet to national defense requirements.

Second, the ownership and the operation of such a merchant fleet by citizens of the United States in so far as may be practicable.

Third, the planning of vessels designed to afford the best and most complete protection for passengers and crew against fire and all marine perils.

Sec. 1151. Construction-Differential Subsidy

Any citizen of the United States may make application to the Federal Maritime Board for a construction-differential subsidy to aid in the construction of a new vessel to be used in the foreign commerce of the United States. No such application shall be approved by the Board unless it determines that (1) the plans and specifications call for a new vessel which will meet the requirements of the foreign commerce of the United States, will aid in the promotion and development of such commerce, and be suitable for use by the United States for national defense or military purposes in time of war or national emergency;...

Sec. 1180. Vessels Eligible for Operating-Differential Subsidy

An operating-differential subsidy shall not be paid under the authority of this subchapter on account of the operation of any vessel which does not meet the following requirements: (1) the vessel shall be of steel or other acceptable metal, shall be propelled by steam or motor, shall be as nearly fireproof as practicable, shall be built in a domestic yard or shall have been documented under the laws of the United States....

SEEKING NEW TRADE ROUTES - S.S. MANHATTAN IN ARCTIC

Courtesy Standard Oil Company (N.J.)

INTERNATIONAL CONVENTION FOR THE SAFETY OF LIFE AT SEA

Signed at London, June 10, 1948 [1]

The Governments of the Argentine Republic, the Commonwealth of Australia, Belgium, the Republic of the United States of Brazil, Canada, the Republic of Chile, the Republic of China, Denmark, Egypt, the Republic of Finland, the French Republic, Greece, the Republic of Iceland, India, Ireland, the Italian Republic, the Netherlands, New Zealand, Norway, Pakistan, the Republic of Panama, the Republic of the Philippines, the Republic of Poland, the Portuguese Republic, the Union of South Africa, Sweden, the United Kingdom of Great Britain and Northern Ireland, the United States of America, the Union of Soviet Socialist Republics and the Federative People's Republic of Yugoslavia, being desirous of promoting safety of life at sea by establishing in common agreement uniform principles and rules directed thereto:... have agreed as follows:-

Article 1

(a) The Contracting Governments undertake to give effect to the provisions of the present Convention and of the Regulations annexed thereto, which shall be deemed to constitute an integral part of the present Convention. Every reference to the present Convention implies at the same time a reference to these Regulations.

(b) The Contracting Governments undertake to promulgate all laws, decrees, orders and regulations and to take all other steps which may be necessary to give the present Convention full and complete effect, so as to ensure that, from the point of view of safety of life,a ship is fit for the service for which it is intended.

Article II

The ships to which the present Convention applies are ships registered in countries the Governments of which are Contracting Governments, the ships registered in territories to which the present Convention is extended under Article XIII.

Article III

Laws, Regulations, Reports

The Contracting Governments undertake to communicate to the Intergovernmental Maritime Consultative Organisation (hereafter called the Organisation) -

(a) the text of laws, decrees, orders and regulations which shall have been promulgated on the various matters within the scope of the present Convention;

(b) all available official reports or official summaries of reports in so far as they show the results of the present Convention, provided always that such reports or summaries are not of a confidential nature; and

(c) a sufficient number of specimens of their Certificates issued under the provisions of the present Convention for circulation to the Contracting Governments for the information of their officers.

Article IV

Cases of Force Majeure

(a) No ship, which is not subject to the provisions of the present Convention at the time of its departure on any voyage, shall become subject to the provisions of the present Convention on account of any deviation from its intended voyage due to stress of weather or any other cause of *force majeure*.

(b) Persons who are on board a ship by reason of *force majeure* or in consequence of the obligation laid upon the master to carry shipwrecked or other persons shall not be taken into account for the purpose of ascertaining the application to a ship of any provisions of the present Convention.

Article V

Carriage of Persons in Emergency

(a) For the purposes of moving persons from any territory in order to avoid a threat to the security of their lives a Contracting Government may permit the carriage of a larger number of persons in its ships than is otherwise permissible under the present Convention.

(b) Such permission shall not deprive other Contracting Governments of any right of control under the present Convention over such ships which come within their ports.

(c) Notice of any such permission, together with a statement of the circumstances, shall be sent to the Organisation by the Contracting Governments granting such permission.

Article VI

Suspension in Case of War

(a) In case of war, Contracting Governments which consider that they are affected, whether as belligerents or as neutrals, may suspend the whole or any part of the Regulations annexed hereto. The suspending Government shall immediately give notice of such suspension to the Organisation.

(b) Such suspension shall not deprive other Contracting Governments of any right of control under the present Convention over the ships of the suspending Governments when such ships are within their ports.

(c) The suspending Government may at any time terminate such suspension and shall immediately give notice of such termination to the Organisation.

(d) The Organisation shall notify all Contracting Governments of any suspension or termination of suspension under this Article.

Article VII

Prior Treaties and Conventions

(a) As between the Contracting Governments the present Convention replaces and abrogates the International Convention for the Safety of Life at Sea which was signed in London on the 31st May,1929.

(b) All other treaties, conventions and arrangements relating to safety of life at sea, or matters appertaining thereto, at present in force between Governments parties to the present Convention,shall continue to have full and complete effect during the terms thereof as regards:-

(i) ships to which the present Convention does not apply;

(ii) ships to which the present Convention applies, in respect of matters for which it has not expressly provided.

(c) To the extent, however, that such treaties, conventions or arrangements conflict with the provisions of the present Convention, the provisions of the present Convention shall prevail.

(d) All matters which are not expressly provided for in the present Convention remain subject to the legislation of the Contracting Governments.

Article VIII

Special Rules Drawn Up by Agreement

When in accordance with the present Convention special rules are drawn up by agreement between all or some of the Contracting Governments, such rules shall be communicated to the Organisation for circulation to all Contracting Governments.

Article IX

Amendments

(a) (i) The present Convention may be amended by unanimous agreement between the Contracting Governments.

(ii) Upon the request of any Contracting Government a proposed amendment shall be communicated by the Organisation to all Contracting Governments for consideration and acceptance under this paragraph.

(b) (i) An amendment to the present Convention may be proposed to the Organisation at any time by any Contracting Government, and such proposal if adopted by a two-thirds majority of the Assembly of the Organisation (hereinafter called the Assembly), upon recommendation adopted by a two-thirds majority of the Maritime Safety Committee of the Organisation... shall be communicated by the Organisation to all Contracting Governments for their acceptance.

(ii) Any such recommendation by the Maritime Safety Committee shall be communicated by the Organisation to all Contracting Governments for their consideration at least six months before it is considered by the Assembly.

(c) (i) A conference of Governments to consider amendments to the present Convention proposed by any Contracting Government shall at any time be convened by the Organisation upon the request of one-third of the Contracting Governments.

(ii) Every amendment adopted by such conference by a two-thirds majority of the Contracting Governments shall be communicated by the Organisation to all Contracting Governments for their acceptance.

(d) Any amendment communicated to Contracting Governments for their acceptance under paragraph (b) or (c) of this Article shall come into force for all Contracting Governments, except those which before it comes into force make a declaration that they do not accept the amendment, twelve months after the date on which the amendment is accepted by two-thirds of the Contracting Governments, including two-thirds of the Governments represented on the Maritime Safety Committee.

(e) The Assembly, by a two-thirds majority vote, including two-thirds of the Governments represented on the Maritime Safety Committee, and subject to the concurrence of two-thirds of the Contracting Governments to the present Convention, or a conference convened under paragraph (c) of this Article by a two-thirds majority vote, may determine at the time of its adoption that the amendment is of such an important nature that any Contracting Government which makes a declaration under paragraph (d) of this Article and which does not accept the amendment within a period of twelve months after the amendment comes into force, shall, upon the expiry of this period, cease to be a party to the present Convention.

(f) Any amendment to the present Convention made under this Article which relates to the structure of a ship shall apply only to ships the keels of which are laid after the date on which the amendment comes into force....

Article X

Signature and Acceptance

(a) The present Convention shall remain open for signature for one month from this day's date and shall, thereafter, remain open for acceptance. ...

Article XII

Denunciation

(a) The present Convention may be denounced by any Contracting Government at any time after the expiry of five years from the date on which the Convention comes into force for that Government.

(b) Denunciation shall be effected by a notification in writing...

(c) A denunciation shall take effect one year, or such longer period as may be specified in the notification, after its receipt by the Organisation.

Article XIII

Territories

(a) (i) The United Nations in cases where they are the administering authority for a territory, or any Contracting Government responsible for the international relations of a territory, may at any time by notification in writing given to the Organisation declare that the present Convention shall extend to such territory ...

1. Department of State, Treaties and Other International Acts Series, No.2495. In force November 19,1952. The detailed Regulations will be found in the official documents.

RULES OF THE ROAD: INTERNATIONAL - INLAND [1]

(Excerpt)

Application of International Regulations for Preventing Collisions at Sea

United States Code
Title 33,
Sec. 1051

The President is authorized to proclaim the regulations set forth in sections 1061-1094 of this title for preventing collisions involving waterborne craft upon the high seas, and in all waters connected therewith. The effective date of such proclamation shall be not earlier than the date fixed by the Inter-Governmental Maritime Consultative Organization for application of such regulations by Governments which have agreed to accept them. Such proclamation, together with the regulations, shall be published in the Federal Register and after the effective date specified in such proclamation such regulations shall have effect as if enacted by statute and shall be followed by all public and private vessels of the United States and by all aircraft of United States registry to the extent therein made applicable. Such regulations shall not apply to the harbors, rivers, and other inland waters of the United States; the Great Lakes of North America and their connecting and tributary waters as far east as the lower exit of the Saint Lambert Lock at Montreal in the Province of Quebec, Canada; to the Red River of the North and the rivers emptying into the Gulf of Mexico and their tributaries; nor with respect to aircraft in any territorial waters of the United States.

Navy and Coast Guard Vessel Exceptions (33 U.S.C. 1052)

Any requirement of such regulations in respect to the number, position, range of visibility, or arc of visibility of the lights required to be displayed by vessels shall not apply to any vessel of the Navy or of the Coast Guard whenever the Secretary of the Navy or the Secretary of the Treasury, in the case of Coast Guard vessels operating under the Treasury Department, or such official as either may designate, shall find or certify that, by reason of special construction, it is not possible for such vessel or class of vessels to comply with such regulations. The lights of any such exempted vessel or class of vessels, however, shall conform as closely to the requirements of the applicable regulations as the Secretary or such official shall find or certify to be feasible. Notice of such findings or certification and of the character and position of the lights prescribed to be displayed on such exempted vessel or class of vessels shall be published in the Federal Register and in the Notice to Mariners and, after the effective date specified in such notice, shall have effect as part of such regulations.

Part A. Preliminary and Definitions

Rule 1 (a) These Rules shall be followed by all vessels and seaplanes upon the high seas and in all waters connected therewith navigable by seagoing vessels, except as provided in Rule 30. Where, as a result of their special construction, it is not possible for seaplanes to comply fully with the provisions of Rules specifying the carrying of lights and shapes, these provisions shall be followed as closely as circumstances permit.

(b) The Rules concerning lights shall be complied with in all weathers from sunset to sunrise, and during such times no other lights shall be exhibited, except such lights as cannot be mistaken for the prescribed lights or do not impair their visibility or distinctive character, or interfere with the keeping of a proper lookout. The lights prescribed by these Rules may also be exhibited from sunrise to sunset in restricted visibility and in all other circumstances when it is deemed necessary.

(c) In the following Rules, except where the context otherwise requires: -

(i) the word "vessel" includes every description of water craft other than a seaplane on the water, used or capable of being used as a means of transportation on water;

(ii) the word "seaplane" includes a flying boat and any other aircraft designed to manoeuvre on the water;

(iii) the term "power-driven vessel" means any vessel propelled by machinery;

(iv) every power-driven vessel which is under sail and not under power is to be considered a sailing vessel, and every vessel under power, whether under sail or not, is to be considered a power-driven vessel;

(v) a vessel or seaplane on the water is "underway" when she is not at anchor, or made fast to the shore, or aground;

(vi) the term "height above the hull" means height above the uppermost continuous deck;

(vii) the length and breadth of a vessel shall be her length overall and largest breadth;

(viii) the length and span of a seaplane shall be its maximum length and span as shown in its certificate of airworthiness, or as determined by measurement in the absence of such certificate;

(ix) vessels shall be deemed to be in sight of one another only when one can be observed visually from the other;

(x) the word "visible", when applied to lights, means visible on a dark night with a clear atmosphere;

(xi) the term "short blast" means a blast of about one second's duration;

(xii) the term "prolonged blast" means a blast of from four to six seconds' duration;

(xiii) the word "whistle" means any appliance capable of producing the prescribed and prolonged blasts;

(xiv) the term "engaged in fishing" means fishing with nets, lines or trawls but does not include fishing with trolling lines...

Part B. Lights and Shapes

Part C. Sound Signals and Conduct in Restricted Visibility

Part D. Steering and Sailing Rules

Part E. Sound Signals for Vessels in Sight of One Another

Part F. Miscellaneous

1. United States Coast Guard, Publication 169, Rules of the Road: International-Inland (Washington: Government Printing Office, September 1, 1965). Also printed in Department of State, Treaties and Other International Acts Series, No. 5813.

AGREEMENT BETWEEN THE GOVERNMENT OF THE UNITED STATES OF AMERICA AND THE GOVERNMENT OF THE KINGDOM OF DENMARK CONCERNING VISITS OF THE N.S. SAVANNAH

Signed at Copenhagen, July 2, 1964;

In Force on Same Date[1]

The Governments of the United States of America and Denmark, having a mutual interest in the peaceful uses of atomic energy, including its application to the merchant marine, have agreed as follows concerning such visits of the N.S. Savannah to Denmark as may be authorized by the Government of Denmark.

Article I. Entry of N.S. Savannah into Ports of Denmark --

(a) Each entry of the N.S. Savannah (hereinafter designated as the "Ship") into Danish ports and territorial waters and the use thereof shall be subject to the prior approval of the Government of Denmark.

(b) The visits of the Ship to Danish ports and territorial waters shall be governed, inter alia but not exclusively, by the principles and procedures set forth in Chapter VIII of the Safety of Life at Sea Convention of 1960 (1) and in the Recommendations Applicable to Nuclear Ships contained in Annex C to the Final Act of the 1960 Safety of Life at Sea Conference. (1)

Article II. Safety Assessment --

(a) To enable the Government of Denmark to consider the grant of approval for entry and use of Danish ports and territorial waters by the Ship, the Government of the United States shall provide a Safety Assessment prepared in accordance with Regulation 7 of Chapter VIII of the Safety of Life at Sea Convention of 1960 and in accordance with Recommendation 9 of Annex C mentioned above.

(b) As soon as practicable after receipt of the Safety Assessment, the Government of Denmark shall notify the Government of the United States whether the Ship can be operated in the ports and territorial waters of Denmark in accordance with this Agreement and the Safety Assessment.

1. Done at London June 17, 1960. Will enter into force May 26, 1965. For text see S. Ex. Doc. K, 87th Cong., 1st sess., pp. 370, 444.

Article III. Ports --

The Government of Denmark shall determine the port or ports to be visited and will designate the authorities responsible for acceptance arrangements and for special control under Regulation 11 of Chapter VIII of the Safety of Life at Sea Convention of 1960.

Article IV. Port Arrangements --

(a) Designated authorities of the Government of Denmark shall make arrangements with appropriate local governmental authorities for entrance of the Ship into Danish ports and the use thereof.

(b) Local governmental authorities shall be responsible for fire and police protection, crowd control and the general preparation of the harbour with respect to acceptance of the Ship.

(c) Control of public access to the Ship shall be the responsibility of the Master of the Ship. Special arrangements relating to such control shall be developed by the Master with the concurrence of designated authorities of the Government of Denmark.

(d) The Master shall comply with local regulations so long as in the opinion of the Master these regulations do not adversely affect the operating safety of the nuclear plant.

Article V. Inspection --

While the Ship is within Danish territorial waters, the designated authorities shall have appropriate inspection access to the Ship and its operating records and program data for purposes of determining whether the Ship has been operating in accordance with the operating manual of the Ship.

Article VI. Radioactive Waste --

The Government of the United States shall ensure that no disposal of radioactive liquid or solid wastes shall take place from the Ship while she is within the territorial waters of Denmark without the specific prior approval of the designated authorities of the Government of Denmark.

Article VII. Casualties --

A report, such as is required by Chapter VIII, Regulation 12 of the Safety of Life at Sea Convention of 1960, shall be made to the designated authorities by the Master of the Ship in the event of any incident, likely to lead to an environmental hazard, while the Ship is in or is approaching the territorial waters of Denmark.

Article VIII. Legal Actions --

The Government of the United States agrees that in any legal action or proceeding brought, in personam, against the United States, in a Danish court of competent jurisdiction, on account of any nuclear incident involving the Ship in a Danish port or in Danish territorial waters or for damage arising out of or resulting from a nuclear incident involving the Ship which is sustained in Denmark, the United States will not interpose the defense of sovereign immunity but will submit to the jurisdiction of such court; and, in such event, the United States will not seek to invoke the provisions of the Danish law, or any other law, relating to the limitations of shipowner's liability.

Article IX. Indemnification --

The Government of the United States represents that there is an agreement in effect between the United States Atomic Energy Commission and the United States Maritime Administration whereunder the Atomic Energy Commission, acting upon the authority of Section 170 of the Atomic Energy Act of 1954 (Public Law 83-703), and amended by Public Law 85-256 and Public Law 85-602, (1) has agreed to indemnify the United States Maritime Administration and other persons indemnified against claims for public liability arising from a nuclear incident in connection with the design, development, construction, operation, repair, maintenance or use of the Ship in the amount of 500 million United States dollars including the reasonable costs of investigating and settling claims and defending suits for damage. This sum represents the maximum amount for which the United States will be liable for a single nuclear incident involving the Ship, regardless of where damage may be suffered. The Government of the United States will promptly notify the Government of Denmark in the event this indemnification is terminated.

Article X. Definitions --

(a) The term "nuclear incident" means any occurrence causing bodily injury, sickness, disease, or death, or loss of or damage to property, or loss of use of property, arising out of or resulting from the radioactive, toxic, explosive, or other hazardous properties of source, special nuclear, or by-product material.

(b) The term "nuclear incident involving the Ship" means any nuclear incident in connection with, arising out of, or resulting from the operation, repair, maintenance or use of the Ship.

(c) The term "person indemnified" means the person with whom an indemnity agreement is executed and any other person who may be liable for public liability for a nuclear incident involving the Ship.

(d) The term "public liability" means any legal liability arising out of or resulting from a nuclear incident, except: (i) claims under United States State or Federal workmen's compensation acts of employees of persons indemnified who are employed at the site of and in connection with the activity where the nuclear incident occurs; and (ii) claims arising out of an act of war. "Public liability" also includes damage to property of persons

(1) 71 Stat. 576; 72 Stat. 525; 42 U.S.C. Sec. 2210.

indemnified, except the Ship and other property which is located at the site of and used in connection with the activity where the nuclear incident occurs.

<u>Article XI.</u> <u>Termination --</u>

Either Government may terminate this Agreement by giving no less than 180 days notice to the other. This Agreement terminates in the event the indemnification specified in Article IX is terminated without being replaced by an arrangement equally acceptable to both Governments.

<u>Article XII.</u> <u>Term of Agreement --</u>

In the event of entry into force of any general multilateral convention relating to the safety and operating procedures or third party liability of nuclear powered merchant ships by which both Governments become bound, this Agreement shall be amended.

1. Department of State, Treaties and Other International Acts Series, No. 5612.

MESSAGE TO THE CONGRESS OF THE UNITED STATES
BY PRESIDENT RICHARD M. NIXON ON
U.S. MERCHANT MARINE

October 23, 1969[1]

To the Congress of the United States:

The United States Merchant Marine--the fleet of commercial ships on which we rely for our economic strength in time of peace and our defense mobility in time of war--is in trouble.

While only one-fourth of the world's merchant ships are more than twenty years old, approximately three-fourths of American trading vessels are at least that antiquated. In the next four years, much of our merchant fleet will be scrapped. Yet we are now producing only a few new ships a year for use in our foreign trade. Building costs for American vessels are about twice those in foreign shipyards and production delays are excessive. Operating expenses also are high by world standards, and labor-management conflicts have been costly and disruptive.

Both government and industry share responsibility for the recent decline in American shipping and shipbuilding. Both government and industry must now make a substantial effort to reverse that record. We must begin immediately to rebuild our merchant fleet and make it more competitive. Accordingly, I am annoucing today a new maritime program for this nation, one which will replace the drift and neglect of recent years and restore this country to a proud position in the shipping lanes of the world.

Our program is one of challenge and opportunity. We will challenge the American shipbuilding industry to show that it can rebuild our Merchant Marine at reasonable expense. We will challenge American ship operators and seamen to move toward less dependence on government subsidy. And, through a substantially revised and better administered government program, we will create the opportunity to meet the challenge.

The need for this new program is great since the old ways have not worked. However, as I have frequently pointed out, our budget constraints at this time are also significant. Our program, therefore, will be phased in such a way that it will not increase subsidy expenditures during the rest of fiscal year 1970 and will require only a modest increase for fiscal year 1971. We can thus begin to rebuild our fleet and at the same time meet our fiscal responsibilities.

The Shipbuilding Industry

Our shipbuilding program is designed to meet both of the problems which lie behind the recent decline in this field: low production rates and high production costs. Our proposals would make it possible for shipbuilders to build more ships and would encourage them to hold down the cost of each vessel. We believe that these two aspirations are closely related. For only as we plan a major long-range building program can we encourage builders to standardize ship design and introduce mass production techniques which have kept other American products competitive in world markets. On the other hand, only if our builders are able to improve their efficiency and cut their costs can we afford to replace our obsolescent merchant fleet with American-built vessels. These cost reductions are essential if our ship operators are to make capital investments of several billion dollars over the next ten years to build new, high-technology ships.

Our new program will provide a substantially improved system of construction differential subsidies, payments which reimburse American shipbuilders for that part of their total cost which exceeds the cost of building in foreign shipyards. Such subsidies allow our shipbuilders--despite their higher costs--to sell their ships at world market prices for use in our foreign trade. The important features of our new subsidy are as follows:

1. We should make it possible for industry to build more ships over the next ten years, moving from the present subsidy of about ten ships a year to a new level of thirty ships a year.

2. We should reduce the percentage of total costs which are subsidized. The government presently subsidizes up to 55 percent of a builder's total expenses for a given vessel. Leaders of the shipbuilding industry have frequently said that subsidy requirements can be reduced considerably if they are assured a long-term market. I am therefore asking that construction differential subsidies be limited to 45 percent of total costs in fiscal year 1971. That percentage should be reduced by 2 percent in each subsequent year

until the maximum subsidy payment is down to 35 percent of total building expenses.

We are confident that the shipbuilding industry can meet this challenge. If the challenge is not met, however, then the Administration's commitment to this part of our program will not be continued.

3. Construction differential subsidies should be paid directly to shipbuilders rather than being channeled through shipowners as is the case under the present system. A direct payment system is necessary if our program is to encourage builders to improve designs, reduce delays, and minimize costs. It will also help us to streamline subsidy administration.

4. The multi-year procurement system which is now used for other government programs should be extended to shipbuilding. Under this system, the government makes a firm commitment to build a given number of ships over a specified and longer period of time, a practice which allows the industry to realize important economies of scale and to receive lower subsidies.

5. The increased level of ship construction will require a corresponding increase in the level of federally insured mortgages. Accordingly, we should increase the ceiling on our present mortgage insurance programs from $1 billion to $3 billion.

6. We should extend construction differential subsidies to bulk carriers, ships which usually carry ore, grain, or oil and which are not covered by our present subsidy program.

7. A commission should be established to review the status of the American shipbuilding industry, its problems, and its progress toward meeting the challenge we have set forth. The Commission should report on its findings within three years and recommend any changes in government policy which it believes are desirable.

The Ship Operating Industry

My comments to this point have related to the building of merchant vessels. The other arm of our maritime policy is that which deals with the operation of these ships. Here too, our new program offers several substantial improvements over the present system.

1. Operating differential subsidies should be continued only for the higher wage and insurance costs which American shipping lines experience. Subsidies for maintenance and repair and for subsistence should be eliminated. Instead of paying the difference between the wages of foreign seamen and actual wages on American ships, however, the government should compare foreign wages with prevailing wage levels in several comparable sectors of the American economy. A policy which ties subsidies to this wage index will reduce subsidy costs and provide an incentive for further efficiencies. Under this system, the operator would no longer lose in subsidies what he saves in costs. Nor would he continue to be reimbursed through subsidies when his wage costs rise to higher levels.

2. At the same time that we are reducing operating subsidies, it is appropriate that we eliminate the "recapture" provisions of the Merchant Marine Act of 1936. These provisions require subsidized lines to pay back to the government a portion of profits. If the recapture provisions are removed, the purposes for which they were designed will be largely accomplished by corporate taxes, which were at much lower rates when these provisions were instituted. We will also save the cost of administering recapture provisions.

3. Many bulk carriers presently receive indirect operating subsidies from the government because of the statutory requirement that certain government cargoes must be shipped in United States vessels at premium rates. When the Department of Agriculture ships grain abroad, for example, it pays higher rates out of its budget than if it were allowed to ship at world market rates. We will propose a new, direct subsidy system for such carriers, thus allowing us to phase out these premium freight rates and reduce the costs of several nonmaritime government programs.

4. Ship operators now receiving operating differential subsidies are permitted to defer Federal tax payments on reserve funds set aside for construction purposes. This provision should be extended to include all qualified ship operators in the foreign trade, but only for well-defined ship replacement programs.

5. Past government policies and industry attitudes have not been conducive to cooperation between labor and management. Our program will help to improve this situation by ending the uncertainty that has characterized our past maritime policy. Labor and management must now use this opportunity to find

ways of resolving their differences without halting operations. If the desired expansion of merchant shipping is to be achieved, the disruptive work stoppages of the past must not be repeated.

6. The larger capital investment necessary to construct a modern and efficient merchant fleet requires corresponding port development. I am therefore directing the Secretary of Commerce and the Secretary of Transportation to work with related industries and local governments in improving our port operations. We must take full advantage of technological advances in this area and we should do all we can to encourage greater use of intermodal transportation systems, of which these high-technology ships are only a part.

Equal Employment Opportunities

The expansion of American merchant shipbuilding which this program makes possible will provide many new employment opportunities. All of our citizens must have equal access to these new jobs. I am therefore directing the Secretary of Commerce and the Secretary of Labor to work with industry and labor organizations to develop programs that will insure all minority groups their rightful place in this expansion.

Research and Development

We will also enlarge and redirect the maritime research and development activities of the Federal government. Greater emphasis will be placed on practical applications of technological advances and on the coordination of Federal programs with those of industry.

* * *

The history of American commercial shipping is closely intertwined with the history of our country. From the time of the Colonial fishing sloops, down through the great days of the majestic clipper ships, and into the new era when steam replaced the sail, the venturesome spirit of maritime enterprise has contributed significantly to the strength of the nation.

Our shipping industry has come a long way over the last three centuries. Yet, as one of the great historians of American seafaring, Samuel Eliot Morrison, has written: "all her modern docks and terminals and dredged channels will avail nothing, if the spirit perish that led her founders to 'trye all ports.'" It is that spirit to which our program of challenge and opportunity appeals.

It is my hope and expectation that this program will introduce a new era in the maritime history of America, an era in which our shipbuilding and ship operating industries take their place once again among the vigorous, competitive industries of this nation.

1. 115 Congressional Record H 9943 (H. Doc. No. 91-183).

CARGO FOR SCIENCE - USCGC EASTWIND IN ANTARCTIC

Courtesy United States Coast Guard

CHAPTER NINE

MODELS FOR THE FUTURE

Introductory Note

The search for new supplies of food and natural resources, for aditional trade and security is fostering fresh activity in the oceans as well as drawing nations into closer contact. Given the differing outlooks, needs and aspirations of states, it is essential that national policy be prepared to deal with a variety of contingencies. This leads to speculation on the models that are available for the guidance of future marine policy.

Extension of National Jurisdiction

The most obvious course for most states to take is to extend their national jurisdiction over wider belts of ocean off their shores. As we have noted in Chapters Two and Three, there has been a tendency to increase territorial limits from three to twelve or even more miles. Thirty-eight countries now claim jurisdictional rights to the twelve mile line, as opposed to thirty-five that adhere to the three mile rule. There are twenty-eight states that claim less than ten miles for territorial waters, but insist upon controlling fishing in contiguous zones extending to twelve miles. To these areas of national jurisdiction are also now added claims to sovereign rights over resources of the continental shelf.

Acting under the principles of the Geneva Convention on the Continental Shelf and the terms of United States law, the U.S. Department of Interior has awarded leases for the drilling of oil in waters as far out as thirty miles and to a depth of 1,800 feet. Permission has also been granted for the extraction of phosphate from sites located forty miles from shore. As man's capability for working in deeper water expands, pressures will undoubtedly rise for the issuance of leases allowing exploitation farther out along the continental shelves. Within the next ten years industry will probably master techniques for drilling in depths of water ranging from 2,000 to 10,000 feet. With advances in technology and increased knowledge of the nature of the sea-beds and subsoil, demands will grow for further extensions of national claims.

The investment of large sums to develop underwater platforms for defense purposes seems also destined to lead to increased claims of national jurisdiction. To the extent that these defense sites are placed beyond the continental shelves and men and vehicles become capable of maneuvering safely in such deeps, moves will be made in some areas to surround these ocean bottom installations with an aura of sovereignty to create so-called national "islands". This could initiate international altercations, depending upon the pacific or threatening nature of the sites and the extent of the claims made.

Predictions as to the types of developments that are likely to occur within the next decade appeared in a news dispatch from Washington during the summer of 1968. This report stated that oceanographers have been investigating the ocean floor more than a mile below surface to determine the practicability of establishing manned research and engineering centers, military installations and submarine detection stations in the deep sea. Defense theorists have for some time considered the idea of constructing manned underwater bases. Studies have shown that the sediments on the floor would be able to support such structures, and that the depth of the water would not interfere with building procedures. However, the economic costs of locating bases in very deep water would be extremely high at the present stage of technology and engineering capability. Yet the possibility of erecting these underwater bases must be sufficiently tangible to have led President Johnson to request that the Geneva disarmament negotiators consider barring the use of the ocean floor for nuclear missiles.

Although talks are proceeding at the United Nations and elsewhere with respect to establishing treaties which would limit further extensions of sovereignty in the seas or confer authority on an international agency to control use of the sea bottom, it would not be wise for states to relinquish the right to extend their jurisdiction in the oceans. Until more knowledge is available of what man can accomplish in deep submergence and states have weighed the pros and cons of such a treaty, nations should maintain their jurisdictional rights for security purposes.

Again, it is conceivable that if a chain of underwater bases were established in the seas, states might apply the sector principle to claim exclusive jurisdiction over waters between the extremities of their coasts and the bases. The Soviet Union has employed this principle to extend its jurisdiction over the waters between its shores and the North Pole. The implications of such "No Trespassing" zones was illustrated in 1967 when the Soviet Union refused to allow two United States Coast Guard cutters to pass from the Barents Sea to Alaska via the Northern Sea Route, notwithstanding a reported announcement that the course had been "opened" to international use.

The United States continues to adhere to the principle of the three mile limit for territorial waters rather than favor wider national belts, save as they may be required for customs and revenue enforcement, security measures, conservation of fisheries, or for such other purposes as may be agreed upon by treaty. Despite disadvantages of claiming such a narrow strip of water, receipt of the reciprocal privilege allowing American vessels to approach within three miles of foreign shores more than offsets the drawbacks. However, often complex difficulties can arise from maintaining this position. For example, several years ago Soviet fishing fleets invaded the fishery just outside of the three mile limit off the edge of Cape Cod and Long Island. This fishing area has long been the preserve and source of livelihood for the local inhabitants. By keeping silent the country would have allowed the Soviets, as well as other foreigners, to establish an historic right to fish these waters. To resolve the issue without proclaiming sovereignty over a greater width of water, the United States demanded its right to restrict use of the fishery within a contiguous zone, thus limiting fishing activity within twelve miles from shore. Despite this move, Soviet fishing vessels have been subsequently allowed in this zone during certain periods of the year. To use the language once employed by the Supreme Court in another context, a scintilla of right is left to foreigners to operate in the contiguous zone which would not exist if these waters were to be assimilated to territorial waters and placed under national sovereignty.

Practice will eventually determine where the limits of national jurisdiction will be drawn. Some further extensions of local claims may continue to be advanced, but reasonable limitations on national jurisdiction in the high seas are in the interest of the majority of states. Yet assurances of long-standing rights to extract minerals or fossil fuels from the sea-bed, to utilize fisheries, and to protect national concerns from foreign interference must be considered in the interest of the public and industry. Conveyance of supranational powers to the United Nations would by no means assure entrepreneurs and the public the same measure of protection and certainty which national rights of sovereignty over the resources of the continental shelves now afford. At the same time it is only fair to recognize the cry uttered by many of the developing countries, which lack the technology and economic strength to explore and exploit the sea beds off their shores, that the present regime of the seas does not allow them equal opportunity to utilize the marine resources needed for their own economic growth. Their argument is real and undeniable. It is questionable, however that the path of progress lies in piling one more layer of authority on top of another, or in restricting marine activities to those who possess the capability to make use of ocean resources. Many factors such as strength, position, economic and political interests, as well as outlooks and strategy must be weighed by those charged with the responsibility of deciding whether to extend national jurisdiction in the seas further, to stand on present policies, or to accept some form of international arrangement and control.

Antarctic and Outer Space Treaties as Models of Cooperation

With pressures mounting for the creation of a new regime of

of the seas, it may be pertinent to consider the Antarctic and Outer Space Treaties as limited models.

The Antarctic Treaty of 1959, proposed by the United States in conjunction with the International Geophysical Year, was designed to reduce conflicting claims in the Antarctic that were threatening to lead to hostilities. Under the terms of the treaty the parties agreed to hold all territorial claims in abeyance. They also consented to allow scientific activity to be conducted freely on the continent, to refrain from introducing armaments or performing nuclear tests in the region, and to exchange scientific information.

This agreement put an end to skirmishes that had been occurring in the Palmer Peninsula and improved the general atmosphere. Scientific investigation has been encouraged, and information has been widely exchanged among the countries working in the Antarctic. No international machinery was established to oversee compliance with the terms of the treaty. None has been needed.

The Antarctic Treaty may offer a precedent for holding claims to the seas in abeyance until more is known about the deep oceans, their resources, and man's underwater engineering capabilities.

The report issued by the Environmental Science Services Administration announcing the U.S.C.G.C. Oceanographer's discovery of several new mountain chains in the South Pacific Ocean not previously recorded on charts, shows how imperfect knowledge still is concerning major bodies of the sea. However, through such collaborative efforts as the International Indian Ocean Expedition, again arranged in conjunction with the International Geophysical Year, information about the marine environment is gradually being obtained. This Expedition gathered a great deal of data pertaining to the bottom profile of the Indian Ocean as well as its currents, salinity, temperatures and resources.

The Treaty Governing Exploration and Use of Outer Space (1966) provides for free investigation and use of outer space and celestial bodies. It stipulates that these places are not to be subjected to national appropriation, that space is to be employed for peaceful purposes, and that weapons of mass destruction shall not be placed there. As in the Antarctic Treaty, no special machinery was created to oversee application of these principles, although the parties did agree to inform the Secretary-General of the United Nations and one another, to the extent feasible, of their space activities.

Differences in the nature of Antarctic, outer space, and the high seas, and the uses to which they can be presently employed, suggest that no single set of terms can be applied interchangeably to both inner and outer space, There is no doubt that states generally wish to retain their right to utilize the ocean for whatever economic, commercial, military, naval, and air usage they consider necessary to advance their interests and to maintain security.

The Antarctic and Outer Space Treaties, as well as the International Indian Ocean Expedition, were acceptable to states precisely because they allowed countries the freedom to experiment and conduct surveys. No supra-national machinery or dictating authority were established, therby giving technology and engineering maximum scope. Generally speaking, the results of these arrangements have been beneficial to the participating nations.

The basic principle of freedom, which has been incorporated into all of these arrangements, may be applicable to the handling of jurisdictional conflicts and activities in the high seas.

A Multilateral Declaration of Principles

In keeping with the United Nations's general attitude toward the use of outer space, the United States Government has suggested that the world body contemplate adopting a broad set of principles relating to the oceans that could serve as a guide to future marine activities. It is thought that such a procedure would help obtain consensus on a new international convention to replace the 1958 instrument. Such a declaration would have moral weight, but would not be legally binding upon parties. A step of this kind would, quite frankly, be a political action.

The United States Government believes that it is possible to seek, through international cooperation, agreed arrangements for use of the deep ocean floor which will benefit all nations, while still taking full account of American interests and the needs of science, technology and engineering. The objective is to ensure that through cooperative measures both Americans and others may be free to utilize the ocean floor and its resources to mutual advantage. The text of the United States proposal is contained in the readings which follow. This undoubtedly will require amendments and changes before it is adopted.

Without going into details at this point, what are the basic considerations that might be expected to be included in a declaration of principles? The following might be considered:

1. The high seas shall remain free and open to the use of all recognized states and their nationals.

2. The right of nations to extend their jurisdiction over the territorial seas and contiguous zone, and over the sea floor, the resources thereon and in the subsoil of the continental shelf, shall be respected.

3. The high seas beyond these limits shall not be subject to appropriation by any state.

4. No state should exercise sovereignty or sovereign rights over the deep ocean floor beyond the outer limits of the continental shelf. The deep ocean floor, like the waters of the high seas, should be open to the exploration and use of all states in accordance with international law.

5. Arrangements should be concluded to govern exploitation of the resources of the deep ocean floor. These should provide for orderly development, ensure respect of the rights of investors to explore and extract, and accommodate commercial and other uses of the ocean floor.

6. Efforts should be made, as soon as practicable, to define the boundary between the national jurisdiction of coastal states in the continental shelf and the deep ocean floor, taking into account the rights and interests of states to exploit the resources situated on and beneath the surface of the continental shelf.

7. For the purposes of furthering international cooperation in the deep ocean environment, states should undertake to exchange information concerning their scientific programs in the deep ocean, and encourage international collaborative scientific investigations.

8. Activities on the deep ocean floor should be of a peaceful

nature. They should respect the rights of others to use the high seas, and should seek to avoid pollution of the ocean environment.

9. States and their national should render all possible assistance in the event of accident, distress, or other emergency occurring in the high seas or on the ocean floor.

A declaration containing such principles would offer several advantages. It would establish a sense of direction and an attitude of cooperation in facing maritime problems. Moreover, it would lay a foundation for future measure, as well as provide certain minimal guidelines for national and private activities on the deep sea-bed. This would give impetus to the proposal made by the President of the United States in 1968 to launch an "historic and unprecedented adventure" through an International Decade of Ocean Exploration.

No provision has been included which would empower the United Nations to license mining or other activities on the deep ocean floor, or to receive fees for leases or the like. It seems questionable that a majority of member states are as yet prepared to give the United Nations such authority. No other machinery has been suggested pursuant to experience with the Antarctic and Outer Space Treaties. Organs of the United Nations are always open for consideration of threats to peace or charges of violations made against international agreements. Bilateral and other instruments of diplomacy, conciliation and arbitration are available for use if needed. And the doors of the International Court of Justice are open in the event of disputes over legal questions.

The United Nations and the Deep Sea

The General Assembly in 1966 requested the Secretary-General to make a survey of marine science and technology activities including resource development, with a view to presenting proposals for increased international cooperation in this sphere. At the 1967 General Assembly the delegate of Malta suggested that a specialized agency should be formed to license exploration and development activities on the sea-bed. Senator Claiborne Pell (Dem., Rhode Island) has called for the establishment of a permanent United Nations Sea Guard to help preserve peace. Although unprepared to take such radical measures at this point, the members of the General Assembly in December 1967 did agree to set up an Ad Hoc Committee of thirty-five to study what should be done with respect to furthering international cooperation in the use of the resources of the deep sea-beds. Some states, including the Soviet Union, have expressed doubts as to whether it is possible at this time to take any additional steps to promote cooperative activities on the seas. They have even questioned the formation of the Ad Hoc Study Committee.

One of the most serious concerns to many governments is the inability of the United Nations to function effectively when peace is threatened and national security is in jeopardy. Others criticize the United Nations for the high degree of emotionalism which at times invades the proceedings of its chief political organs, and for the inclination of its members to act as blocs without always paying due regard to the rights and interests of others. Nevertheless, it does seem clear that the world body can be useful in precipitating issues, and at times in assisting the growth of consensus. These perhaps will be the most useful attributes of the United Nations in connection with encouraging peaceful use of the deep ocean floor.

The Community Concept

One alternative for coping with maritime issues is to utilize the community concept as has been developed among the six Western European states who have joined to form the Common Market. The Common Market rests upon the principle that mutual concern for a particular situation or set of problems gives rise, under appropriate circumstances, to a sense of community.

The European Economic Community of the Six is comprised of three separate but inter-related arrangements -- a Coal and Steel Community, the Common Market, and the European Atomic Community. These states have agreed by treaty to forge unified policies applying to the production of coal and steel, trade, agriculture, transport, finance and the use of nuclear energy. Certain common institutions have been established to ensure attainment of these goals. A Commission or High Authority is given executive powers and responsibilities. Interlocking Councils of Ministers determine policy questions. A Common Assembly or Parliament debates general issues and may overrule the executive by a vote of censure or lack of confidence. A Court of Justice hears cases involving states, community institutions, associations and individuals. It may even declare acts of other organs unconstitutional if it finds them in excess of their powers. Perhaps eventually states will be agreeable to forming similar institutions for regulating use of the oceans. For the moment it seems more likely that they will limit their efforts to the creation of consultative bodies such as the Commission for the Northwest Atlantic Fisheries (ICNAF), or the Organization for Economic Cooperation and Development (OECD) which seeks to assure that each country is aware of the implications of its policies for others.

There is room for action, and no lack of models, whenever states are ready to conclude and implement new agreements for the oceans.

Conclusion

The world is moving to a point where new treaty arrangements will soon be needed for the oceans due to the racing pace of technological innovation. Various alternatives for meeting this need are available both within and outside of the United Nations; collectively, unilaterally and bilaterally. At present it seem desirable to hold all options open until further applications of marine engineering and technology have indicated more clearly what can actually be achieved with deep submergence, and until something more is known about the extent of the resources on the ocean floor and their usefulness to industry. Thoughtful consideration of future steps, rather than a hasty plunge ahead before there is full knowledge of what is feasible, is probably the wiser course for public policy at this juncture.

Thus far neither the United States nor other principal powers are convinced that control of the seas should be conferred upon an international body. Nor are they ready to endow an organization with supra-national authority to dictate marine activities. Enlightened conceptions of national interest remain the surest guide for policy. Little confidence can be reposed in fickle voting majorities which rest upon large numbers of countries that have little power or responsibility and no appreciable experience in utilizing technology for investing the properties of the deep oceans.

Until much more is known about the marine environment in terms of what may may accomplished there, what the potentialities of resources are, and what military measures can be taken in the deeps, it is best to move circumspectly. Few nations are likely to appropriate large areas of the seas or ocean floor prematurely.

Experience may show that the adoption of principles similar to those embodied in the Treaties on Antarctica and Outer Space would be advantageous. This can be explored through negotiation. Although this can be a laborious, time-consuming process, espe cially where new and complex questions are at issue, it is still the surest way toward increased cooperation among states.

The readings which follow illustrate some of the considerations and models that are available for seeking a new regime of the seas.

For additional references see Assistant Secretary of State Joseph J. Sisko, "Recent International Developments Concerning the Ocean and Ocean Floor," Department of State Bulletin, Vol. LVIII, No. 1488, January 1, 1968, pp. 17-19; Interim Report on the United Nations and the Issue of Deep Ocean Resources, together with Hearings by the Subcommittee on International Organizations and Movements of the Committee on Foreign Affairs, U.S. House of Representatives, House Report No. 999, 90th Congress, 1st Session, December 7, 1967; Philip C. Jessup and Howard J. Taubenfeld,

Controls for Outer Space (New York, Columbia University Press, 1959, Part I; Lewis M. Alenander (ed.), The Law of the Sea: Off-Shore Boundaries and Zones (Columbus, Ohio State University Press, 1967); ibid., The Law of the Sea: The Future of the Sea's Resources, Proceedings of the Second Annual Conference on the Law of the Sea Institute (Kingston, University of Rhode Island, 1968); Marine-Science Affairs - A Year of Plans and Progress, Second Report of the President to the Congress on Marine Resources and Engineering Development, March 1968 (Washington, Government Printing Office, 1968).

ANTARCTIC TREATY

Signed at Washington, December 1,1959 [1]

The Governments of Argentina, Australia, Belgium, Chile, the French Republic, Japan, New Zealand, Norway, the Union of South Africa, the Union of Soviet Socialist Republics, the United Kingdom of Great Britain and Northern Ireland, and the United States of America,

Recognizing that it is in the interest of all mankind that Antarctica shall continue forever to be used exclusively for peaceful purposes and shall not become the scene or object of international discord;

Acknowledging the substantial contributions to scientific knowledge resulting from international cooperation in scientific investigation in Antarctica;

Convinced that the establishment of a firm foundation for the continuation and development of such cooperation on the basis of freedom of scientific investigation in Antarctica as applied during the International Geophysical Year accords with the interests of science and the progress of all mankind;

Convinced also that a treaty ensuring the use of Antarctica for peaceful purposes only and the continuance of international harmony in Antarctica will further the purposes and principles embodied in the Charter of the United Nations;

Have agreed as follows:

Article I

1. Antarctica shall be used for peaceful purposes only. There shall be prohibited , *inter alia*, any measures of a military nature, such as the establishment of military bases and fortifications, the carrying out of military maneuvers, as well as the testing of any type of weapons.

2. The present treaty shall not prevent the use of military personnel or equipment for scientific research or for any other peaceful purpose.

Article II

Freedom of scientific investigation in Antarctica and cooperation toward that end, as applied during the International Geophysical Year, shall continue, subject to the provisions of the present treaty.

Article III

1. In order to promote international cooperation in scientific investigation in Antarctica, as provided for in Article II of the present treaty, the Contracting Parties agree that, to the greatest extent feasible and practicable:

(a) information regarding plans for scientific programs in Antarctica shall be exchanged to permit maximum economy and efficiency of operations;
(b) scientific personnel shall be exchanged in Antarctica between expeditions and stations;
(c) scientific observations and results from Antarctica shall be exchanged and made freely available.

2. In implementing this article, every encouragement shall be given to the establishment of cooperative working relations with those Specialized Agencies of the United Nations and other international organizations having a scientific or technical interest in Antarctica.

Article IV

1. Nothing in the present treaty shall be interpreted as:

(a) a renunciation by any Contracting Party of previously asserted rights of or claims to territorial sovereignty in Antarctica;
(b) a renunciation or diminution by any Contracting Party of any basis of claim to territorial sovereignty in Antarctica which it may have whether as a result of its activities or those of its nationals in Antarctica, or otherwise;
(c) prejudicing the position of any Contracting Party as regards its recognition or non-recognition of any other State's rights of or claim or basis of claim to territorial sovereignty in Antarctica.

2. No acts or activities taking place while the present treaty is in force shall constitute a basis for asserting, supporting or denying a claim to territorial sovereignty in Antarctica or create any rights of sovereignty in Antarctica. No new claim, or enlargement of an existing claim, to territorial sovereignty in Antarctica shall be asserted while the present treaty is in force.

Article V

1. Any nuclear explosions in Antarctica and the disposal there of radioactive waste material shall be prohibited.
2. In the event of the conclusion of international agreements concerning the use of nuclear energy, including nu-

clear explosions and the disposal of radioactive waste material, to which all of the Contracting Parties whose representatives are entitled to participate in the meetings provided for under Article IX are parties, the rules established under such agreements shall apply in Antarctica.

Article VI

The provisions of the present treaty shall apply to the area south of 60° South Latitude, including all ice shelves, but nothing in the present treaty shall prejudice or in any way affect the rights, or the exercise of the rights, of any state under international law with regard to the high seas within that area.

Article VII

1. In order to promote the objectives and ensure the observance of the provisions of the present treaty, each Contracting Party whose representatives are entitled to participate in the meetings referred to in Article IX of the treaty shall have the right to designate observers to carry out any inspection provided for by the present article. Observers shall be nationals of the Contracting Parties which designate them. The names of observers shall be communicated to every other Contracting Party having the right to designate observers, and like notice shall be given of the termination of their appointment.

2. Each observer designated in accordance with the provisions of paragraph 1 of this article shall have complete freedom of access at any time to any or all areas of Antarctica.

3. All areas of Antarctica, including all stations, installations and equipment within those areas, and all ships and aircraft at points of discharging or embarking cargoes or personnel in Antarctica, shall be open at all times to inspection by any observers designated in accordance with paragraph 1 of this article.

4. Aerial observation may be carried out at any time over any or all areas of Antarctica by any of the Contracting Parties having the right to designate observers.

5. Each Contracting Party shall, at the time when the present treaty enters into force for it, inform the other Contracting Parties, and thereafter shall give them notice in advance, of

(a) all expeditions to and within Antarctica, on the part of its ships or nationals, and all expeditions to Antarctica organized in or proceeding from its territory;

(b) all stations in Antarctica occupied by its nationals; and

(c) any military personnel or equipment intended to be introduced by it into Antarctica subject to the conditions prescribed in paragraph 2 of Article I of the present treaty.

Article VIII

1. In order to facilitate the exercise of their functions under the present treaty, and without prejudice to the respective positions of the Contracting Parties relating to jurisdiction over all other persons in Antarctica, observers designated under paragraph 1 of Article VII and scientific personnel exchanged under subparagraph 1(b) of Article III of the treaty, and members of the staffs accompanying any such persons, shall be subject only to the jurisdiction of the Contracting Party of which they are nationals in respect of all acts or omissions occurring while they are in Antarctica for the purpose of exercising their functions.

2. Without prejudice to the provisions of paragraph 1 of this article, and pending the adoption of measures in pursuance of subparagraph 1(e) of Article IX, the Contracting Parties concerned in any case of dispute with regard to the exercise of jurisdiction in Antarctica shall immediately consult together with a view to reaching a mutually acceptable solution.

Article IX

1. Representatives of the Contracting Parties named in the preamble to the present treaty shall meet at the City of Canberra within two months after the date of entry into force of the treaty, and thereafter at suitable intervals and places, for the purpose of exchanging information, consulting together on matters of common interest pertaining to Antarctica, and formulating and considering, and recommending to their governments, measures in furtherance of the principles and objectives of the treaty, including measures regarding:

(a) use of Antarctica for peaceful purposes only;
(b) facilitation of scientific research in Antarctica;
(c) facilitation of international scientific cooperation in Antarctica;
(d) facilitation of the exercise of the rights of inspection provided for in Article VII of the treaty;
(e) questions relating to the exercise of jurisdiction in Antarctica;
(f) preservation and conservation of living resources in Antarctica.

2. Each Contracting Party which has become a party to the present treaty by accession under Article XIII shall be entitled to appoint representatives to participate in the meetings referred to in paragraph 1 of the present article,

during such time as that Contracting Party demonstrates its interest in Antarctica by conducting substantial scientific research activity there, such as the establishment of a scientific station or the despatch of a scientific expedition.

3. Reports from the observers referred to in Article VII of the present treaty shall be transmitted to the representatives of the Contracting Parties participating in the meetings referred to in paragraph 1 of the present article.

4. The measures referred to in paragraph 1 of this article shall become effective when approved by all the Contracting Parties whose representatives were entitled to participate in the meetings held to consider those measures.

5. Any or all of the rights established in the present treaty may be exercised as from the date of entry into force of the treaty whether or not any measures facilitating the exercise of such rights have been proposed, considered or approved as provided in this article.

Article X

Each of the Contracting Parties undertakes to exert appropriate efforts, consistent with the Charter of the United Nations, to the end that no one engages in any activity in Antarctica contrary to the principles or purposes of the present treaty.

Article XI

1. If any dispute arises between two or more of the Contracting Parties concerning the interpretation or application of the present treaty, those Contracting Parties shall consult among themselves with a view to having the dispute resolved by negotiation, inquiry, mediation, conciliation, arbitration, judicial settlement or other peaceful means of their own choice.

2. Any dispute of this character not so resolved shall, with the consent, in each case, of all parties to the dispute, be referred to the International Court of Justice for settlement; but failure to reach agreement on reference to the International Court of Justice shall not absolve parties to the dispute from the responsibility of continuing to seek to resolve it by any of the various peaceful means referred to in paragraph 1 of this article.

Article XII

1 (a) The present treaty may be modified or amended at any time by unanimous agreement of the Contracting Parties whose representatives are entitled to participate in the meetings provided for under Article IX. Any such modification or amendment shall enter into force when the depositary government has received notice from all such Contracting Parties that they have ratified it.

(b) Such modification or amendment shall thereafter enter into force as to any other Contracting Party when notice of ratification by it has been received by the depositary government. Any such Contracting Party from which no notice of ratification is received within a period of two years from the date of entry into force of the modification or amendment in accordance with the provisions of subparagraph 1(a) of this article shall be deemed to have withdrawn from the present treaty on the date of the expiration of such period.

2 (a) If after the expiration of thirty years from the date of entry into force of the present treaty, any of the Contracting Parties whose representatives are entitled to participate in the meetings provided for under Article IX so requests by a communication addressed to the depositary government, a conference of all the Contracting Parties shall be held as soon as practicable to review the operation of the treaty.

(b) Any modification or amendment to the present treaty which is approved at such a conference by a majority of the Contracting Parties there represented, including a majority of those whose representatives are entitled to participate in the meetings provided for under Article IX, shall be communicated by the depositary government to all the Contracting Parties immediately after the termination of the conference and shall enter into force in accordance with the provisions of paragraph 1 of the present article.

(c)If any such modification or amendment has not entered into force in accordance with the provisions of subparagraph 1(a) of this article within a period of two years after the date of its communication to all the Contracting Parties, any Contracting Party may at any time after the expiration of that period give notice to the depositary government of its withdrawal from the present treaty; and such withdrawal shall take effect two years after the receipt of the notice by the depositary government.

Article XIII

1. The present treaty shall be subject to ratification by the signatory states. It shall be open for accession

by any state which is a member of the United Nations, or by any other state which may be invited to accede to the treaty with the consent of all the Contracting Parties whose representatives are entitled to participate in the meetings provided for under Article IX of the treaty.

2. Ratification of or accession to the present treaty shall be effected by each state in accordance with its constitutional processes.

3. Instruments of ratification and instruments of accession shall be deposited with the Government of the United States of America, hereby designated as the depositary government...

1. Department of State Bulletin, Vol. 41 (1959), p. 912.

DRAFT TREATY GOVERNING EXPLORATION OF OUTER SPACE

December 8, 1966[1]

The States Parties to this Treaty,

Inspired by the great prospects opening up before mankind as a result of man's entry into outer space,

Recognizing the common interest of all mankind in the progress of the exploration and use of outer space for peaceful purposes,

Believing that the exploration and use of outer space should be carried on for the benefit of all peoples irrespective of the degree of their economic or scientific development,

Desiring to contribute to broad international cooperation in the scientific as well as the legal aspects of the explorations and use of outer space for peaceful purposes,

Believing that such co-operation will contribute to the development of mutual understanding and to the strengthening of friendly relations between States and peoples,

Recalling resolution 1962 (XVIII), entitled "Declaration of Legal Principles Governing the Activities of States in the Exploration and Use of Outer Space", which was adopted unanimously by the United Nations General Assembly on 13 December 1963,

Recalling resolution 1884 (XVIII), calling upon States to refrain from placing in orbit around the earth any objects carrying nuclear weapons or any other kinds of weapons of mass destruction or from installing such weapons on celestial bodies, which was adopted unanimously by the United Nations General Assembly on 17 October 1963,

Taking account of United Nations General Assembly resolution 110 (II) of 3 November 1947, which condemned propaganda designed or likely to provoke or encourage any threat to the peace, breach of the peace or act of aggression and considering that the aforementioned resolution is applicable to outer space,

Convinced that a Treaty on Principles Governing

the Activities of States in the Exploration and Use of Outer Space, including the Moon and Other Celestial Bodies, will further the Purposes and Principles of the Charter of the United Nations,

Have agreed on the following:

Article I

The exploration and use of outer space, including the moon and other celestial bodies, shall be carried out for the benefit and in the interests of all countries, irrespective of their degree of economic or scientific development, and shall be the province of all mankind.

Outer space, including the moon and other celestial bodies, shall be free for exploration and use by all States without discrimination of any kind, on a basis of equality and in accordance with international law, and there shall be free access to all areas of celectial bodies.

There shall be freedom of scientific investigation in outer space, including the moon and other celestial bodies, and States shall facilitate and encourage international co-operation in such investigation.

Article II

Outer space, including the moon and other celestial bodies, is not subject to national appropriation by claim of sovereignty, by means of use or occupation, or by any other means.

Article III

States Parties to the Treaty shall carry on activities in the exploration and use of outer space, including the moon and other celestial bodies, in accordance with international law, including the Charter of the United Nations, in the interest of maintaining international peace and security and promoting international co-operation and understanding.

Article IV

States Parties to the Treaty undertake not to place in orbit around the earth any objects carrying nuclear weapons or any other kinds of weapons of mass destruction, install such weapons on celestial bodies, or station such weapons in outer space in any other manner.

The moon and other celestial bodies shall be used

by all States Parties to the Treaty exclusively for peaceful purposes. The establishment of military bases, installations, and fortifications, the testing of any type of weapons and the conduct of military manoeuvres on celestial bodies shall be forbidden. The use of military personnel for scientific research or for any other peaceful purposes shall not be prohibited. The use of any equipment or facility necessary for peaceful exploration of the moon and other celestial bodies shall also not be prohibited.

Article V

States Parties to the Treaty shall regard astronauts as envoys of mankind in outer space and shall render to them all possible assistance in the event of accident, distress, or emergency landing on the territory of another State Party or on the high seas. When astronauts make such a landing, they shall be safely and promptly returned to the State of registry of their space vehicle.

In carrying on activites in outer space and on celestial bodies, the astronauts of one State Party shall render all possible assistance to the astronauts of other State Parties.

States Parties to the Treaty shall immediately inform the other States Parties to the Treaty or the Secretary-General of the United Nations of any phenomena they discover in outer space, including the moon and other celestial bodies, which could constitute a danger to the life or health of astronauts.

Article VI

States Parties to the Treaty shall bear international responsibility for national activities in outer space, including the moon and other celestial bodies, whether such activities are carried on by governmental agencies or by non-governmental entities, and for assuring that national activities are carried out in conformity with the provisions set forth in the present Treaty. The activities of non-governmental entities in outer space, including the moon and other celestial bodies, shall require authorization and continuing supervision by the State concerned. When activities are carried on in outer space, including the moon and other celestial bodies, by an international organization, responsibility for compliance with this Treaty shall be borne both by the international organization and by the States Parties to the Treaty participating in such organization.

Article VII

Each State Party to the Treaty that launches or procures the launching of an object into outer space, including the moon and other celestial bodies, and each State Party from whose territory or facility an object is launched, is internationally liable for damage to another State Party to the Treaty or to its natural or juridical persons by such object or its component parts on the Earth, in air space or in outer space, including the moon and other celestial bodies.

Article VIII

A State Party to the Treaty on whose registry an object launched into outer space is carried shall retain jurisdiction and control over such object, and over any personnel thereof, while in outer space or on a celestial body. Ownership of objects launched into outer space, including objects landed or constructed on a celestial body, and of their component parts, is not affected by their presence in outer space or on a celestial body or by their return to the Earth. Such objects or component parts found beyond the limits of the State Party to the Treaty on whose registry they are carried shall be returned to that State, which shall, upon request, furnish identifying data prior to their return.

Article IX

In the exploration and use of outer space, including the moon and other celestial bodies, States Parties to the Treaty shall be guided by the principle of co-operation and mutual assistance and shall conduct all their activities in outer space, including the moon and other celestial bodies, with due regard to the corresponding interests of all other States Parties to the Treaty. States Parties to the Treaty shall pursue studies of outer space, including the moon and other celestial bodies, and conduct exploration of them so as to avoid their harmful contamination and also adverse changes in the environment of the Earth resulting from the introduction of extra-terrestrial matter and, where necessary, shall adopt appropriate measures for this purpose. If a State Party to the Treaty has reason to believe than an activity or experiment planned by its or its nationals in outer space, including the moon and other celestial bodies, would cause potentially harmful interference with activities of other States Parties in the peaceful exploration and use of outer space, including the moon and other celestial bodies, it shall undertake appropriate international consultations before proceeding with any such activity or experiment. A State Party to the Treaty which has reason to believe that an activity or experiment planned by another State Party in outer space, including the moon and other celestial bodies, would cause potentially harmful interference with activities in the peaceful exploration and use of outer space, including the moon and other celestial bodies, may request consultation concerning the activity or experiment.

Article X

In order to promote international co-operation in the exploration and use of outer space, including the moon and other celestial bodies, in conformity with the purposes of this Treaty, the States Parties to the Treaty shall consider on a basis of equality any requests by other States Parties to the Treaty to be afforded an opportunity to observe the flight of space objects launched by those States.

The nature of such an opportunity for observation and the conditions under which it could be afforded shall be determined by agreement between the States concerned.

Article XI

In order to promote international co-operation in the peaceful exploration and use of outer space, States Parties to the Treaty conducting activities in outer space, including the moon and other celestial bodies, agree to inform the Secretary-General of the United Nations as well as the public and the international scientific community, to the greatest extent feasible and practical, of the nature, conduct, locations and results of such activities. On receiving the said information, the Secretary-General of the United Nations should be prepared to disseminate it immediately and effectively.

Article XII

All stations, installations, equipment and space vehicles on the moon and other celestial bodies shall be open to representatives of other States Parties to the Treaty on a basis of reciprocity. Such representatives shall give reasonable advance notice of a projected visit, in order that appropriate consultations may be held and that maximum precautions may be taken to assure safety and to avoid interference with normal operations in the facility to be visited.

Article XIII

The provisions of this Treaty shall apply to the activities of States Parties to the Treaty in the exploration and use of outer space, including the moon and other celestial bodies, whether such activities are carried on by a single State Party to the Treaty or jointly with other States, including cases where they are carried on within the framework of international inter-governmental organizations.

Any practical questions arising in connexion with activities carried on by international inter-governmental organizations in the explorations and use of outer space, including the moon and other celestial bodies, shall be resolved by the States Parties to the Treaty either with the appropriate international organization or with one or more States members of that international organization, which are Parties to this Treaty.

Article XIV

1. This Treaty shall be open to all States for signature. Any State which does not sign this Treaty before its entry into force in accordance with paragraph 3 of this article may accede to it at any time.

2. This Treaty shall be subject to ratification by signatory States. Instruments of ratification and instruments of accession shall be deposited with the Governments of the Union of Soviet Socialist Republics, the United Kingdom of Great Britain and Northern Ireland and the United States of America, which are hereby designated the Depositary Governments.

3. This Treaty shall enter into force upon the deposit of instruments of ratification by five Governments including the Governments designated as Depositary Governments under this Treaty.

4. For States whose instruments of ratification or accession are deposited subsequent to the entry into force of this Treaty, it shall enter into force on the date of the deposit of their instruments of ratification or accession.

5. The Depositary Governments shall promptly inform

all signatory and acceding States of the date of each signature, the date of deposit of each instrument of ratification of and accession to this Treaty, the date of its entry into force and other notices.

6. This Treaty shall be registered by the Depositary Governments pursuant to Article 102 of the Charter of the United Nations.

Article XV

Any State Party to the Treaty may propose amendments to this Treaty. Amendments shall enter into force for each State Party to the Treaty accepting the amendments upon their acceptance by a majority of the States Parties to the Treaty and thereafter for each remaining State Party to the Treaty on the date of acceptance by it.

Article XVI

Any State Party to the Treaty may give notice of its withdrawal from the Treaty one year after its entry into force by written notification to the Depositary Governments. Such withdrawal shall take effect one year from the date of receipt of this notification.

Article XVII

This Treaty, of which the Chinese, English, French, Russian and Spanish texts are equally authentic, shall be deposited in the archives of the Depositary Governments. Duly certified copies of this Treaty shall be transmitted by the Depositary Governments to the Governments of the signatory and acceding States.

IN WITNESS WHEREOF the undersigned, duly authorized, have signed this Treaty.

DONE in ______________________, at the cities of London, Moscow and Washington, the _______ day of ________ one thousand nine hundred and ___________________.

1. Department of State Bulletin, December 26, 1966, pp. 953-955.

UNITED NATIONS GENERAL ASSEMBLY

PROPOSAL FOR A DECLARATION AND TREATY RESERVING THE SEA BED AND OCEAN FLOOR BEYOND TERRITORIAL LIMITS FOR PEACEFUL PURPOSES AND USE IN THE INTERESTS OF MANKIND

Note Verbale from the Permanent Mission of Malta to the United Nations addressed to the Secretary-General[1]

August 17, 1967

The Permanent Mission of Malta to the United Nations presents its compliments to the Secretary-General of the United Nations and has the honour to propose under rule 14 of the rules of procedure of the General Assembly the inclusion of the following item in the agenda of the twenty-second session of the General Assembly: "Declaration and treaty concerning the reservation exclusively for peaceful purposes of the sea-bed and of the ocean floor, underlying the seas beyond the limits of present national jurisdiction, and the use of their resources in the interests of mankind."

An explanatory memorandum is attached in accordance with rule 20 of the Rules of Procedure.

MEMORANDUM

1. The sea-bed and the ocean floor are estimated to constitute approximately five-sevenths of the world's area. The sea-bed and ocean floor, underlying the seas outside present territorial waters and/or the continental shelves, are the only areas of our planet which have not yet been appropriated for national use, because they have been relatively inaccessible and their use for defence purposes or the economic exploitation of their resources was not technologically feasible.

2. In view of the rapid progress in the development of new techniques by technologically advanced countries, it is feared that the situation will change and that the sea-bed and the ocean floor, underlying the seas beyond present national jurisdiction, will become progressively and competitively subject to national appropriation and use. This is likely to result in the militarization of the accessible ocean floor through the establishment of fixed military installations and in the exploitation and depletion of resources of immense potential

benefit to the world, for the national advantage of technologically developed countries.

3. It is, therefore, considered that the time has come to declare the sea-bed and the ocean floor a common heritage of mankind and that immediate steps should be taken to draft a treaty embodying, _inter alia_, the following principles:

(a) The sea-bed and the ocean floor, underlying the seas beyond the limits of present national jurisdiction, are not subject to national appropriation in any manner whatsoever;
(b) The exploration of the sea-bed and of the ocean floor, underlying the seas beyond the limits of present national jurisdiction, shall be undertaken in a manner consistent with the Principles and Purposes of the Charter of the United Nations;
(c) The use of the sea-bed and of the ocean floor, underlying the seas beyond the limits of present national jurisdiction, and their economic exploitation shall be undertaken with the aim of safeguarding the interests of mankind. The net financial benefits derived from the use and exploitation of the sea-bed and of the ocean floor shall be used primarily to promote the development of poor countries;
(d) The sea-bed and the ocean floor, underlying the seas beyond the limits of present national jurisdiction, shall be reserved exclusively for peaceful purposes in perpetuity.

4. It is believed that the proposed treaty should envisage the creation of an international agency (a) to assume jurisdiction, as a trustee for all countries, over the sea-bed and the ocean floor, underlying the seas beyond the limits of present national jurisdiction; (b) to regulate, supervise and control all activities thereon; and (c) to ensure that the activities undertaken conform to the principles and provisions of the proposed treaty.

1. U.N. Document A/6695. 18 August 1967.

STATEMENT BY AMBASSADOR ARTHUR J. GOLDBERG,

U.S. REPRESENTATIVE TO THE UNITED NATIONS,

ON RESERVATION OF SEA-BED AND OCEAN FLOOR

December 18, 1967[1]

Mr. President, the resolution before us marks the first major step by the United Nations in a realm of great significance to all members of this Organization. I would like to take this opportunity to reemphasize the position of my country on this very important matter.

First, we believe that the prospects of rich harvest and mineral wealth both in the deep oceans and on the deep ocean floors must not be allowed to create a new form of competition among marine nations.

Second, my nation believes that the nations of the world should take steps to assure that there will be no race among nations to grab and hold the lands under the high seas. The deep ocean floor should not be allowed to become a stage for competing claims of national sovereignty.

Third, we must ensure that the oceans and the deep ocean bottoms remain, as they are, the legacy of all human beings; and that the deep ocean floor will be open to exploration and use by all states, without discrimination.

Fourth, my nation stands ready to join with all other nations to achieve these objectives in peace and under law.

My country supports the resolution to establish an *ad hoc* committee as a first step in this direction.

We believe that the study which the committee is asked to prepare will constitute a most useful basis for future decisions of the General Assembly. We particularly hope that the 23rd General Assembly, as the result of the work of this *ad hoc* committee, will be in a position to establish a Committee on the Oceans with a broad mandate to develop law and to promote international cooperation with respect to the ocean and ocean floor. There is no question that there are many complex and difficult problems -- political, legal, scientific, and economic -- which are involved in this matter. But I want to make it clear to the General Assembly that I believe the members of the United Nations, working together, can overcome these problems, just as they have overcome equally complex problems in similar areas in the past.

When we made our first proposal for an Outer Space Committee in 1958, there were also many complexities involved. But we now have an important treaty in this area, the Outer Space Treaty, which is the result of the work of the Outer Space Committee. And we now have before us the report of this Committee recommending a second important agreement to this Assembly for approval -- the Agreement on Assistance to and Return of Astronauts and Space Vehicles.

This agreement is another major accomplishment, and a testimonial to what the members of the United Nations can achieve, working together, on even the most difficult problems.

In reviewing the debate leading to the draft resolution calling for an _ad hoc_ committee to study matters relating to the sea-bed and ocean floor, I should like to note several points which emerged from the extensive discussions of the matter in the First Committee.

There is a common appreciation of the complexity of this question and of the importance of the General Assembly proceeding with care in addressing the scientific, technical, legal, economic and arms control issues involved. There is also a general appreciation of the importance of advancing international cooperation in the exploration and use of the ocean and ocean floor. These realizations should permit us to move ahead, carefully but with all deliberate speed -- just as we moved ahead carefully but surely in our consideration of Outer Space.

Finally, because it marks the first step by the General Assembly in a highly complex field, and because the question of the future regime of the ocean floor is a matter of great concern to all nations, we believe it is generally agreed that the principle of consensus be established from the outset. I am sure all members will recall that this was the procedure followed by the Outer Space Committee -- and that this procedure has not precluded steady progress, important agreements, and beneficial results.

In mentioning the achievements of the Outer Space Committee, I would not wish to imply that the problems and opportunities of the oceans and of outer space are perfectly analogous. Obviously, they are not. The oceans are close at hand; outer space extends beyond us to infinity. Man has travelled and fished on the surface of the oceans since the earliest days of history; outer space, until recently, has remained totally unexplored. And the oceans, which are already being used commercially by man, with rich prospects of food and mineral wealth awaiting further exploration and development, are far more valuable economically than outer space.

Yet both outer space and the sea, through science and technology, promise much to mankind; and both require, the fulfillment of that promise, that we the nations of this world, through this Organization, address ourselves to our tasks in cooperation and not in conflict.

For this reason my Delegation strongly supports the resolution to establish this _ad hoc_ committee, as the first major step by the United Nations -- a step of historical importance -- to help mankind develop and make full use of the great benefits which lie in and under the great oceans of the earth.

In closing, my Delegation would like to pay tribute to the Government of Malta and to its distinguished representative, whose initiative brought this important matter to the attention of the Assembly.

1. Press Release, United States Mission to U.N., No. 250, December 18, 1967.

U.S. DRAFT RESOLUTION OF PRINCIPLES FOR DEEP OCEAN FLOOR

United Nations General Assembly, 1968 [1]

The General Assembly,

Desiring to encourage the exploration, use and development of the deep ocean floor to the fullest extent possible for the benefit and in the interest of all mankind,

Believing that such exploration and use of the deep ocean floor will contribute to international co-operation and understanding,

Convinced that no nation, regardless of geographical location, level of economic development, or technological capability, should be denied the opportunity to participate in the exploration and use of the deep ocean floor,

Conscious of the importance of promoting the general welfare of all peoples, and of furthering scientific study and the conservation of resources,

Reaffirming the traditional freedoms of the high seas under international law,

Recalling its resolution 2340 (XXII) of 18 December 1967,

Commends to States for their guidance the following principles concerning the deep ocean floor:

1. No State may claim or exercise sovereignty or sovereign rights over any part of the deep ocean floor. There shall be no discrimination in the availability of the deep ocean floor for exploration and use by all States and their nationals in accordance with international law;

2. There shall be established, as soon as practicable, internationally agreed arrangements governing the exploitation of resources of the deep ocean floor. These arrangements shall reflect the other principles contained in this Statement of Principles concerning the Deep Ocean Floor and shall include provision for:

(a) the orderly development of resources of the deep ocean floor in a manner reflecting the interest of the international community in the development of these resources;

(b) conditions conducive to the making of investments necessary for the exploration and exploitation of resources of the deep ocean floor;

(c) dedication as feasible and practicable of a portion of the value of the resources recovered from the deep ocean floor to international community purposes;

(d) accomodation among the commercial and other uses of the deep ocean floor and marine environment;

3. Taking into account the Geneva Convention of 1958 on the Continental Shelf, there shall be established, as soon as practicable, an internationally agreed precise boundary for the deep ocean floor - the sea-bed and subsoil beyond that over which coastal States may exercise sovereign rights for the purpose of exploration and exploitation of its natural resources;

Exploitation of the natural resources of the ocean floor that occurs prior to establishment of the boundary shall be understood not to prejudice its location, regardless of whether the coastal State considers the exploitation to have occurred on its "continental shelf";

4. States and their nationals shall conduct their activities on the deep ocean floor in accordance with international law, including the Charter of the United Nations, and in the interest of maintaining international peace and security and promoting international co-operation, scientific knowledge, and economic development;

5. In order to further international co-operation in the scientific investigation of the deep ocean floor, States shall:

(a) disseminate, in a timely fashion, plans for and results of national scientific programmes concerning the deep ocean floor;

(b) encourage their nationals to follow similar practices concerning dissemination of such information;

(c) encourage co-operative scientific activities regarding the deep ocean floor by personnel of different States;

6. In the exploration and use of the deep ocean floor States and their nationals:

(a) shall have reasonable regard for the interests of other States and their nationals;

(b) shall avoid unjustifiable interference with the exercise of the freedom of the high seas by other States and their nationals, or with the conservation of the living resources of the seas, and any interference with fundamental scientific research carried out with the intention of open publication;

(c) shall adopt appropriate safeguards so as to minimize pollution of the seas and disturbance of the existing biological, chemical and physical processes and balances;

Each State shall provide timely announcement and any necessary amplifying information of any marine activity or experiment planned by it or its nationals that could harmfully interfere with the activities of any other State or its nationals in the exploration and use of the deep ocean floor. A State which has reason to believe that a marine activity or experiment planned by another State or its nationals could harmfully interfere with its activities or those of its nationals in the exploration and use of the deep ocean floor may request consultation concerning the activity or experiment;

7. States and their nationals shall render all possible assistance to one another in the event of accident, distress or emergency arising out of activities on the deep ocean floor.

1. U.N. Doc. A/AC,135/25. 28 June 1968. Ad Hoc Committee to Study the Peaceful Uses of the Sea-Bed and the Ocean Floor beyond the Limits of National Jurisdiction.

UNITED NATIONS RESOLUTION ESTABLISHING A COMMITTEE ON PEACEFUL USES OF THE SEA-BED AND THE OCEAN FLOOR BEYOND THE LIMITS OF NATIONAL JURISDICTION

United Nations General Assembly, December 21, 1968[1]

The General Assembly,

Recalling the item entitled "Examination of the question of the reservation exclusively for peaceful purposes of the sea-bed and the ocean floor, and the subsoil thereof, underlying the high seas beyond the limits of present national jurisdiction, and the use of their resources in the interests of mankind",

Having in mind its resolution 2340 (XXII) of 18 December 1967 concerned with the problems arising in the area to which the title of the item refers,...

Considering that it is important to promote international cooperation for the exploration and exploitation of the resources of this area,

Convinced that such exploitation should be carried out for the benefit of mankind as a whole, irrespective of the geographical location of States, taking into account the special interests and needs of the developing countries,

Considering that it is essential to provide, within the United Nations system, a focal point for the elaboration of desirable measures of international cooperation, taking into account alternative actual and potential uses of this area, and for the coordination of the activities of international organizations in this regard,

1. Establishes a Committee on the Peaceful Uses of the Sea-Bed and the Ocean Floor beyond the Limits of National Jurisdiction, composed of forty-two States;

2. Instructs the Committee:

(a) To study the elaboration of the legal principles and norms which would promote international cooperation in the exploration and use of the sea-bed and the ocean floor and the subsoil thereof beyond the limits of national jurisdiction and to ensure the exploitation of their resources for the benefit of mankind, and the economic and other requirements which such a regime should satisfy in order to meet the interests of humanity as a whole;

(b) To study the ways and means of promoting the exploitation and use of the resources of this area, and of international cooperation to that end, taking into account the foreseeable development of technology and the economic implications of such exploitation and bearing in mind the fact that such exploitation should benefit mankind as a whole;

(c) To review the studies carried out in the field of exploration and research in this area and aimed at intensifying international cooperation and stimulating the exchange and the widest possible dissemination of scientific knowledge on the subject;

(d) To examine proposed measures of cooperation to be adopted by the international community in order to prevent the marine pollution which may result from the exploration and exploitation of the resources of this area;

3. Also call upon the Committee to study further, within the context of the title of the item, and taking into account the studies and international negotiations being undertaken in the field of disarmament, the reservation exclusively for peaceful purposes of the sea-bed and the ocean floor without prejudice to the limits which may be agreed upon in this respect;

4. Requests the Committee:

(a) To work in close cooperation with the specialized agencies, the International Atomic Energy Agency and the intergovernmental bodies dealing with the problems referred to in the present resolution, so as to avoid any duplication or overlapping of activities;

(b) To make recommendations to the General Assembly on the questions mentioned in paragraphs 2 and 3 above;

(c) In cooperation with the Secretary-General, to submit to the General Assembly reports on its activities at each subsequent session;

5. Invites the specialized agencies, the International Atomic Energy Agency and other intergovernmental bodies,

including the Intergovernmental Oceanographic Commission of the United Nations Educational, Scientific and Cultural Organization, to cooperate fully with the Committee in the implementation of the present resolution.

1. U.N. Document 2467 A (XXIII). Adopted by a vote of 112 in favour to none against, with 7 abstentions, December 21, 1968.

UNITED NATIONS RESOLUTION FOR STUDY OF MACHINERY ON USE OF RESOURCES OF THE SEA-BED AND OCEAN FLOOR

United Nations General Assembly, December 21, 1968[1]

The General Assembly,

Having Considered the item entitled "Examination of the question of the reservation exclusively for peaceful purposes of the sea-bed and the ocean floor, and the subsoil thereof, underlying the high seas beyond the limits of present national jurisdiction, and the use of their resources in the interests of mankind,"

Reaffirming that exploration and exploitation of the resources of the sea-bed and the ocean floor, and the subsoil thereof, should be carried out for the benefit of mankind as a whole, taking into special consideration the interests and needs of the developing countries,

Recalling that international cooperation in this field is of paramount importance,...

1. Requests the Secretary-General to undertake a study on the question of establishing in due time appropriate international machinery for the promotion of the exploration and exploitation of the resources of this area, and the use of these resources in the interests of mankind, irrespective of the geographical location of States, and taking into special consideration the interests and needs of the developing countries, and to submit a report thereon to the Committee on the Peaceful Uses of the Sea-bed and the Ocean Floor beyond the Limits of National Jurisdiction for consideration during one of its sessions in 1969;

2. Calls upon the Committee to submit a report on this question to the General Assembly at its twenty-fourth session.

1. U.N. Document 2467 C (XXIII). Adopted by a vote of 85 in favour to 9 against, with 25 abstentions, December 21, 1968. The Soviet Union voted against the resolution; the United States and other principal maritime states abstained.

UNITED NATIONS RESOLUTION ENDORSING INTERNATIONAL DECADE OF OCEAN EXPLORATION

United Nations General Assembly, December 21, 1968[1]

The General Assembly,

Convinced that the nations of the world should join together, with due respect for national jurisdiction, in a common long-term programme of exploration of the ocean as a potential source of resources, which should eventually be used for meeting the needs of all mankind with due recognition of those of developing countries and irrespective of the geographical location of States,

Recalling also that in its resolution 2172 (XXI) of 6 December 1966 it requested the Secretary-General to prepare proposals for ensuring the most effective arrangements for an expanded programme of international cooperation to assist in a better understanding of the marine environment through science, and to initiating and strengthening marine education and training programmes,...

1. Welcomes the concept of an International Decade of Ocean Exploration to be undertaken within the framework of a long-term programme of research and exploration, including scientific research and exploration of the sea-bed and the ocean floor, under the aegis of the United Nations, on the understanding that all such activities falling under the national jurisdiction of a State shall be subject to the previous consent of such State, in accordance with international law;

2. Invites Member States to formulate proposals for national and international scientific programmes and agreed activities to be undertaken during the Decade with due regard to the interests of developing countries, to transmit these proposals to the United Nations Educational, Scientific and Cultural Organization for the Intergovernmental Oceanographic Commission in time to begin the Decade in 1970, and to embark on such activities as soon as practicable;

3. Urges Member States to publish as soon as practicable the results of all activities which they will have undertaken within the framework of the Decade as part of a long-term coordinated programme of scientific research and exploration, and at the same time to communicate these results to the Intergovernmental Oceanographic Commission;...

1. U.N. Document 2467 D (XXIII). Adopted by the General Assembly without objection, December 21, 1968.

DRAFT TREATY BANNING NUCLEAR WEAPONS ON THE OCEAN FLOOR

Joint Proposal of the United States and the Soviet Union to the United Nations General Assembly, 1969[1]

The states parties to this treaty, recognizing the common interest of mankind in the progress of the exploration and use of the seabed and the ocean floor for peaceful purposes;

Considering that the prevention of a nuclear arms race on the seabed and the ocean floor serves the interests of maintaining world peace, reduces international tensions, and strengthens friendly relations among states;

Convinced that this treaty constitutes a step toward the exclusion of the seabed, the ocean floor and the subsoil thereof, from the arms race, and determined to continue negotiations concerning further measures leading to this end;

Convinced that this treaty constitutes a step toward a treaty on general and complete disarmament under strict and effective international control, and determined to continue negotiations to this end;

Convinced that this treaty will further the purposes and principles of the Charter of the United Nations, in a manner consistent with the principles of international law and without infringing the freedoms of the high seas;

Have agreed as follows:

ARTICLE I

1. The states parties to this treaty undertake not to emplant or emplace on the seabed and the ocean floor and in the subsoil thereof beyond the maximum contiguous zone provided for in the 1958 Geneva Convention on the Territorial Sea and the Contiguous Zone any objects with nuclear weapons or any other types of weapons of mass destruction, as well as structures, launching installations or any other facilities specifically designed for storing, testing or using such weapons.

2. The states parties to this treaty undertake not to assist, encourage or induce any state to commit actions prohibited by this treaty and not to participate in any other way in such actions.

ARTICLE II

1. For the purpose of this treaty the outer limit of the contiguous zone referred to in Article I shall be measured in accordance with the provisions of Section II of the 1958 Geneva Convention on the Territorial Sea and the Contiguous Zone and in accordance with international law.

2. Nothing in this treaty shall be interpreted as supporting or prejudicing the position of any state party with respect to rights or claims which such state party may assert, or with respect to recognition or non-recognition of rights of claims asserted by any other state, related to waters off its coasts, or to the seabed and the ocean floor.

ARTICLE III

1. In order to promote the objectives and insure the observance of the provisions of this treaty, the states parties to the treaty shall have the right to verify the activities of other states parties to the treaty on the seabed and the ocean floor and in the subsoil thereof beyond the maximum contiguous zone, referred to in Article II, if these activities raise doubts concerning the fulfillment of the obligations assumed under this treaty, without interfering with such activities or otherwise infringing rights recognized under international law, including the freedoms of the high seas.

2. The right of verification recognized by the states parties in Paragraph 1 of this article may be exercised by any state party using its own means or with the assistance of any other state party.

3. The states parties to the treaty undertake to consult and to cooperate with a view to removing doubts concerning the fulfillment of the obligations assumed under this treaty.

ARTICLE IV

Any state party to the treaty may propose amendments to this treaty. Amendments must be approved by a majority of the votes of all the states parties the the treaty, including those of all the states parties to this treaty possessing nuclear weapons, and shall enter into force for each state party to the treaty accepting such amendments upon their acceptance by a majority of the states parties to the treaty, including the states which possess nuclear weapons and are parties to this treaty. Thereafter the amendments shall enter into force for any other party to the treaty after it has accepted such amendments.

ARTICLE V

Each party to this treaty shall in exercising its national sovereignty have the right to withdraw from this treaty if it decides that extraordinary events related to the subject matter of this treaty have jeopardized the supreme interests of its country. It shall give notice of such withdrawal to all other parties to the treaty and to the United Nations Security Council three months in advance. Such notice shall include a statement of the extraordinary events it considers to have jeopardized its supreme interests.

ARTICLE VI

1. This treaty shall be open for signature to all states. Any state which does not sign the treaty before its entry into force in accordance with Paragraph 3 of this Article may accede to it at any time.

2. This treaty shall be subject to ratification by signatory states. Instruments of ratification and of accession shall be deposited with the governments of ..., which are hereby designated the depositary governments.

3. This treaty shall enter into force after the deposit of instruments of ratification by twenty-two governments, including the governments designated as depositary governments of this treaty.

4. For states whose instruments of ratification or accession are deposited after the entry into force of this treaty it shall enter into force on the date of the deposit of their instruments of ratification or accession.

5. The depositary governments shall forthwith notify the governments of all states signatory and acceding to this treaty of the date of each signature, of the date of deposit of each instrument of ratification or of accession, of the date of the entry into force of this treaty, and of the receipt of other notices.

6. This treaty shall be registered by the depositary governments pursuant to Article 102 of the Charter of the United Nations.

ARTICLE VII

This treaty, the English, Russian, French, Spanish and Chinese texts of which are equally authentic, shall be deposited in the archives of the depositary governments.

Duly certified copies of this treaty shall be transmitted by the depositary governments to the governments of the states signatory and acceding thereto.

IN WITNESS WHEREOF the undersigned, being duly authorized thereto, have signed this treaty.

DONE in ___________ at ___________ this __________ day of _________.

1. Text from Department of State Bulletin, Vol. XLI, No. 1584, November 3, 1969, pp. 367-368.

NEED FOR COASTAL ZONE MANAGEMENT - NEW PROBLEM FOR POLICY

Photo by Author

CHAPTER TEN

POLITICAL PROCESS AND THE FUTURE OF NATIONAL OCEAN POLICY

Introductory Note

The preceding chapters have dealt with a series of questions relating to increased utilization of the oceans.

Many activities concerning the seas are responses to historic policies. They seek to learn more about the forces at work within the oceans, to obtain larger yields of food, and to promote commerce.

Activities involving extensive applications of modern technology are more especially associated with recently crystalized objectives. These speak to the need to supplement dwindling mineral resources on land, to advance economic growth, and to further national security.

The different capabilities of states to apply modern technology and engineering to the use of the oceans represent another dimension of the problem at the international level. This is expressed in the demand voiced by many developing countries to have the United Nations take control of the deep sea beds, to license exploitation of mineral resources found therein, and to require a sharing either of the resources extracted therefrom or of the income received with the poorer countries for their advancement.

We have endeavored in each chapter to relate the clusters of issues arising from renewed interest and activity in the sea to national policies and international agreements. The ocean engineer cannot afford to overlook these associations, for he operates in an environment that is uniquely sensitive to national interest and the exercise of power. Wherever he functions, whether in territorial waters, on the continental shelf, or on the high seas, his installations, designs and structures must conform to standards laid down by states. They can be subjected to inspections and procurement of approval. And some body of national or international law will follow the engineer wherever he goes. Furthermore, activities leading to exploitation of the resources of the sea, harnessing the forces of the oceans, or simply experimenting with new installations, craft or structures, are usually encompassed within the general framework of policy interests of his own or other states.

As a national of one country he may be excluded from working in the territorial waters or on the continental shelf of another country without its consent. Upon and under the high seas he remains subject to the laws of his own country. His vessels are obliged to navigate according to agreed rules of the road, to observe safety, registration and inspection requirements. He may be penalized for failing to observe the terms of treaties which his government has entered into with others. He is liable for torts committed upon the seas and may be brought before courts of admiralty of his own or other countries into which he may go for damages resulting from marine accidents in which he has been involved.

The jurisdictional bounds of states are often not defined with precision at the sea frontier where contiguous zones merge into the high seas. There is likewise a considerable measure of uncertainty surrounding the limits of national jurisdiction on the continental shelves. Lawyers and engineers continue to debate whether the "outer edge" of the shelf is to be regarded as the point at which the land dips off sharply into the abyssal deep, or whether it is where the shelf land mass touches the deep ocean floor. The issue is not likely to be resolved soon due to the fundamental differences of viewpoint that prevail with respect to the treatment of this geosubmarine feature. Delimitation of the boundary by treaty is admittedly the desirable course. This will probably be delayed, however, until practice has revealed further the nature of the assets located on the outer slope and rise. Meanwhile, this is an issue of some urgency for national policy while debate continues at the United Nations.

As the United States moves to achieve the objectives set forth in the Marine Resources and Engineering Development Act, and other legislation, it is necessary to view these activities in the perspective of overall policy objectives, and to order priorities.

Some of the activities undertaken since 1966 are basically continuations of activities begun long ago. These include such things as surveying the seas, placing aids to navigation, encouraging commercial fisheries, promoting the construction of a fast, efficient merchant fleet, strengthening the national defense, and negotiating treaties to assure Americans most favored nation treatment. Other activities represent attempts to capitalize upon targets of opportunity. These include support for education and training under the Sea Grant Projects, and establishing fish protein processing plants. Still others speak to longer run objectives such as supplementing supplies of strategic and critical raw materials, developing capability for living and working in the cold, dark environment of the deep seas, learning how to build and maintain platforms and structures in the ocean abyss, perfecting new means of propulsion and carriage of goods by sea, and multiplying the production of edible living resources of the sea.

In looking forward to the progressive achievement of these and other objectives of national policy, it is essential to bear in mind that this policy does not stand alone. It is in continual competition with other Government enterprises for funds, trained manpower, authorizations, and equipment. It functions in the marketplace of politics for Presidential and public backing,and for Congressional approval of needed legislation and funds. Although it is sure to have backing from some quarters, it is nonetheless a rival to other major projects which enjoy strong backing from other quarters. Seemingly unrelated matters such as housing and poverty, urban renewal, agricultural support, foreign aid and national defense all operate in the same mart and must compete for portions of the national income.

Gaining and holding the necessary support within Government requires much thought and the cultivation of carefully planned contacts. Furthermore, the program must anticipate needs several years in advance and demonstrate bold leadership. Success in the political process depends upon having a firm groundwork of support when hearings are held and crucial votes are called for on the floor of Congress. Courtesies to key members of the Congress, letters to professional friends and associates, performance of missions for influential clients, care in responding to Presidential requests for information, invitations to vital officials and Congressmen to visit new installations or to journey on new vessels. - All these are important steps to cultivating a favorable climate of opinion that will help carry votes in the right directions when the tallies are taken. To insure the maximum measure of continuity attention must also be given to the press and to a high level of publications.

To maintain progress amid the foibles of such a process requires the mounting of a major effort each year. Imaginative, well-reasoned suggestions must be forwarded to the White House for inclusion in the annual State of the Union address of the President. Exhaustively-prepared estimates must be submitted for the Budget message and defended before the Director of the Budget. Subsequently, administrators must testify before Congressional hearings on their programs, on requests for appropriations and authorizations, and on proposals for additional legislative enactments.

Emerging successfully from this array of reviews entails having taken a prior long look at where an agency or program is going, what it seeks to attain, and how the various parts mesh together. Emphasis must be placed on the most important items to enable the leadership of the country to chart a reasonable course over a period of several years.

The readings that follow have been chosen for their emphasis upon items which their authors believe merit priority over the next decade. Different viewers are bound to see matters from somewhat different perspectives depending upon the guidlines of their choice.

As we survey the ocean scene from the present stance, it appears to us that the following elements of the national program merit priority treatment during the next decade:

1. Study of deep ocean use, including vehicles, structures and platforms of various kinds; metals and their reactions to sea floor forces; power for deep water tasks;

life support and rescue systems; improved search and recovery capabilities.

2. Continental shelf utilization, including accurate mapping; investigation of mineral and fossil fuel properties and potentials; developing of mining techniques and equipment; study of the legal and political problems associated with use of the shelves and enaction of necessary additional legislation; consideration of the questions of a new ocean regime.

3. Atlantic Ridge surveys to determine in detail the properties of this significant phenomenon; examination of signs of continental drift and plotting of future estimated movements, if any.

4. Marine biology,including the effects of mining operations and pollutants of various kinds upon marine life; experimentation with aquaculture and various types of electronic and sonic "fences" for retaining fish within fixed bounds.

5. Communications within the seas, as well as study of submarine sounds.

6. Underwater soil mechanics studies on the effects of earthquakes, tidal waves, and seismic forces; study of the formation of seamounts.

7. Improved weather and tsunami forecasting, together with coastal protections from the destructive effects of waves and storms.

8. Promotion of graduate education in ocean engineering,

and advanced research on oceanology with large Federal inputs.

9. Extended study of ocean currents, their regenerative forces, and the problems of beach and estuarial erosion.

10. Air-sea interchanges and the forces affecting the paths of storms, the shifting of currents, and the modifications of climates.

Finally, no catalogue of priority items would be complete without suggesting the need for on-going research on the oldest aspects of marine engineering, namely, the improvement of harbor and docking facilities; advancement in ship design; experiment with new forms of propulsion and radically new concepts of hull and superstructures; investigation of the possibilities of establishing port facilities on artificial islands; and research and development on problems associated with naval defense forces.

We assume that the seas will continue to serve mankind as they have for centuries through commerce, fishing, and as a base for sea power. Innovations in technology are bound, nevertheless, to alter the underpinning of concepts of the roles of the sea and the effects of new devices upon the relative power of nations.

Seen in the large, the political process is both an instrumentality for producing change, and a medium for gaining strength with which to shape the future.

EFFECTIVE USE OF THE SEA

Report of the Panel on Oceanography

President's Science Advisory Committee

June 1966

Findings and Recommendations

National Goals. The oceans' importance to national security, considered in the widest possible sense, requires that goals for the Nation's ocean program be clearly stated and that the program be oriented toward meeting these goals. The Panel therefore recommends that the President state the ultimate objective of the national ocean program as being effective use of the sea by man for all purposes currently considered for the terrestrial environment: commerce; industry, recreation and settlement; as well as for knowledge and understanding. This objective implies four specific goals:

1. Acquiring the ability to predict and ultimately control phenomena affecting the safety and economy of seagoing activities.

2. Undertaking measures required for fullest exploitation of resources represented by, in and under the sea.

3. Utilizing the sea to enhance national security.

4. Pursuing scientific investigations for describing and understanding marine phenomena, processes and resources.

Role of the Federal Government. Great concern was evident within the private sector as to the Federal Government's proper role in developing the nation's ocean program. The Panel believes that division of effort among government, industry, and universities appropriate to land-based activities is advisable for the oceans and that the Federal Government should not preempt these activities to the extent it has, for example, in space. We recommend that the Government perform four functions in achieving the goals of the national ocean program:

1. Enunciate national policies concerning the marine interests of the United States.

2. Foster exploration, development and use of oceans and their resources through establishment of appropriate financial, legal, regulatory, enforcement and advisory institutions and measures.

3. Promote description and prediction of the marine environment and development of capabilities for its modification.

4. Initiate, support, and encourage programs of education, training, and research and provide technical services and facilities related to activities in pertinent sciences and technology.

These Federal functions are not new; however, only the last two functions are to any degree developed and coordinated across existing agency lines. Systematic development and application by a more centralized authority are required for efficient implementation of the first two functions.

Oceans and National Security. Increased Federal participation in ocean activities is required for national security. The developing strategic situation, which may require a much improved undersea deterrent force, coupled with the need for defenses against missile-launching submarines, implies that the Navy must develop the capability to operate anywhere within the oceans at any time. The Navy has underway a Deep Submergence Systems Project. This effort as presently constituted is insufficient if the Navy is to meet its goals in a reasonable time period. The Panel therefore recommends expansion of activities which will permit operation at any location and time within the oceans. It is recommended that a continuing, special effort be made by the Navy to utilize personnel, facilities and know-how of the private sector in achieving its objectives in the Deep Submergence Systems and Man in the Sea Projects. Navy technological results in these programs should be made available to industry upon acquisition.

The Navy presently has primary responsibility for development of capability for using man at depths in the oceans. The general level of research in the Man in the Sea Project is inadequate. Insufficient attention has been given to biomedical problems of survival in the wet, cold, dark, high-pressure environment, and our efforts in this field lag well behind those of other countries. If the goals of the Man in the Sea Project are to be achieved, adequate opportunities must be provided for basic studies by a variety of institutions. In particular we recommend establishment of a major shore facility fully equipped for the range of basic studies required by Man in the Sea. This facility should be associated with a university or medical research center. Navy efforts may need to be complemented through instrumented, movable, submersible laboratories for basic studies on man living beneath the sea's surface for extended periods. These laboratories should be available to a wide community of scholars outside the Navy who are interested in biomedical problems of man in the deep sea.

The Panel recognizes that development of adequate programs in undersea technology and Man in the Sea may be hampered by traditional views within the Navy to the effect that the Navy is primarily an operating force at or near the surface. If the Navy does not adequately pursue programs recommended in this report, program responsibilities for Man in the Sea and undersea technology should be shifted to a civilian agency.

The Thresher experience in 1963 and the recent lost nuclear weapon incident off the Spanish coast clearly illustrate the continuing importance of search-and-recovery capabilities. We recommend that ocean search-and-recovery missions related in any way to national security be the Navy's responsibility. However, the technology developed through such programs should be made available to industry on a current basis.

The Navy should have broad responsibilities in furthering ocean science and technology in addition to its problem-oriented research. Most of the technology developed for undersea operations within the Government will result from the Navy's efforts. An important need is development of a test range equipped with standardized stations at which components, systems, concepts, and materials can be critically tested. Such a range will be an expensive undertaking, though of great value to private industry and university research. We therefore recommend that a supporting role of the Navy should be provision of test facilities that are open to scientific and technological communities. Users would be expected to pay a prorated share of operating costs and depreciation, as is the case in other national facilities.

The Navy has maintained good relations with the academic oceanographic community, and, in turn, the community has frequently responded to the Navy's needs in rapid and effective manner. The successful bomb recovery operations off the Spanish coast are a recent, dramatic but typical example of this cooperation. Long-term support of academic oceanography through the ONR has been fruitful in the past, and we recommend that the Navy continue these programs. The total Navy commitment to ocean science and technology has almost doubled in fiscal year 1965-67, yet Navy support of basic research has remained constant. This situation cannot continue if the Navy is to make adequate use of new developments in ocean science and technology; therefore, the Panel recommends that Navy support of basic research in the oceans increase at a rate consonant with the total Navy program in ocean science and technology.

Marine Food Resources. In the civilian sector economic analyses --admittedly crude because of lack of adequate data and previous analyses -- suggest that activities related to improved weather prediction and the near-shore environment can be justified on economic grounds. No similar economic justification for development of marine food resources exists; however, the Panel recommends that development of marine food resources be given very high priority for other vitally important reasons.

A great public health problem is protein deficiency (it is the leading cause of death in the period between weaning and 5 years of age in certain countries). Proper long-range development of marine food resources requires numerous studies in marine biology. The protein-deficiency problem is so acute that efforts should be made to bypass therequirement for detailed understanding of means to obtain more food from the sea. New advances in development of marine food can greatly alleviate this problem, and we recommend expansion and improvement in technology for developing these resources and Government approval for human use of marine protein concentrate. Emphasis should be placed on development of this technology for export to underdeveloped countries in which malnutrition exists.

A program for the development of marine food resources offers a major opportunity for substantive international cooperation. Several countries, including Japan, U.S.S,R., and Norway, have advanced technologies for fishing. An international effort to further this technology and expand it to other marine food resources for the benefit of underdeveloped nations could be of major importance in achieving peace on earth. Such a program might be developed through auspices of the United Nations.

Preserving the Near-Shore Environment. Almost half our population lives near the margins of the oceans or the Great Lakes. The near-shore environment is thus of critical importance. This environment is being modified rapidly, by human activities, in ways that are unknown in detail but broadly are undesirable. Pollution, which renders beaches unsafe for swimmers, destroys valuable fisheries and generally degrades the coastline, is the chief modification. This problem is urgent, and dangers have not been adequately recognized. Specific recommendations cannot be made for solution of this serious problem because the research to date has been largely ineffectual.Therefore, the Panel recommends intensification of research in the area of pollution and pollution control.

Recommendations with regard to marine biology affect both the long-range goal of increasing marine food resources and preserving the near-shore environment. Specific recommendations are:

1. Intensive multidisciplinary studies of biological communities in marine habitats subject to human influence and exploitation. Such studies should include estuaries and the continental shelf.A very important, special case is the proposed sea level canal to join the Atlantic and Pacific Oceans.

2. Establishment of marine wilderness preserves to provide a baseline for future studies.

3. Construction of facilities needed for studying organisms in special marine environments such as the deep sea and tropics.

4. Increased encouragement and support of identification and use of marine organisms as tools for biomedical research and as potential sources of drugs.

5. Establishment of a national center for collection, maintenance, and distribution of living marine organisms for use in marine and biological research.

Unity of Environmental Sciences. Throughout its investigations the Panel has been impressed by the unity of environmental sciences. Methods of investigation, intellectual concepts and ways of analyzing data are remarkably alike in oceanography, meteorology and solid-earth physics. Educational, industrial, and governmental organizations for the most part have not taken advantage of this unity in developing their programs. The Panel's recommendations have been influenced to a large extent by similarities among these fields.

Research in Oceanography. The Panel finds that much research effort in marine biology and physical oceanog-

ADDITIONAL RESEARCH VESSELS NEEDED - ATLANTIS II

Courtesy Woods Hole Oceanographic Institution

raphy during the last 10 years has concerned surveys of the ocean, measuring "classical" quantities. Such surveys were important 50 and even 20 years ago in defining problems: however, the subject has advanced to the stage that well-defined problems are known to exist. The Panel recommends that emphasis be shifted from surveys to solutions of these problems. In section 6 a number of problems related to physical oceanography and marine biology are considered. A problem of great importance in physical oceanography both because of intrinsic scientific interest and possible contributions to security and commerce within the oceans is that of oceanic weather, weather being defined as fluctuations of temperature, pressure and current over a wide range of time and length scales. Major progress in this area can result from implementation of any of several buoy programs proposed heretofore. The Panel therefore recommends initiation of a step-by-step buoy program from detailed studies of limited regions to larger scale studies. A step-by-step program is necessary because buoy technology is not well developed.

Development of undersea technology will depend on understanding the boundary between the oceans and the solid earth. Recent studies show that physical processes at this boundary are complex, and there is little understanding of them. The Panel recommends that high priority be given to benthic-boundary study.

Education in Oceanography. Oceanographic education has been narrowly conceived and does not adequately recognize the importance of fundamental sciences in the subject's long-range development. The intellectual isolation of many oceanographic institutions needs to be corrected. Attempts should be made to associate oceanographic institutions with groups of universities to permit easy access by scientists and engineers throughout the country for work in ocean activities. The Panel questions the wisdom of granting Ph.D.'s in oceanography per se and feels education should be focused on a broad spectrum of environmental sciences, incorporating basic sciences. Many of the most active contributors to oceanography entered from other fields. This practice should be encouraged in the future, perhaps through special efforts in developing postdoctoral programs in oceanography.

As activities in the oceans increase, it is clear that there will be interaction between those interested in the science and technology of the sea and those interested in legal, social, and economic aspects. We therefore recommend establishment and funding of Marine Study Centers to examine a wide range of problems associated with activities in the sea but not to be degree-granting organizations. Research is particularly needed on economic aspects of ocean science and technology.

Ships for Oceanographic Research. A substantial portion of the personnel in numerous oceanographic institutions is concerned with administration and operation of ships. Ship time is more readily available to members of an institution than to scientists at universities and other organizations not directly connected with such an institution.

Within the institutions ship operations are no longer as flexible or as responsive to scientific objectives as they were 5 or 10 years ago. Operating costs of many ships are met by a conglomeration of grants and contracts. Because of administrative difficulties, we recommend comprehensive block-funding for oceanographic vessels. The funding should imply a commitment for the operating cost of the ship for its expected life. Operating moneys should be funded separately from the oceanographic project for which the ship is used.

Block-funding will facilitate more effective planning and scheduling of oceanographic ships. It does not, however, solve the problem of access to ships by qualified scientists regardless of institutional affiliations. Therefore, we recommend that oceanographic ships be grouped generally into regional fleets of reasonable size. Perhaps three or four such fleets would serve the Nation's needs. Fleets should be assigned to independent regional organizations representing user groups from oceanographic laboratories and universities. Every effort should be made to include in user groups those institutions which at present do not have formal activity in ocean science and technology.

Organization of Oceanography Within the Federal Government. No natural advocate for oceanography was found within the Federal establishment; responsibility for oceanography is diffused through a number of agencies. The Navy, of course, must maintain a strong oceanographic effort in order to meet its mission requirements. However, if the goal of effective use of the sea for all purposes now pursued on land is to be achieved, present methods of supporting civilian portions of the program are inadequate to the task, and basic revision of the system is necessary. In particular the Panel recommends that activities now in cluded in the Environmental Science Services Administration, Geological Survey (regarding land and ocean activities), Bureau of Commercial Fisheries, oceanographic activities of the Bureau of Mines, and a portion of the oceanographic activities of the Coast Guard be combined in a single agency. Such an agency would be competent to deal with the four governmental functions specified earlier. A reorganization of this type would recognize the fact that Federal activities related to description and prediction of the environment are very closely related, and one cannot sensibly separate the atmosphere from the oceans or the oceans from land. In addition, the ability to develop ocean resources and to use the oceans for commerce depends very heavily on our ability to describe and predict. There is thus an intimate connection between environmental sciences in providing services and development and use of ocean resources.

The Panel recommends that the Nation's oceanographic activities be supported in five ways:

1. By the NSF in its traditional role of supporting fundamental studies through grants and fellowships, with special emphasis on aspects that contribute to manpower education for ocean science and technology.

2. By the new agency in carrying out its responsibility for management of environment and ocean resources and for providing description and prediction services through a balanced program of direct participation and support of industry and universities.

3. By the Navy in discharging its mission of national security through its laboratories and industry and through ONR support of civilian institutions, as well as by its supporting role in the development of undersea technology and provision of national test facilities.

4. By agencies such as AEC and HEW in carrying out their missions.

5. By the Smithsonian Institution in fulfilling its major obligation to systematic biology.

Creation of a mission-oriented agency, with major responsibilities as previously stated, does not by itself provide a clear mechanism for coordination, planning and budgeting. Several agencies, the Navy and NSF in particular, will continue to have major responsibilities in ocean-oriented activities. The need for information interchange and dissemination now discharged by ICO will continue, and we recommend formation of an interagency group under the Federal Council for Science and Technology to provide services now rendered by ICO and the Interagency Committee on Atmospheric Sciences. This group should also have responsibilities for information interchange related to solid-earth sciences. It would thus link environmental science activities within the new agency to those in other agencies.

Budget allocations among the new agency, NSF, and the Navy would be made on a competitive basis, recognizing the mission responsibilities of the new agency and the Navy. The Federal Council, Bureau of the Budget, and Congress would all participate in the budgeting process. Although the proposed agency would not solve all problems of budgeting, it will provide a centralized authority with major mission responsibility.

Cost of Recommendations. We have not attempted to estimate costs of individual recommendations contained herein because more detailed studies will be required before such determinations can be made. Instead, we recommend a general increase of the nondefense component of the national oceaographic program from the present $120 million to $210 million by fis-al year 1971. This is based on foreseeable national needs for Federal services and support of marine science and technology. We do not propose a uniform expansion of the existing program; indeed, we believe some parts should be curtailed. We particuzrly recommend an increase in basic research and education support from about $15 million to at least $25 million by fiscal year 1971; these figures do not include cost of ships or other platforms.

The defense component of the oceanographic program will probably increase more than nondefense expenditures if these recommendations are implemented. The Navy needs large, expensive facilities for its program. Furthermore, we have charged it with construction and operation of facilities for other agencies, industry, and private research, and with continuing support of education and research. Under the circumstances a doubling of the present program by fiscal year 1971 would not be unexpected.

The total, therefore, would increase from $310 million in fiscal year 1967 to roughly $600 million in fiscal year 1971. Much of the nondefense increase would be devoted to economically promising programs or would support socially crucial ones.. ...

Priorities

The Panel has not attempted to offer a detailed blueprint of the national program from the oceans but believes it is essential to recognize a long-term goal which has been identified as the effective use of the sea. The Panel has examined opportunities in technology, science, education, and management vital to attaining this goal.

Ocean Science and Technology

The Panel assigns highest priority to those efforts in oceanography that deal with national security. The problems outlined in Section 5 [not reproduced here] clearly indicate need for developing the capability of operating anywhere in the oceans, either by manned or unmanned vehicles, at any time. We are a long way from achieving this capability. The Navy should continue to be the lead agency for that part which pertains to national security.

The Navy in its Deep Submergence Systems Project is making an intensive effort at achieving part of this capability. We give this program a high priority, and we feel it should be expanded, including extramural consultation and participation. The requirements for achieving the capability include:

1. Development of large working volumes at atmospheric pressure.

2. Development of tools, manipulators, and semi-remote-control power tools and support structures.

3. Development of small underwater systems having power plants in the 10- to 100-kw. range, which will require a greater emphasis on fuel-cell power systems than the Navy has so far supported.

4. Knowledge about the long-term effects of high pressures on man.

In terms of national security we feel high priority should be given to studies of the benthic boundary, since weapon systems of the future may be deployed on the ocean floor, and to basic studies of weather in the oceans at all scales. These studies are needed for construction and operation of undersea structures and are critical to the ASW problem.

We recommend that the Navy continue and expand its support of basic research through ONR. It has made highly successful contributions through research and education in the past, and we expect it to continue to do so in the future.

In the civilian sector the Panel gives highest priority to two related problem areas: Development of food resources and development of capability for environmental prediction.

The economic analysis in Section 7 suggests that greatest economic returns can be expected from progress in environmental prediction and control. For the oceans the field is still in the research stage, although sound conditions can be predicted to a limited degree in connection with ASW problems. The buoy programs... are given high priority by the Panel. This is based on scientific interest and on environmental-prediction need.... Buoys and related instrument development will provide essential data regarding weather in the oceans and the nature of the ocean-atmosphere interaction.

While development of food resources does not rate high on an economic basis, viewed strictly in domestic terms, it can contribute in a very major way to the Nation's international position.

The Panel assigns a very high priority to development of coastal regions for recreation and commerce; these functions will be possible only if the quality of the near-ocean environment is maintained and improved. The problems here are unusually complex, since they involve badly understood science, engineering with a high failure rate and a variety of legal and social problems. The Panel believes that standards of coastal engineering can be raised only by active participation of university groups. There is need to enhance research at CERC as well as at other laboratories.

The Panel gives low priority to continuing hydrographic surveys in their present form. Methods employed are outmoded, slow and are not responsive to user requirements. We believe that high priority should be assigned to development of survey technology ...

In the area of management the Panel believes the present administration of the Federal program is unacceptable, and major revisions are required if the country is to progress toward the goal of effective use of the sea. The Panel has outlined ... one possible reorganization scheme. This scheme appears logical to the Panel in view of the close interdependence of environmental sciences, resource development, use of the ocean and environmental description, and prediction. Because the proposed reorganization may create severe political problems, the Panel wishes its major recommendations to stand apart from those regarding reorganization. However, the Panel assigns a very high priority to questions about present administration of the Nation's ocean program.

In the field of education the Panel assigns highest priority to developing means by which scientists from a wide variety of fields and institutions can be brought into research in the oceans. It is important to develop cooperative arrangements between universities throughout the country with oceanographic facilities.

In particular the Panel views its recommendations with regard to ship provision as a major step in furthering the goal of effective use of the sea. The heavy overburden of bureaucracy associated with ship management deadens the intellectual life of laboratories and should be lessened. Our solution is to provide block-funding for the ships and organize the ships into regional operating fleets under "user group" management.

Ocean Science and Technology in Comparison with Other Fields

It is difficult in dealing with such complex subjects as oceanography to list priorities within the subject. Even more difficult is the task of comparing oceanography with other fields of science and technology, although this kind of comparison is essential in developing a total national plan.

Oceanography in the nondefense agencies is characterized by the fact that the percentage of total budget devoted to research and development is high; the percentage devoted to basic research is similarly high. In terms of total expenditures for the national oceanographic program, basic research makes up about 10 percent; whereas in other fields of science and technology the percentage devoted to basic research is 10 percent of research and development, rather than of the total program.

We cannot compare oceanography, for example, with the high energy physics program, since that program is devoted entirely to science and is thus 100 percent basic research. Perhaps a large governmental program most nearly paralleling oceanography is the space program, which is something like 90-95 percent research and development and, like oceanography, has a similarly high percentage of basic research.

We believe the present oceanographic program can be justified to a large extent on the basis of its contributions to national security and to civilian economy. We feel that a much stronger program can be developed along the lines outlined in our report and that oceanography should receive a higher priority in the national planning than it has in the past. For example in any competition for funds with the space program the case for oceanography would be very good. In making this statement we recognize many intangibles which are often used to justify programs.

It is far more difficult to compare expenditures in oceanography with expenditures in Great Society programs whose science and technology component is relatively smaller. ... In any event oceanography as conceived in this report supplements many facets of Great Society programs.

IMPROVED STORM PREDICTION NEEDED - HURRICANE CAMILLE, AUGUST 17, 1969

Courtesy Environmental Science Services Administration

MESSAGE TO THE CONGRESS OF THE UNITED STATES BY PRESIDENT LYNDON B. JOHNSON ON INTERNATIONAL DECADE OF OCEAN EXPLORATION [1]

The seas are the world's oldest frontiers. As Longfellow observed, they not only separate -- but unite-- mankind.

Even in the Age of Space, the sea remains our greatest mystery. But we know that in its sunless depths, a richness is still locked which holds vast promise for the improvement of men's lives -- in all nations.

Those ocean roads, which so often have been the path of conquest, can now be turned to the search for enduring peace.

The task of exploring the ocean's depth for its potential wealth -- food, minerals, resources -- is as vast as the seas themselves. No one nation can undertake that task alone. As we have learned from prior ventures in ocean exploration, cooperation is the only answer.

I have instructed the Secretary of State to consult with other nations on the steps that could be taken to launch an historic and unprecedented adventure -- an International Decade of Ocean Exploration for the 1970's.

Together the countries which border the seas can survey the ocean's resources, reaching where man has never probed before.

We hope that those nations will join in this exciting and important work.

Already our marine technology gives us the ability to use the ocean as a new and promising source of information on weather and climate. We can now build and moor electronic buoys in deep water. Unattended, these scientific outposts can transmit to shore data for accurate long-range forecasts.

The benefits will be incalculable ....

1. White House Press Release, March 8, 1968.

STATEMENT BY RICHARD M. NIXON

THE SEA: OUR LAST UNEXPLORED FRONTIER[1]

Since earliest times, two aspects of nature have commanded the awe and intrigued the curiosity of man. The first is the heavens: the night sky led men to wonder, then to think, then to chart the stars in their courses....The power to determine accurately the movements of the stars across the heavens meant the power to navigate accurately, to expand the economic, social and intellectual horizons of the ancient civilizations.

...Space exploration has followed the same path — from wonder to idea to action -- that marked the ancients' interest in the heavens....

But the second aspect of nature explored by the ancients is only now beginning to receive attention from the modern world. I speak of the sea.

Man has never conquered the sea in the same way he has conquered the land. Mysterious, unknown except in part, the sea has long been the unexplored frontier. Although it lies as close as the nearest beach, the sea in its mystery and its promise is as distant as the stars. The fringes of outer space have already been visited by man; the depths of inner space await our first tentative, courageous investigations.

It is this unknown frontier -- the sea with its inexhaustible riches -- that will be the scene of the next great adventure of the American people. What little we know about the sea suggests that here is a source of benefits so vast, opportunities so diverse, and power so immense that it rivals our previous frontiers of the land and the heavens.

To most of us the sea is the tiny fraction of it we enjoy at ocean resorts. But to a new generation of oceanographers and marine scientists the sea is food for starving millions, power for new technologies, medecine for the sick, water for the arid regions of the world, new kinds of recreation, and whole new fields of industrial and technological progress.

The Fifties were the start of the Outer Space Age; the Seventies will be the start of the Inner Space Age, an Age that will be unmatched in history for challenge to man's ingenuity, benefits for the people of the world, and the sense of wonder that many have feared is lost in the modern age.

Three questions must be answered before we can realistically begin the exploration of inner space:

--First, what can we expect to find there?

--Second, how much of what we find there can we realistically expect to exploit for man's use?

--Third, what policies must we pursue to carry out best a program of exploration and investigation?

The answer to the first question is as complex as it is exciting. From sources of power to sources of food, the sea promises an abundance of riches:

--The oil resources on our continental shelf are estimated at 2.5 trillion barrels -- more than equal to our known land reserves. We are pumping oil as far as 87 miles off-shore and exploring at depths down to 640 feet.

--Vast stores of minerals lie beneath the ocean floor waiting for the ingenuity and courage and determination of man to extract them. The ocean waters themselves contain dissolved elements of great value. Even now the United States obtains 80 percent of its magnesium and most of its bromine from the waters of the ocean, and Great Britain has developed a technique for extracting dissolved uranium from ocean waters.

But like the iceberg that floats more hidden than visible, there is far more to discover in the seas than we have yet discovered. The sea has been called our greatest neglected medical resource. Specialists in the field of biomedical research have found substances in marine plant and animal life unknown on land and of great potential benefit in fighting many of the serious diseases of mankind.

Waves, currents, the ocean tides, and temperature differentials offer sources of energy largely untapped but before we will be able to use these sources of energy for our benefit, we will have to understand them better.

In another area the House Committee on Science and Astronautics has estimated that even a 10 percent improvement in predicting weather conditions from studying the sea could save hundreds of millions of dollars every year.

We may discover beneath the sea a food supply that will satisfy the growing needs of humanity, but before the food resources of the sea become fully available to us, we need to know far more than we do now.

The ocean is a world system, and neither its waters nor its marine life respect national boundaries. A long and complex food chain sustains the living creatures of the sea--a food chain so complex that scientists differ widely in their estimates of the available yield now being fished from the sea.

In spite of their differences all agree that with greater knowledge and understanding of oceanographic conditions and the migratory habits of fish, we could increase greatly our use of the sea as a source of food without reducing its future productivity. Such knowledge will also provide a more rational base for effective national and international fishing policies.

We have only begun to apply our technological skills in electronics and chemistry to the problems of locating and attracting fish. Aquaculture, the science of marine farming, is also in its infancy and is now limited to high-value products found in the shallow waters of bays and estuaries.

The United States fishing industry has deteriorated, and I have spoken before of the failure of our existing Federal programs to encourage the fishing industry to modernize fast enough to counter foreign competition. But fleet modernization is only one of the many types of technological advances that can bring the United States back to a position of leadership in the fishing industry -- and enable us to reap a harvest from the sea that will provide an inexpensive source of protein for the malnourished peoples of the world.

In other areas also, the sea is ready to provide whenever we are able to meet its challenge. A limited supply of water is now one of the pressing problems in the world and could become a severe problem in America. A breakthrough in desalination methods could make fresh water available to coastal and surrounding areas throughout the world. Desalination offers an exciting possibility of greater output at much lower, perhaps even competitive, prices. We must stop talking about the future of water preservation and development and start doing the research and studies that will bring the future to us.

The oceans also offer great recreational potential. Underwater national parks have been established in Florida and the Virgin Islands. Pollution control and shoreline reclamation will greatly expand the availability of the ocean front for recreational purposes.

The interest of private enterprise in the marine environment has expanded rapidly in recent years. Over 1,000 U.S. firms are interested in the field. One of them is now working on a research vessel that could dive to depths of 20,000 feet -- and would thus be capable of exploring all but 2 percent of the ocean floor. Another will explore ways to build underwater shelters for as many as 1,000 men and as deep as 6,000 feet. Still another is developing anchored or mobile underwater spheres that can be used as laboratories or living quarters.

These, then, are what we can expect to find in the frontier of inner space; no other frontier has ever promised more, no other unknown world has ever challenged us more greatly.

But what we can expect to find there is only a part of the story. Our imagination can soar, but if we fail to follow our hopes and dreams with realistic appraisals of possible methods by which to exploit these riches, the sea will remain a mystery instead of a new challenge to man's courage and ingenuity.

We need the poet and the dreamer in oceanography. But we need this in combination with a well-organized and steadily funded national program, utilizing our finest scientific and management talent -- for the ocean is a world that will not be easy to conquer.

Darkness, pressure, cold, subsurface waves, corrosion, and lack of oxygen await us under the sea.

To tap its riches and explore its frontiers, we will need greatly improved undersea instruments and methods of ocean engineering and navigation. We will need better techniques of undersea rescue. We will need sophisticated -- probably electronic -- methods of fighting corrosion. We will need to know far more than we do now about how man can live and work in the depths.

The benefits of the sea will come to us only from sustained and precise investigation of this complex and hostile environment. The well-springs of the benefits we will reap from the sea are not only our vision of its potential and our courage, but the hard-headed application of our scientific, technological, and economic abilities and wisdom.

Some worthwhile steps toward the development of a sound national program have already been taken, and we will build on them.

The National Sea Grant College and Program Act of 1966 will further university research and the education of oceanographers. Under the Marine Resources and Engineering Development Act of 1966, a Cabinet-level Council and study Commission were established. Plans for an International Decade of Ocean Exploration are also underway.

Nevertheless, we still lack a unified effort in the field of marine sciences and engineering.

Our national oceanography effort is fragmented and confused, overlapping and lacking in direction. An astonishing number of Federal agencies, departments, and bureaus are involved, and many Congressional committees and subcommittees must consider oceanographic problems and programs.

Only recently have we been spending on ocean exploration even a tenth of what we have been spending on space exploration. Yet our continental shelf is far closer to us than the moon and potentially far more beneficial to man.

In spite of the steps taken by Congress toward a more effective oceanographic effort, the current Administration has frittered away time and failed to offer the nation the kind of oceanographic program it needs....

Meanwhile, the Soviet Union is reportedly far ahead of us in using underwater vehicles to develop information about fisheries and marine resources. Almost two hundred Soviet ships collect oceanographic information, and the Soviet fleet is growing more rapidly than ours. Soviet submarine technology is advancing faster than we expected -- in the speed of submarines, the control of noise made by the power plant and hull construction, Soviet scientists publish as many papers in the field of oceanography as our own scientists do.

If we do not take steps soon to upgrade and organize our

national oceanographic effort, we will not only delay the economic benefits the sea can bring us -- we may also find ourselves in second place in underwater security.

Making full use of the 1966 Act, it will be a first priority of my Administration to present to the Congress an integrated and comprehensive program in oceanography. The purposes of this program will be to:

--Establish national goals for our oceanographic effort.

--Provide a more effective framework for coordinating the work of private industry, of the universities, and of government at all levels. Consideration should be given to establishing a Sea Exploration Agency, with responsibility for coordinating our activities in oceanography.

--Ensure that the effects of one type of use of the ocean and the seabed do not preclude the benefits that could be realized by the sea's other users. Destruction of ocean life from underwater blasting or chemical pollution and damage to recreation possibilities by industrial use are examples of the types of problems that can arise from multiple use of the sea.

--Provide incentives for the participation of private industry.

--Ensure that research funds are properly allocated to oceanographers and institutions most capable of doing sound work in this field.

--Provide a framework for approaching the national and international problems associated with exploitation of the sea's resources.

--Promote international cooperation when such cooperation is in the best interests of the United States.

--Eliminate wasteful duplication of effort in the government's oceanographic projects and planning.

In developing this program my Administration will make sure that it has available to it the best counsel and advice in this field that industry, the scientific community, and the legal profession have to offer.

Man crossed the frontiers of space in the Fifties.

The Seventies can be the decade when Americans not only reach for the stars, but dive for the riches of the sea -- not for the traditional sunken treasures, but for protein to feed the world, raw materials to supply our industries, chemicals to cure diseases, and knowledge of many varieties to make nature work in the service of man....

1. Press Release, Miami, Florida, October 30, 1968.

Printed by Libri Plureos GmbH in Hamburg,
Germany

9 780262 660013